The Politics of Eurozone Reforms

ECPR Press

ECPR Press is an imprint of the European Consortium for Political Research. It publishes original research from leading political scientists and the best among early career researchers in the discipline. Its scope extends to all fields of political science, international relations and political thought, without restriction in either approach or regional focus. It is also open to interdisciplinary work with a predominant political dimension.

ECPR Press Editors
Editors
Ian O'Flynn is Senior Lecturer in Political Theory at Newcastle University, UK.
Laura Sudulich is Reader in Public Policy at the University of Essex, UK. She is also affiliated to Cevipol (Centre d'Étude de la vie Politique) at the Université libre de Bruxelles, Belgium.

Associate Editors
Andrew Glencross is Senior Lecturer in the Department of Politics and International Relations at Aston University, UK.
Liam Weeks is Lecturer in the Department of Government and Politics, University College Cork, Ireland, and Honorary Senior Research Fellow, Department of Politics and International Relations, Macquarie University, Australia.

The Politics of Eurozone Reforms

Edited by
Zdenek Kudrna, Sonja Puntscher Riekmann,
and Fabio Wasserfallen

Published by ECPR Press

European Consortium for Political Research, Harbour House, 6–8 Hythe Quay, Colchester, CO2 8JF, United Kingdom

© Zdenek Kudrna; Sonja Puntscher Riekmann; and Fabio Wasserfallen, 2021

All rights reserved. No part of this book may be reproduced in any form or by any electronic or mechanical means, including information storage and retrieval systems, without written permission from the publisher, except by a reviewer who may quote passages in a review.

British Library Cataloguing in Publication Data

Library of Congress Cataloging-in-Publication Data on File

ISBN 978-1-9102-5976-4
ISBN 978-1-5381-5153-2 (cloth : alk. Paper)
ISBN 978-1-5381-5155-6 (electronic)

Printed by Lightning Source

Contents

1. The Politics of the Eurozone: Analyses of New Data from Multiple Methodological and Theoretical Perspectives ... 1
   Zdenek Kudrna, Sonja Puntscher Riekmann, and Fabio Wasserfallen

2. Preference Formation and Decision-Making in the Reform of the Eurozone ... 13
   Stefanie Bailer, Jonas Tallberg, and Fabio Wasserfallen

3. Preference Formation During the Eurozone Crisis: A Cross-National Comparison ... 33
   Sabine Saurugger, Thomas Warren, Hussein Kassim, Shaun P. Hargreaves Heap, and Scott James

4. Southern Europe and the Eurozone Crisis Negotiations: Preference Formation and Contested Issues ... 57
   Leonardo Morlino and Cecilia Emma Sottilotta

5. National Constitutional Law as Manifold Steeplechase for Fiscal Integration ... 81
   Elisabeth Lentsch

6. Studying Integration and EMU's Choices ... 103
   Dirk Leuffen and Uwe Puetter

7. Eurozone Politics and Its Implications for Further Reforms ... 123
   Zdenek Kudrna and Sonja Puntscher Riekmann

Appendix	153
Index	159
About the Editors and Contributors	165

Chapter 1

The Politics of the Eurozone

Analyses of New Data from Multiple Methodological and Theoretical Perspectives

Zdenek Kudrna, Sonja Puntscher Riekmann, and Fabio Wasserfallen

1.1 INTRODUCTION

The euro has survived, and against all odds, no member state has left the Eurozone. When the wicked financial and fiscal crisis engulfed the monetary union in the aftermath of the collapse of Lehman Brothers in 2008, many economists predicted dangers and doom for the euro. Yet, despite the vulnerabilities of the monetary union, which includes a diverse set of economies, the Eurozone has not disintegrated, but deepened.

The creators of the euro sought to forestall some asymmetries and macroeconomic imbalances by treaty clauses on debt, deficit and no bailout as well as the rules enshrined in the Stability and Growth Pact, combined with repeated commitments to structural reforms and support for economic convergence. This stance was qualified as the result of 'a gargantuan misreading of the laws of economics' (Marsh 2011, 7). When member states came to realise the weakness of their toolbox, they sharpened them considerably and added new rules and institutions to supervise their implementation. In emergency circumstances, member states agreed on rescue funds, such as the European Stability Mechanism (ESM), fiscal discipline legislation, such as the Two- and Six-Pack, and banking regulations that were previously beyond reach. Despite different initial interpretations of the causes and consequences of the crisis, decision-makers from the member states and EU institutions eventually took collective action to rescue the euro and reduce risk for national financial sectors.

The contributions to this book summarise the main findings of the Horizon 2020 project *EMU Choices*, which started in the wake of the reform process and lasted from 2015 to 2019. The consortium of political scientists and legal scholars analysed manifold measures that were enacted between 2010 and 2015 to refine our understanding of the reform processes and to identify insights into future reforms. While recent reforms of the Economic and Monetary Union (EMU) mark the most profound deepening of European integration since Maastricht, important elements of a sustainable architecture for a single currency are still missing. Therefore, a refined understanding of political and legal constraints on EMU reform politics remains an important prerequisite for future progress.

This book puts member states' preferences, positions and strategies front and centre of our research, while not neglecting the role of supranational agents such as the Commission, the European Council, the ECOFIN, the Eurogroup or the European Central Bank (ECB). Our research questions are, *first*, how preferences of EU member states on EMU reforms were formed, and, *second*, how the European decision-making produced the reform outcomes that were enacted during the Eurozone Crisis.

To answer these questions, we have built four new datasets based on the analysis of more than 5,000 documents, 200 expert interviews and the review of constitutional court cases in all 28 EU countries. First, the *EMU Positions* dataset collects comprehensive and systematic data on the bargaining positions of each EU member state and six EU institutions during all Eurozone reforms enacted between 2010 and 2015. Second, the *EMU Historical* dataset provides a long-term perspective of these positions. Third, the *EMU Formation* dataset codes which actors were most influential in the domestic formation of member state positions. Finally, the *EMU Legal Index* maps the procedural hurdles imposed by national and EU legal systems on the process of EMU-induced constitutional change or treaty change, respectively. Relying on these unique datasets, we were able to analyse our questions systematically and comprehensively.

While most chapters of this book present research exploring these datasets, we maintain methodological pluralism throughout the book. Some contributions focus on the quantitative analysis of preference formation and EU-level bargaining; others develop comparative case studies or employ systematic legal analysis. Moreover, we build on and advance different theoretical approaches to EU decision-making and preference formation. The organisation of the broader *EMU Choices* research project follows the two-stage model of European integration, which dissects EU policymaking into, first, preference formation at the national level and, second, interstate bargaining at the European level (Moravcsik 1993, 2018). We use this two-stage model as a structuring framework. Accordingly, our research focuses on the study of how preferences are formed and how political conflicts among member states on the European level shape the reform outcomes. In the spirit of academic pluralism, the various strands of our research project extend several analytical accounts (see chapter 6), typically evaluating theoretical conjectures with rigorous empirical testing using the new data gathered in the project.

The relentless focus on data collection combined with methodological pluralism defines the main contribution of this book and served as the baseline on which all scholars of the *EMU Choices* project collaborated. The wealth of new data enables us to refine and evaluate insights into the reform politics of the Eurozone. Unlike earlier literature, we are not limited to a handful of policy issues and the analysis of major member states. Rather, we provide a comprehensive account of dozens of policy issues, all member states and key EU institutions. Indeed, some of our key findings, such as the single-dimensional structure of the policy conflict or the dominant role of financial stability concerns in preference formation, cannot be established without access to comprehensive datasets. Moreover, the systematic empirical analysis also supported the choices of key topics for case studies that provide more detailed insights into the dynamics of preference formation, EU-level bargaining or the role of constitutional courts. The comparative chapters on major EU economies and Southern member states complement and challenge key findings of existing empirical analyses. They also shape our contribution to multiple stands of EU-focused literature.

The EMU is the topic of abundant and rather specialised economic literature focusing on efficient system design. Studies in this tradition analyse existing Eurozone arrangements in relation to economic models and make proposals for reforms from an economic perspective (Sinn 2014; de Grauwe 2016; Cardinale et al. 2017; Schelkle 2017). This strand of research provides important baseline knowledge on the economics of a monetary union on which the *EMU Choices* project and book rely. At the same time, we complement this discussion with a systematic mapping of political and legal constraints that often prevent the adoption of its recommendations. Our data and insights guide reform proposals that are more compatible with dominant constraints and improve the odds of securing political compromise on their adoption and implementation.

Our focus on policy conflicts among political actors on national and European levels is based, among others, on the extensive political economy literature on the Eurozone Crisis. We work from studies showing how imbalances in competitiveness and in current accounts shape political conflicts (Copelovitch et al. 2016; Armingeon and Cranmer 2018). Important points of our orientation came from Brunnermeier et al. (2016), who stress the power of economic ideas and underlying economic philosophies in shaping policy preferences. Our focus, however, is on actors and institutions. Furthermore, our conclusions advance earlier accounts of the Eurozone Crisis, discussed in Caporaso and Rhodes (2016), as we provide more systematic insights on political and legal constraints to their observations of economic and political dynamics among key member states.

Apart from that, our analysis of the Eurozone crisis also speaks to a larger literature that explores how the various crises of European integration shaped the process of integration from the empty-chair crisis in the mid-1960s to the immigration crisis and Brexit. At the time of the final editing of this book, politics in the EU and all member states are entirely focused on the COVID-19 crisis. The distributional conflicts on the European level in this crisis are very similar to the conflicts analysed in this book. Again, Southern member states call for solidarity and burden sharing, while Northern member states, like the Netherlands and Austria, oppose unconditional financial support. Unfortunately, we had no time, given the publication timeline of this book, to incorporate these current developments more fully. The only two things we can state at the time of finalising this book are that our analyses of Eurozone reform politics explain, to a large extent, the current political divides and that the next crisis – which may lead to further common action – has already hit Europe.

In this broader context of integration through crises, the Eurozone Crisis is one instance in a series of crises that have often led to increased integration. By exploring its political dimension, we also hope to contribute to this broader understanding of how crises shape European integration (Majone 2014; Fabbrini 2015; Matthijs and Blyth 2015; Dinan et al. 2017; Caporaso 2018; Schlosser 2019). Particularly important in that respect is Jones et al. (2016) and the special issue edited by Ioannou et al. (2015), which connect the Eurozone Crisis to other crises and situate this case in the broader debate on the drivers of integration.

In sum, by presenting a comprehensive analysis of the politics of Eurozone reform, we engage with a large set of literature. The individual chapters of this book summarise and synthesise findings of more than 80 research papers and reports written in the context of the *EMU Choices* research project. Each chapter connects to different literatures in more detail. For example, chapter 3 engages with findings on the question of leadership in the Eurozone (Schoeller 2019; Howarth and Quaglia 2016) and chapter 5 furthers the existing analyses of legal impacts of EMU reforms on national legal systems and vice versa (Beukers et al. 2017; Woźniakowski 2018). The theoretical lenses of individual chapters – contrasted and summarised in chapter 6 – build on the state-of-the-art scholarship explaining EU policy and decision-making (Hix and Høyland 2011; Cini and Pérez-Solórzano Borragán 2016) as well as specialised studies of EU legislative politics (Thomson 2011) and high politics of intergovernmental conferences (Moravcsik 1998; König and Hug 2006).

Last but not least, this book derives implications for the policy debates on the future reforms of the Eurozone. We summarise proposals from Presidents' Reports, discuss their feasibility under prevailing political and legal constraints and reconcile them with a survey of expectations conducted at national representations in Brussels. In the concluding chapter, we also outline two reform scenarios and map them on to recent reform experience, which is going to shape the outlook for the new Commission, headed by Ursula von der Leyen.

1.2 MAIN FINDINGS

The comprehensive and data-driven analyses allow us to evaluate and refine some common wisdom about Eurozone politics established in academic literature as well as media discourses on the Eurozone Crisis. Our findings confirm the North–South divide, while also providing novel insights on the positions of individual member states on specific policy issues. Similarly, we can confirm the important role of Germany and France, while also pointing out that no member state was able to dominate legislative politics in Brussels. The prominent role of concerns about the stability of the banking sector in the decisions of national government is also well known. Yet, we add systematic evidence that it dominated the position taking of governments in Eurozone politics. The role of the German constitutional court in shaping some EMU reform decisions is also often listed as common wisdom, corroborated by the ruling on PSPP of 5 May 2020; however, we provide an overview of constitutional cases in all member states and also derive some implications for future reforms, taking all other EU member states into account. In short, while the headline features of Eurozone politics will be familiar to informed readers, their empirically substantiated refinements are new and important for the discussion of future EMU reforms.

The shock unleashed by the global financial crisis hit the divergent economies of the Eurozone unequally. They were also differently prepared to cope with the consequences (another parallel to the COVID-19 crisis of 2020). When constructing the Eurozone, member state representatives were well aware of their economic diversity, but – against the warning of numerous economists (see Feldstein 2012; Krugman 2013) – preferred to rely on the deficit and debt regime and the no-bailout clause, rather than put more emphasis on automatic stabilisers or risk-sharing. Hence, in the crisis, the lack of stabilisation mechanisms was the key problem underlying the institutional structure of the Eurozone.

The asymmetry of the impact of the economic crisis gave rise to the most obvious feature of Eurozone politics, typically referred to as the North–South divide. Inevitably, it is a simplifying metaphor that is neither geographically correct nor fully congruent with the distribution of policy preferences. As chapter 2 demonstrates in detail, the preferences of some Eurozone countries clearly cluster at opposite camps across all policy issues, while the rest of the EU is closer to the median position than either extreme as their preferences vary on specific issues. Nonetheless, the North–South categorisation became a major point of reference for Eurozone politics because, indeed, the political divide was most acute between the Northern Eurozone core and the Mediterranean periphery.

The less obvious aspect of the North–South divide is the question of what forced both sides to agree on the EMU reforms. After all, governments from both sides agreed on handing out loans and credits through provisional mechanisms and, later, the permanent ESM as well as the Banking Union with new supervision and resolution mechanisms. In chapter 2, Bailer, Tallberg and Wasserfallen conclude that exposure to financial markets was a major explanatory factor for variation in member states' approaches and positions with respect to euro rescue operations. A major reason why member states tolerated the ECB's non-standard measures, such as Mario Draghi's announcement of OMT, the execution of QE and the zero-bound interest rate policy, was that the alternative – the dissolution of the euro – would have had detrimental consequences, not only in the Southern economies but also in the financial sectors of the Eurozone core member states.

Dramatic pronouncements, such as German chancellor Angela Merkel's famous dictum 'if the euro fails, Europe fails',[1] were an important part of the story. However, the detailed analysis of preferences indicates that the exposure to other Eurozone banking sectors (Târlea et al. 2019) brought countries together. Also, stabilisation funding came with strings attached. The credits for ailing countries were disbursed on austerity conditions, which is in line with the Maastricht narrative of no-bailout and strict rules for national deficit and debt. This approach was defined in the Memoranda of Understanding between the Troika composed of the Commission, ECB and IMF and the recipient state. Common debt management was ruled out to stifle moral hazard. Solidarity and austerity became twin arguments fuelling deep resentments on both sides and thus further enhancing the polarisation of decision-making on EMU reforms. Our findings are in line with the argument that solidarity is a 'by-product' of self-interest rather than of normative considerations (Schelkle 2017, 12).

The quantitative analysis of member states preferences summarised in chapter 2 also reveals unusual single-dimensionality of the North–South divide. In a nutshell, a coalition of predominantly Southern member states prefers fiscal transfers against the opposition of Northern member states, who support fiscal discipline. This is distinct to most other cases of EU politics, as there is no discernible evidence of other dimensions, such as the left–right ideological orientation of governments or their general preference for more or less integration (Marks and Steenbergen 2002). The absence of additional dimensions precludes a formulation of package deals, whereby member governments are prepared to make concessions on EMU reforms as long as they are aligned with their political orientation or in exchange for benefits in other policy domains. The conflict constellation in Eurozone politics requires mutual concessions between the North and South coalitions.

Our empirical findings also refine the common wisdom about the German or Franco–German dominance of the EMU reform process. While the two countries are central to the respective coalitions and, in some important cases, were able to set the agenda by excluding measures such as Eurobonds or a common deposit insurance (Degner and Leuffen 2019), overall, they were not disproportionally successful in achieving their policy preferences (Lundgren et al. 2019). Germany was neither capable of pursuing its primary goal of highly conditional engagement ('member states have to do their homework before receiving help') nor of imposing its policy preferences on the rest of the EU. When EMU reform proposals entered the EU legislative process – mostly via the ordinary legislative procedure – the success in achieving policy preference was broadly comparable across all member states. Balanced legislative compromises indicate that the decisions taken to resolve the crisis left no states as unequivocal winners or losers of EU legislative bargaining. At the same time, however, the economic consequences of the crisis were very unevenly distributed, as the Southern member states were much more affected by the Euro Crisis with deep economic and social disruptions.

Moving to the domestic level, the analyses of the preference formation reveal strong centralisation as national governments and EU institutions were by far the most influential actors in all member states (Kudrna et al. 2019). The EMU Formation data indicates that national parliaments played some balancing role in some member states, but media, public opinion or business actors had very limited influence in shaping government preference. Chapter 3 by Saurugger et al. refines this observation with a more detailed, comparative analysis of Germany, France and the UK. They confirm a strong centralisation of preference formation and subsequent decision-making in the hands of a narrow political elite dominated by the offices of the heads of government and treasuries. At the same time, they also unveil differences between France and the UK, on the one hand, and Germany, on the other. The German case is marked by differences between the ministries of finance and economy, and by a greater role of the Bundestag in preference formation. Moreover, German politicians need to develop preferences and positions in the shadow of the Federal Constitutional Court, which has repeatedly ruled on the implications of EMU reform for German democracy and the budgetary autonomy of the Bundestag. Chapter 3 also identifies the circular preference formation between France and Germany, whereby the administrations of both countries internalise each other's red lines. This is also facilitated by a longstanding and ongoing informal conversation between ministerial actors. The UK case is special in the sense that the British administration was keen to participate in this conversation to safeguard its interests as a non-euro member and cooperated accordingly in the elaboration of the Banking Union.

In chapter 4, Morlino and Sottilotta provide a comparative analysis of the Southern member states during the crisis. They challenge the view that shared preferences on EMU reforms were rooted in similar political and economic constellations. With the exception of Malta, Southern member states were deeply affected by the crisis, but for quite different reasons. Spain and Cyprus had low public debt before the crisis, contrary to Greece, Portugal and Italy. While Italy had been plagued by high public debt for decades, it also had a good reputation for debt management. Moreover, in the negotiations on measures to combat the crisis effects, Southern member states only gradually came to accept the main thrust of solidarity-cum-austerity measures. To avoid EU rescue operations, Italy, in particular, opted for internalising structural reforms to maintain its refinancing capacity on financial markets. Others manifested oscillating positions between imputing responsibilities for national woes to the respective governments and eventual support for multilateral aid to avoid contagion. While Southern member states chose different approaches to accept austerity conditions, they agreed to EU decisions based on their preference to stay in the Eurozone.

Chapter 5 by Elisabeth Lentsch points out the common wisdom that recent Eurozone reforms increased the activity of national constitutional courts. She refines this observation by a systematic overview of all relevant cases, arguing that rulings provide important information on relevant constitutional options, limits and obstacles that constrain any further transfers of competences to the supranational level. She finds marginal progress in recent changes to the EU treaties as well as secondary legislation as an 'embryonic' fiscal union, which emphasise the view of the euro area as a 'single and distinct entity'. Chapter 5 complements the findings from recent constitutional case law with a systematic analysis of procedural requirements on both EU treaty change and EU-induced constitutional amendments. The latter are presented in the form of the *EMU Legal Index* dataset. The data of this index reinforces the expectation that a treaty change is an unlikely option for reform. The member states do not seem to be prepared to sacrifice constitutional principles. Rather, they remain capable of accepting some modifications. As in the last crisis, further reforms are likely to be based on existing treaty elements.

As mentioned, the *EMU Choices* project used liberal intergovernmentalism as a baseline theory structuring the data collection process, and much of the subsequent analysis of E(M)U decision-making. However, the methodological pluralism of the project led to challenges and refinements of this approach and some of its key assumptions. Chapter 6 by Leuffen and Puetter discusses our theoretical and methodological choices by reviewing the most pertinent publications of the *EMU Choices* project. They show that the diverse approaches generated more encompassing perspectives on the politics of EMU reform by inviting controversial debates and helping to identify the scope of conditions under which different theories perform best.

As also argued in chapters 3 and 4, preferences and positions, as key analytical variables, need a wider and more differentiated perspective. Another important question concerns the stability of preferences tackled by various scholars of the project. Most concluded that stability may vary, but also that it is important to clarify when, why and how preferences and subsequent positions are likely to change. Other questions address the role of EU-level discussions as input into national preference formation and its 'destabilising' force of previously formed preferences. In that respect, our project research shows that in the iterative nested bargaining games, which became so frequent during the financial and fiscal crisis, the independence assumption between the two levels of integration is an assumption with clear limitations.

1.3 THE FUTURE OF EUROZONE REFORMS

The last chapter by Kudrna and Puntscher Riekmann summarises key policy-relevant findings of this book (see table 7.2), reconciles them with the current reform agenda and develops a gradual outlook for further EMU reforms. The common wisdom of the North–South divide, refined with the insight of the single-dimensional policy conflict, presents the most important stumbling block for future reforms. However, the dominant role of financial stability concerns in the preference formation provides an opening for preference convergence on further reforms. During the crisis, this concern helped to forge crucial compromises across the North–South divide, while currently, it motivates Northern governments to delay reforms until the legacy losses in Southern financial sectors are resolved. Nonetheless, as the latter makes progress in reducing these risks, the former will have fewer reasons to oppose reforms, and their preferences may gradually converge into viable compromises.

As chapter 7 documents, there is some evidence of very gradual convergence, such as agreements on the fiscal backstop for the Single Resolution Fund or the development of the Budgetary Instrument for Convergence and Competitiveness. While these steps tap into existing risk-sharing mechanisms – the ESM and EU budget, respectively – they still demonstrate a willingness to develop the missing parts of the Eurozone architecture. If nothing else, they can be scaled up quickly in crisis circumstances.

The very limited progress until the end of 2019, combined with the results of our survey of expectations conducted at national representations in Brussels, indicates that the horizon for gradualist strategy goes well beyond the mandate of the next Commission. While political leaders, such as President Macron or German finance minister Scholz, occasionally attempt to intensify reform debates, the stronger impetus is more likely to come from the next crisis, which has already hit the EU in the form of the COVID-19 crisis. In any case, a shift from the gradual to the crisis-driven scenario is inherently risky, as there is no guarantee that member states and EU institutions will be able to orchestrate the turning-point agreement that stops further escalation. Moreover, if the crisis is to enable any reform progress, it needs to change the single-dimensionality of Eurozone politics by rearranging the North–South coalitions along additional dimensions and by opening space for some kind of package deal or grand bargain.

The gradualist reform strategy puts the stability of the EMU at the mercy of the economic cycle. As long as future recessions and financial shocks remain mild and do not escalate to a crisis, testing the new policy mechanisms of the EMU, the EU may have enough time to complete gradual reforms. At the same time, the Eurozone is better prepared for the next crisis than for the last one. The ESM, the Banking Union or the extraordinary intervention tools of the ECB make the EMU more resilient, despite the prevailing incompleteness of its crisis-management framework.

Only the future will tell whether the gradualist approach in the spirit of muddling through (Schlosser 2019) and 'governing the commons' without a clear hierarchy of responsibilities (Schelkle 2017) are conducive to the preservation of the euro, which is and remains an extraordinary experiment of regional integration. While the question of democratic legitimacy is here to stay, the current large support from EU citizens for a common currency should bode well.

NOTE

1. German chancellor Angela Merkel's speech in Bundestag on 19 May 2010 on the approval of the 123 billion share in the rescue package of (at the time) €750 billion.

REFERENCES

Armingeon, K. and S. Cranmer. 2018. "Position-taking in the Euro Crisis." *Journal of European Public Policy* 25, no. 4: 546–66.

Beukers T., B. de Witte, and C. Kilpatrick. 2017. *Constitutional Change through Euro-Crisis Law*. Cambridge: Cambridge University Press.

Brunnermeier, M.K., H. James, and J.P. Landau. 2016. *The Euro and the Battle of Ideas*. Princeton: Princeton University Press.

Caporaso, J.A. 2018. "Europe's Triple Crisis and the Uneven Role of Institutions: The Euro, Refugees, and Brexit." *Journal of Common Market Studies* 56, no. 6: 1345–61.

Caporaso, J.A. and M. Rhodes. 2016. *Political and Economic Dynamics of the Eurozone Crisis*. Oxford: Oxford University Press.

Cardinale, I., D. Coffman, and R. Scazzieri. 2017. *The Political Economy of the Eurozone*. Cambridge: Cambridge University Press.

Cini, M. and N. Pérez-Solórzano Borragán. 2016. *European Union Politics*. Oxford: Oxford University Press.

Copelovitch, M., J. Frieden, and S. Walter. 2016. "The Political Economy of the Euro Crisis." *Comparative Political Studies* 49, no. 7: 811–40.

De Grauwe, P. 2016. *Economics of Monetary Union*. Oxford: Oxford University Press.

Degner, H. and D. Leuffen. 2019. "Franco–German Cooperation and the Rescuing of the Eurozone." *European Union Politics* 20, no. 1: 89–108.

Dinan, D., N. Nugent, and W.E. Paterson. 2017. *The European Union in Crisis*. Houndmills: Palgrave Macmillan.

Fabbrini, S. 2015. *Which European Union? Europe after the Euro Crisis*. Cambridge: Cambridge University Press.

Feldstein, M. 2012. "The Failure of the Euro. The Little Currency that Couldn't." *Foreign Affairs* 91, no. 1: 105–16.

Hix, S. and B. Høyland. 2011. *The Political System of the European Union*. Houndmill: Palgrave Macmillan.

Howarth, D. and L. Quaglia. 2016. *The Political Economy of European Banking Union*. Oxford: Oxford University Press.

Ioannou, D., P. Leblond, and A. Niemann. 2015. "European Integration and the Crisis: Practice and Theory." *Journal of European Public Policy* 22, no. 2: 155–76.

Jones, E., D.R. Kelemen, and S. Meunier. 2016. "Failing Forward. The Euro Crisis and the Incomplete Nature of European Integration." *Comparative Political Studies* 49, no. 7: 1010–34.

König, T. and S. Hug. 2006. *Policymaking Processes and the European Constitution*. Abingdon: Routledge.

Krugman, P.R. 2013. "Revenge of the Optimum Currency Area." *NBER Macroeconomics Annual 2012*, no. 27: 439–48.

Kudrna, Z., S. Bailer, S. Târlea, and F. Wasserfallen. 2019. "Three Worlds of Preference Formation in European Union Politics: Evidence from New Data on Eurozone Reforms." *EMU Choices Working Paper*, March, 2019. https://emuchoices.eu/wp-content/uploads/2019/03/2018WP_Kudrna_et_al_EMUfpaper.pdf.

Lehner, T. and F. Wasserfallen. 2019. "Political Conflict in the Reform of the Eurozone." *European Union Politics* 20, no. 1: 45–64.

Lundgren, M., S. Bailer., L.M. Dellmuth, J. Tallberg, and S. Târlea. 2019. "Bargaining Success in the Reform of the Eurozone." *European Union Politics* 20, no. 1, 65–88.

Majone, G. 2014. *Rethinking the Union of Europe Post-Crisis. Has Integration Gone Too Far?* Cambridge: Cambridge University Press.

Marks, G. and M. Steenbergen. 2002. "Understanding Political Contestation in the European Union." *Comparative Political Studies* 35, no. 8: 879–92.

Marsh, D. 2009. *The Euro: The Battle for the New Global Currency.* New Haven: Yale University Press.

Matthijs, M. and M. Blyth. 2015. *The Future of the Euro.* Oxford: Oxford University Press.

Moravcsik, A. 1993. "Preferences and Power in the European Community: A Liberal Intergovernmentalist Approach." *Journal of Common Market Studies* 31, no. 4: 473–524.

Moravcsik, A. 2018. "Preferences, Power and Institutions in 21st-century Europe." *Journal of Common Market Studies* 56, no. 7: 1648–74.

Schelkle, W. 2017. *The Political Economy of Monetary Solidarity: Understanding the Euro Experiment.* Oxford: Oxford University Press.

Schlosser, P. 2019. *Europe's New Fiscal Union.* London: Palgrave Macmillan.

Schoeller, M.G. 2019. *Leadership in the Eurozone: The Role of Germany and EU Institutions.* London: Palgrave Macmillan.

Sinn, H.-W. 2014. *The Euro Trap. On Bursting Bubbles, Budgets and Beliefs.* Oxford: Oxford University Press.

Târlea, S., S. Bailer, H. Degner, L.M. Dellmuth, D. Leuffen, M. Lundgren, J. Tallberg, and F. Wasserfallen. 2019. "Explaining Governmental Preferences on Economic and Monetary Union Reform." *European Union Politics* 20, no. 1: 24–44.

Thomson, R. 2011. *Resolving Controversy in the European Union. Legislative Decision-Making before and after Enlargement.* Cambridge: Cambridge University Press.

Woźniakowski, T.P. 2018. "Why the Sovereign Debt Crisis Could Lead to a Federal Fiscal Union: The Paradoxical Origins of Fiscalization in the United States and Insights for the European Union." *Journal of European Public Policy* 25, no. 4: 630–49.

Chapter 2

Preference Formation and Decision-Making in the Reform of the Eurozone

Stefanie Bailer, Jonas Tallberg, and Fabio Wasserfallen

2.1 INTRODUCTION

The reforms of the Economic and Monetary Union (EMU) represent the most profound deepening of European integration in modern times, and they offer a unique opportunity to study all aspects of European Union (EU) decision-making during a period in which stakes were at their highest. For a rigorous analysis of this integration step, we collected two encompassing datasets in the *EMU Choices* project: the *EMU Positions* and *EMU Formation* datasets. Both datasets are based on information from the analysis of 5,000 documents and more than 160 expert interviews conducted in Brussels and across all EU member states. They provide detailed empirical information on the formation of member state preferences at the domestic level as well as bargaining and decision-making at the European level. This chapter summarises and synthesises the most pertinent findings of the project research derived from the analysis of this data.

The *EMU Choices* project research builds on the baseline model of European integration, which dissects EU policymaking into a first step of national preference formation and a second step of interstate bargaining (Moravcsik 1993, 2018). Accordingly, the analyses of the two datasets investigate various steps of EU decision-making: from preference formation to agenda setting, bargaining dynamics and decision-making. The *EMU Positions* dataset reports the positions of all twenty-eight EU member states and six EU institutions, covering forty-seven contested issues negotiated in the Eurozone reforms between 2010 and 2015. It includes policies of the Greek assistance programmes, European Financial Stability Facility, European Stability Mechanism, Six-Pack, Two-Pack, Fiscal Compact and the Banking Union (for a more detailed discussion of these negotiations and issues, see Wasserfallen et al. 2019). The *EMU Formation* dataset covers fewer policy positions but is more detailed on the preference formation step by coding the domestic and supranational actors that were most influential in the formation of member states' preferences for each of the twenty-eight EU member states (Kudrna et al. 2019).

Among others, the analyses of these datasets show that (a) the preference formation in most EU member states was dominated by the governments, with little responsiveness to public opinion and marginal involvement of other political and social actors, besides the heads of governments and finance ministries (Kudrna et al. 2019); (b) the governments, by and large, defended the economic interests of their country in the negotiations on the European stage (Târlea et al. 2019); (c) in the interstate bargaining at the European level, two larger coalitions, led by France and Germany, opposed one another (Lehnert and Wasserfallen 2019); and (d) neither of the two opposing coalitions dominated the bargaining outcomes. Rather, the negotiations were characterised by reciprocity and compromise (Lundgren et al. 2019).

As far as the supranational influence in the reform of the Eurozone is concerned, we find that EU institutions shaped the preferences of the member states and that particularly the Commission influenced the negotiation outcomes (Lundgren et al. 2020; Kudrna et al. 2019; Finke and Bailer 2019). Thus, while the key role of the European Central Bank, with its activist monetary policy, has been widely acknowledged, more recent research shows that the Commission also was highly influential in EMU decision-making.

Taken together, these findings make three substantial contributions to both academic literature and public debate. First, the very government-centred preference formation process follows, to a large extent, economic interests and is neither responsive to public opinion nor involves multiple political and social actors. This points to a lack of domestic deliberation and democratic anchoring of governments' actions at the European level. Second, the research on intergovernmental bargaining shows that the negotiations are structured by a very polarised setting, where concessions are negotiated across two stable coalitions confronting one another. Third, the finding that the Commission was highly influential adds to the classic debate in European integration studies, which centres around the question of how and when supranational institutions and interests shape EU policymaking (Haas 1958; Hoffmann 1966; Moravcsik 1999; Sandholtz and Stone Sweet 1998; Tallberg 2002; Pollack 2003). All of these results on EMU decision-making are also relevant for ongoing and future EMU reform attempts, as they point to systematic dynamics in preference

2.2 EMU DECISION-MAKING IN TWO STAGES: PREFERENCE FORMATION AND INTERSTATE BARGAINING

The *EMU Choices* project's research organisation follows the two-stage model of European integration, which dissects EU policymaking into the two steps of preference formation at the national level and interstate bargaining at the European level (Moravcsik 1993, 2018). Of course, the processes of domestic preference formation and interstate bargaining are not strictly unidirectional. Member states also change positions during negotiations at the European level, and the formation of national positions is influenced by discussions within European institutions (Csehi and Puetter 2017). However, the representatives of member states defend distinct national interests, and they have formulated policy stances before negotiations start at the European level.

Like any other model, the two-stage model builds on an analytical abstraction. We believe that the theoretical distinction into a domestic and a European stage is very useful for elaborating theoretical and empirical insights on EU and EMU politics. However, to explore the interactions between the domestic and European levels, several studies of the project go beyond this model, analysing how EU institutions shaped member state preferences and decision-making outcomes (Csehi and Puetter 2017; Lundgren et al. 2020).

During the Eurozone Crisis, one of the major crises of the EU in the last decades, member states experienced how weak economic policy coordination and loose fiscal oversight destabilised the monetary union, which was originally intended to further unite the internal market. As a reaction to this major economic crisis, EU governments opted for an even more integrated EU, involving further economic coordination, to avoid similar crises in the future. To understand this rather unexpected move towards more economic integration, just after having experienced the pitfalls of the monetary union, we study in detail which factors determined the preferences of EU governments.

2.3 PREFERENCE FORMATION

To analyse the first step of the two-stage model – member state preference formation – the project researchers conducted several systematic studies building on the two major datasets, *EMU Positions* and *EMU Formation*. Târlea et al.

(2019) examine national preference formation with regard to the Eurozone reforms, analysing the determinants of member state positions in the negotiations. Among others, the authors investigate the following questions: What were the factors that shaped government preferences in the EMU reforms? Did concerns about countries' structural economic vulnerability matter, or was it rather fluctuations in public support for the Eurozone, or possibly other factors?

Since we still have rather limited knowledge of the political and economic determinants of government positions (Copelovitch et al. 2016), this study takes up an ongoing debate. Particularly, international relations and political economy literatures state the importance of economic factors for determining a country's preferences (Frieden 1999; Moravcsik 1997; Bailer et al. 2015; Wasserfallen 2014), in contrast to approaches which underline that government preferences in international negotiations are strongly influenced by public opinion (Hagemann et al. 2017; Aldrich et al. 2006), the partisan orientation of governments (Hagemann and Hoyland 2008) and interest groups (Schneider and Baltz 2003).

Târlea et al. (2019) rely on the *EMU Positions* dataset to empirically analyse the economic and political factors that informed national preference formation during the Eurozone Crisis. Member state positions are coded in this study on a scale from the least ambitious to the most ambitious reform proposal, seeking to capture the willingness of a member state to support further fiscal, economic and financial integration (please note that this is not the same as the divide between supporters and opponents of fiscal discipline as investigated by, for instance, Schlipphak and Treib (2017) or Armingeon and Cranmer (2018)). This approach allows for a structural analysis of whether member state positions on further EMU integration are better explained by variations in economic profiles, public opinion, political systems or party conflicts.

The main finding of the study suggests that the domestic level of economic integration is the strongest predictor of the willingness of a member state to advocate further economic, fiscal and financial integration – more specifically, the level of financial integration, measured as financial liabilities of a country's banking sector vis-à-vis all other EU member states. While other economic variables also explain some variation in positions, it is striking that the extent of financial interconnectedness is the most powerful predictor of support for further integration. This finding indicates that a government is more willing to increase the prerogative of European institutions if its economy has an oversized financial sector that would be difficult to control (or bailout) domestically. If a financial sector is multiple times larger than the entire GDP of a country, this is perceived as too great a risk to be dealt with just at the domestic level, implying that governments prefer greater supranational integration through reforms to the EMU.

In contrast, the study finds no support for arguments that public opinion, the partisan conflict structure or the vote share of EU-sceptic parties contribute to explaining variation among the positions of member states. This is not to say that domestic politics do not matter at all, but, according to this broader comparative analysis, we cannot detect systematic differences in the willingness of member states to support further integration based on such political variables. This further emphasises that governments primarily act based on national, economic interests in EU negotiations, rather than domestic party politics or public opinion (see also Armingeon and Cranmer 2018).

It is up for further debate to which degree the dominance of economic factors holds. While some previous research on preferences (Bailer 2011) or votes (Bailer et al. 2015) in the EU Council confirm the importance of economic rules, other studies have detected which domestic political actors play an important role, such as public opinion (Hagemann et al. 2017) and national parliaments (Hagemann et al. 2019; Auel and Christiansen 2015). Most prominently, national parliaments have pushed for more oversight and control at the EU level in recent decades (Winzen 2012), which can be detected in the negotiation behaviour of states in the EU Council of Ministers dealing with EU legislation (Hagemann et al. 2019). As for the EU crisis, qualitative studies looking at individual countries and the interplay between parliaments and governments did detect an impact of the legislators on their government in specific cases (Puntscher Riekmann and Wydra 2013; Auel and Höing 2014, 2015; Auel and Christiansen 2015).

The influence of national parliaments does not seem to be based on an established connection between a government and its legislature, which means that we cannot yet speak of democratisation of EU negotiations in that respect. Rather, the national legislatures need to push for a larger say: necessary is the combination of attentive parliamentarians with an Eurosceptic public to motivate a national parliamentary debate about EU affairs (Winzen et al. 2018). This highlights that further research needs to pay more attention to the interplay of domestic actors and the question of how they increase each other's power to influence the government's position in EU negotiations. For too long, domestic actors were considered as unconnected actors. Future studies need to develop models studying how they interact.

In contrast to Târlea et al. (2019), Kudrna et al. (2019) analyse domestic preference formation with a focus on agency rather than structure. Their study builds on the EMU Formation dataset, which codes the involvement of all potentially relevant actors in the formation of positions, based on 141 expert interviews conducted in all 28 EU member states (more than 160 interviews were conducted for both datasets). This comparative dataset codes the extent to which the preferences of the governments were shaped by the finance ministries, parliaments, parties, national central banks, public opinion, media, banking sector associations, employers' associations, trade unions and external EU actors, such as the European Central Bank, European Council, European Commission, European Parliament, Eurogroup, and Economic and Financial Committee.

With this approach, Kudrna et al. (2019) are the first to assess systematically and comparatively for all 28 EU member states the influence of national and supranational actors on national governments' negotiation positions. While previous studies have combined data on governments' negotiation positions with data that measured domestic preferences on other issues (Bailer 2011; Armingeon and Cranmer 2018), or on only a subset of countries (Schneider and Baltz 2005; Schneider et al. 2007; Hagemann et al. 2017), the combination of the *EMU Positions* and the *EMU Formation* datasets allows for a thorough study of the factors influencing negotiation positions, using data on the same negotiation issues.

The analysis of the data clearly shows that national governments and finance ministries were the key – and in many countries exclusive – domestic actors in the formation of member states' preferences. As far as the influence at the European level is concerned, the positions of EU institutions were, for most governments, an important point of orientation in the formation of preferences. In the majority of countries, national parliaments have also shaped (to varying extents) the negotiation positions of member states, while the media, public opinion and social partners were only in very few countries relevant in the formation of preferences (and, even then, to a rather marginal extent), which also holds for business interests. These findings are in line with more detailed qualitative findings on preference formation in Southern countries (Morlino and Sottilotta 2019). The result that each member state's position was formed almost exclusively by its government suggests that member states' governments have not reacted to the pressure from organised, domestic interests. Rather, the governments seem to have internalised the focus on the domestic, economic interests of their own country as a key point of orientation in EMU politics.

Based on the analyses of these novel datasets, it was possible to contribute to an ongoing debate on the influence of national parliaments, public opinion, interest groups and the media on foreign policy and negotiation positions. While research on foreign policy assumed for a long time that public opinion hardly matters (Aldrich et al. 2006), more recent studies recognise that voters care about international politics (Gelpi et al. 2007) and that they can exert some pressure in international and EU negotiations (Hagemann et al. 2017). While voters are simply not sufficiently informed about EU legislative negotiations of average salience (Bailer et al. 2015), it is a different matter in negotiations receiving attention in the media, giving rise to different dynamics (Hagemann et al. 2017; Hobolt and Wratil, 2020).

Particularly during and after the Eurozone Crisis, much scholarly attention was paid to public opinion on the Euro and the EU (Hobolt and Wratil 2015; Cramme and Hobolt 2015). However, even in this case, we could not find clear evidence for the impact of public opinion on government behaviour. Germany appears to have been an exception in this regard (see Degner and Leuffen 2018).

The lack of evidence that public opinion and interest groups matter is fascinating and troubling since both factors are usually considered influential for guaranteeing the success and survival of governments. During the Eurozone Crisis, neither the mass protests in Southern European member states (Altiparmakis and Lorenzini 2018) nor the intense politicisation of EU affairs or the rise of challenger parties in debtor countries (Hernandez and Kriesi 2016) seems to have directly impacted national preferences and negotiation positions. Possibly, the impact of these factors on government preference formation could have been captured using a research design that is more sensitive to underlying processes and time dynamics.

With regard to the impact of interest groups on a government's foreign policy, the international relations literature has developed a more thorough understanding in recent years (Jacobs and Page 2005; Mearsheimer and Walt 2006), while this issue has always attracted extensive interest in the EU literature (Dür and Mateo 2013; Dür et al. 2015; Klüver 2009, 2013). However, the evidence for interest groups' influence on national negotiation positions is scarce (for an exception see Schneider and Baltz 2003 or Schneider et al. 2007). Similarly, the study of Kudrna et al. (2019) could not show that interest groups play an important role in determining a government's negotiation position on EMU reforms. Therefore, it remains to be established whether interest groups manage to impact their national governments' positions in EU negotiations or whether they rather lobby directly EU institutions such as the Commission and the Parliament.

Likewise, understanding of the media's impact on EU negotiations is so far rather limited, apart from studies by Hagemann et al. (2017) and Hobolt and Wratil (2020), which find an impact of greater media attention in national politics on government behaviour in the Council. Closer media attention is associated with the saliency of a policy proposal; often, they are considered the same concept. Saliency or media attention may also increase the impact of public opinion and strengthen the voice of voters or even play an independent role in influencing a government's foreign policy decision (Aday 2017; Iyengar and Simon 1993; Iyengar et al. 1982). However, our knowledge regarding the impact of media and saliency on national preference formation is extremely limited: while we could expect that more media attention leads to more voters paying attention to a government's actions at the international stage, we simply cannot identify this effect in our studies. Although various interview partners did talk about the effect of mass media, the economic variables seem to matter far more (Târlea et al. 2019).

Taken together, our research on preference formation suggests that national governments were only to a very limited extent responsive to domestic political actors and the opinion of the public in EMU reforms. Rather, the governments acted based on their domestic economic interests and the fear of economic consequences related to a country's financial exposure and interconnectedness. Interestingly, the analysis of the data suggests that this is not necessarily a function of intense and successful lobbying by economic interest groups, but seems to be internalised as national interest by the governments themselves. While domestic actors beyond the government were not of great relevance in the formation of member state preferences, the executives of EU member states took the stances of the EU institutions into account when they formed and prepared their positions for European negotiations.

2.4 INTERGOVERNMENTAL BARGAINING

A further focal point of the *EMU Choices* project is the analysis of intergovernmental bargaining on the European level – the second step in the two-stage model of European integration. Following the outbreak of the Eurozone Crisis in late 2009, European policymakers agreed to a string of reforms that together amounted to a profound deepening of fiscal and monetary cooperation in the Eurozone. Battling the crisis, EU governments created joint resources for Eurozone states in fiscal stress (European Financial Stability Facility and European Stability Mechanism), strengthened the Stability and Growth Pact through multiple sets of reforms (Six-Pack and Two-Pack), agreed on a new treaty to force a balancing of government budgets (Fiscal Compact) and adopted measures to establish a Banking Union. These reforms did not come about lightly. On the contrary, they typically resulted from an intense battle against the raging crisis and arduous negotiations among the governments. Several studies in the project investigate the processes and outcomes of the interstate bargaining resulting in these reforms.

Lehner and Wasserfallen (2019) analyse which conflict dimension(s) structured the contestation among governments in the Eurozone reform. The classic dimensions of conflict in EU politics are between more vs. less integration and the left vs. right of the political spectrum (Marks and Steenbergen 2002; Hooghe et al. 2002; Hix 1999). The political economy literature on the Eurozone Crisis adds the divide between advocates of fiscal transfer and fiscal discipline as a key dimension of conflict (Armingeon and Cranmer 2018; Beramendi and Stegmueller 2017; Frieden and Walter 2017). Lehner and Wasserfallen (2019) consider the possibility that each of these conflict dimensions structures the politics of EMU reform in a one-dimensional conflict space – or, alternatively, that different combinations of these underlying conflicts span over a two-dimensional space. They empirically investigate the dimensionality of political conflict during the Eurozone Crisis with dimension-reduction methods using the *EMU Positions* dataset. Based on Bayesian IRT and other scaling methods, they reduce the forty-seven contested negotiation issues into underlying conflict dimensions.

In contrast to most analyses of EU politics, the findings show that the politics of EMU reform are not multi-dimensional (e.g., a combination of left–right and pro–anti EU), although they cover a broad range of fiscal, economic, financial and institutional reform proposals. Rather, a one-dimensional conflict between countries advocating for more fiscal transfers vs. countries prioritising fiscal discipline dominated the EMU negotiations.

On this single conflict dimension, Lehner and Wasserfallen (2019) estimate the aggregated positioning of each member state. Figure 2.1 shows the ideal point estimates from this analysis. France advocated the most extreme positions on the fiscal transfer side, followed by Greece and supported by the other Southern European member states and Belgium. At the other end of the spectrum, the Netherlands and Finland were the most pronounced advocates of fiscal discipline, followed by Germany. On the fiscal discipline side, yet closer to the middle, is a large group of Northern, Central and Eastern European member states. The fiscal transfer and discipline coalitions both seek the support of the actors positioned in the middle. Here, we find most EU institutions, Ireland, Cyprus, Luxembourg and Slovenia.

In sum, the scaling analysis points to a very profound and historically rooted divide between advocates of fiscal discipline and countries that support more transfers within the Eurozone, which is consistent with the findings of other studies (Armingeon and Cranmer 2018; Brunnermeier et al. 2016). The enlargements of the EU to Central and Eastern Europe have strengthened the fiscal discipline coalition. However, this has not strongly affected the negotiation dynamics. In essence, member states are still divided over two different macroeconomic concepts for the EMU, while the diverging

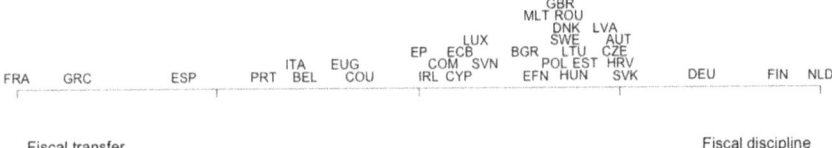

Figure 2.1 Ideal Points of Member States and EU Institutions on the One-dimensional Conflict Space Estimated with Bayesian Ordinal IRT Models. Source: Lehner and Wasserfallen (2019, 55).

preferences for these concepts reflect ideational, economic and institutional differences among EU member states (Brunnermeier et al. 2016). Within this clear divide, opposing narratives and analyses of the causes and consequences of the challenges of the Eurozone persist – if anything, the crisis has deepened this divide further.

Going a step further, Lundgren et al. (2019) analyse the relative bargaining success of EU member states in the EMU reforms negotiations. They start from a typical observational stance of pundits: that Germany was successful in getting its way in the Eurozone negotiations (Bernhard and Leblang 2016). From the discussions on bailouts in 2010 to negotiations of successive Eurozone reforms and the talks on Greece's macroeconomic adjustment, Germany was seen to prevail. Against this backdrop, Lundgren et al. (2019) offer the first systematic analysis of bargaining success in the reform of the Eurozone. They consider whether the narrative of German dominance holds up to the empirical evidence, or whether the pattern of bargaining success is more multifaceted.

Empirically, Lundgren et al. (2019) map and explain the bargaining success of member states on the most fundamental proposals for Eurozone reform from 2010 to 2015. They estimate bargaining success through spatial analysis, calculating the distance between member states' positions at the beginning of negotiations and the final outcome. Theoretically, they advance an argument about preferences and institutions as determinants of bargaining success. They submit that bargaining success is explained by conditions of the strategic setting as determined by the positioning of actor preferences and the applicable decision rules. They contrast this argument with an alternative account that privileges member states' power resources.

Contrary to the narrative of German dominance, their analysis shows that the EMU negotiations produced no clear winners and losers, confirming previous findings (Arregui and Thomson 2009; Bailer 2004). Holding preferences that were centrist or close to those of the European Commission favoured bargaining success, particularly when the adoption of policy reform did not require unanimity among member states. The analysis of bargaining success suggests that the two opposing coalitions, identified by Lehner and Wasserfallen (2019), negotiated with one another in a dynamic of compromise and reciprocity, where gains and concessions appear to have been traded both within and across issues. Importantly, the findings reported in figure 2.2 show that the two most powerful countries of the EU, Germany and France, did not dominate the negotiation outcomes at the bargaining stage.

Lundgren et al. (2019) offer three complementary interpretations for why these findings run counter to prevailing power-orientated narratives. First, the influence of larger member states was partly neutralised by their commitment to the Euro, which opened them up for exploitation by other parties. Second,

Preference Formation and Decision-Making 23

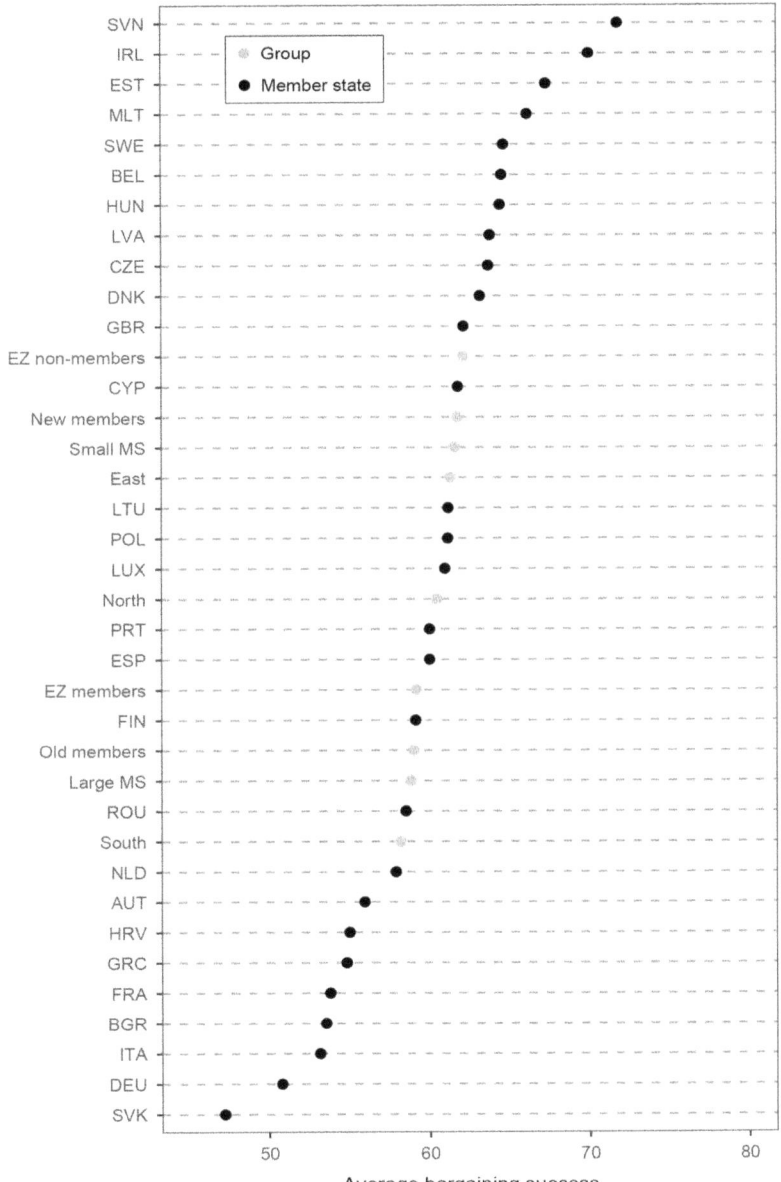

Figure 2.2 **Mean Bargaining Success by Country and Group.** Note: Higher values indicate greater preference attainment. Source: Lundgren et al. (2019, 74).

larger member states partly exercised influence by shaping the issues for negotiation, even if they were less successful at the negotiation table. Third, larger member states often held extreme preferences, forcing them to give more ground as the parties converged on compromises.

These findings carry three broader implications for our understanding of negotiations and politics in the EU. First, they suggest that the EU is a bargaining setting in which economic power does not dictate outcomes at the negotiation table. While the EU's larger member states may have influenced what issues came up for negotiation, the results are consistent with earlier studies finding evidence against superior bargaining success for the most resourceful states in EU legislative negotiations (Cross 2013; Arregui and Thomson 2009; Bailer 2004; Golub 2012). Second, and related, the results suggest that a spatial approach anchored in rational choice institutionalism can take us far in understanding the nature of EU negotiations. Third, the findings speak to concerns about legitimacy in Eurozone reform. Some researchers have pointed to the potentially detrimental consequences for the legitimacy of the EU if some states were disproportionately more influential in determining policy outcomes (Golub 2012; Arregui and Thomson 2009). However, the discussed empirical findings shed a different light on this issue and do not display dominance of one group of member states. While the economic woes of the crisis were certainly highly unevenly distributed, the steps taken to resolve the crisis reflected a balancing of gains and concessions that left no states as unequivocal winners or losers.

Taken together, the results of the studies by Lehner and Wasserfallen (2019) and Lundgren et al. (2019) suggest that the advantage of a one-dimensional conflict structure is a setting that provides a straightforward negotiation space for reciprocity and compromise with the median position as an equilibrium solution. In practice, France and Germany act as the leaders of two opposing camps among EU governments. Collectively, the preference distribution among EU member states with the two major countries, France and Germany, as leaders of the two opposing coalitions, provides an ideal setting for joint German–French initiatives, proposals and compromises.

Focusing specifically on this issue, Degner and Leuffen (2019) provide a detailed analysis of the Franco–German cooperation during the Eurozone Crisis. To this end, they explore three mechanisms linking Franco–German cooperation to EMU decision-making. The first mechanism refers to the elimination of proposals or issues from the European negotiation agenda; by casting a joint veto, France and Germany are argued to have reduced the choice set available to all other member states. The second mechanism suggests that these two countries broker solutions that are acceptable for other member states. France and Germany seem to form an inner negotiation circle, developing compromises and proposing compensation measures. Thus, they reduce the transaction costs of EU decision-making. According to the third mechanism, France and Germany constitute a power duo that imposes its preferred solutions on other member states.

To test the effects of Franco–German cooperation on EMU decision-making, Degner and Leuffen (2019) apply process tracing to proposals contained in the EMU Positions dataset. The analyses reveal that France and Germany, indeed, jointly affected EMU reforms between 2010 and 2015, even beyond their individual weights as large, powerful member states. In particular, they show that these two countries together eliminated several issues from the official negotiation table, which substantially impacted the final negotiation outcomes. The power of issue selection and agenda control may account for the limited bargaining power of Germany and France documented by Lundgren et al. (2019). In addition, their case studies highlight that France and Germany repeatedly identified compromise solutions or compensations, and thus facilitated the adoption of key reforms. The case studies do not find evidence, however, that France and Germany were able to impose their preferred policy solutions for EMU reforms on the other member states. They conclude that France and Germany possess the negative power of the veto but cannot independently shape EMU reforms. However, due to their strong resource endowments and their joint interests in rescuing the Eurozone, they have contributed to brokering viable solutions for larger European majorities.

Finke and Bailer (2019) offer an additional analysis of the determinants of bargaining outcomes in the Eurozone reform, focusing specifically on the predictive power of multiple bargaining models. Drawing on the *EMU Positions* dataset, they locate actors' positions on three reform dimensions, namely the level of fiscal discipline, transfer payments and institutionalisation. On this basis, they test three established models of decision-making: the Symmetric and Asymmetric Nash Bargaining Model, as well as an Agenda Setting Model. The graphical illustration and the comparison of the predictions with actual outcomes show that models, which consider formal decision rules and asymmetric market pressure, perform best in predicting negotiation outcome. Pressures from financial markets on member states with high debts weakened the bargaining power of debtor countries. Accordingly, they argue that the dominance of fiscal discipline and austerity in the reform approach (Frieden and Walter 2017) – compared to other measures, such as debt reliefs and transfer payments – is a function of asymmetric economic exposure and pressure. The dominance of economic explanations is also due to the crisis nature of the reforms: decisions taken at the height of the crisis are not to the advantage of countries that are most affected and in need of reforms.

Finally, Lundgren, Tallberg and Wasserfallen (2020) move beyond intergovernmental bargaining by studying the influence of the European Commission on EMU reforms. They conceptualise the power of this supranational institution as the extent to which the Commission is able to pull the negotiation outcomes towards its own positions, away from what is to be expected based on the broader intergovernmental power structure. Lundgren, Tallberg and Wasserfallen (2020) develop theoretical expectations about the determinants of the Commission's differentiated influence by analysing on which member states the Commission exerts bargaining influence. Empirically, they draw on data from the *EMU Positions* dataset, including thirty-nine contested policy issues negotiated during the Eurozone Crisis. Methodologically, they pioneer a novel relational measure of supranational influence vis-à-vis individual member states, which they analyse with cross-nested hierarchical models.

The central findings of their analysis are that the Commission greatly influenced negotiated outcomes and, most importantly, that Commission exerted influence by pulling closer to its own position member states with greater voting power, less network capital, higher economic vulnerability and lower issue salience. These findings suggest that supranational influence remains an important feature of EU politics, even on a highly contested issue such as Eurozone reform.

These insights indicate that the Commission played a more central role in Eurozone reform than recognised by earlier research, which has tended to focus on the struggle between creditor and debtor countries (Brunnenmeier et al. 2016; Frieden and Walter 2017). When supranational institutions are discussed in that respect, it is typically with a focus on the activist role of the European Central Bank. The finding that the Commission was highly influential in the negotiations of policy solutions is all the more important because the Eurozone reforms present a hard case for supranational influence in EU politics, particularly as far as the influence of the Commission is concerned. While the Commission conventionally is regarded as powerful in everyday agenda setting and implementation and on issues of low politics (Sandholtz and Stone Sweet 1998; Lelieveldt and Princen 2015; Nugent and Rhinard 2016), the Eurozone reforms represented the exact opposite: hard bargaining on a highly contested political issue. In this contested setting, the Commission successfully pushed for solutions closer to its own preferences (without simply assuming the role of an honest broker).

2.5 CONCLUSION

The EMU reforms represent a unique opportunity to study EU decision-making during a period in which stakes were at their highest. Drawing on the novel *EMU Formation* and *EMU Positions* datasets, the *EMU Choices* project has engaged in comprehensive analyses of the preference formation and negotiations at the European level.

As described in this chapter, the analyses offered a range of novel results, many of which cut against conventional accounts about domestic preference formation and interstate bargaining in Eurozone reform. In the broader context of EU politics, several of these results also further nuance previous findings with regard to the dominance of economic factors in preference formation, the conflict and bargaining dynamics among member states in negotiations and the role of supranational actors, such as the Commission. That said, future research needs to tackle several questions yet unanswered.

To begin with, we need to study in more detail whether the negotiation behaviour of member states can be explained by domestic actors, for example, parliaments, interest groups, public opinion or the media, and what the exact interplay is between them. In which instances does the role of public opinion or interest groups matter, and can they reinforce each other's impact? Moreover, several aspects of the analysis of national preference formation deserve further scrutiny. How does time pressure impact the number of actors able to influence a government? In which instances does it matter to have a partisan, technocrat or populist government negotiating (Târlea and Bailer 2020)? How does salience and media attention influence the formation of a government's negotiation position? Only case studies such as Miklin's (2009) analysis have so far paid attention to the various stages of this process; further research should explore how representative such illustrations are. Until now, we could hardly detect an impact on the choice of negotiation strategies: not only technocratic but also partisan governments are driven more by the economic interests of the member states and not by their political orientation.

Additionally, more research is needed to fully understand the stage of interstate bargaining, for example, by integrating the bargaining conditions in more detail. We still know little about the following questions: How do negotiations and their course change according to the actor setting as well as the timing of the negotiations? Do states choose negotiation behaviour also depending on the number of actors opposing or supporting them? How does negotiation strategy vary over time and during negotiations?

REFERENCES

Aday, S. 2017. "The US Media, Foreign Policy, and Public Support for War." In *The Oxford Handbook of Political Communication*, edited by K. Kenski and K. Hall Jamieson, 315–37. Oxford and New York: Oxford University Press.

Aldrich, J.H., C. Gelpi, P. Feaver, J. Reifler, and K.T. Sharp. 2006. "Foreign Policy and the Electoral Connection." *Annual Review of Political Science* 9, no. 1: 477–502.

Altiparmakis, A. and J. Lorenzini. 2018. "Disclaiming National Representatives: Protest Waves in Southern Europe During the Crisis." *Party Politics* 24, no. 1: 78–89.

Armingeon, K. and S. Cranmer. 2018. "Position-taking in the Euro Crisis." *Journal of European Public Policy* 25, no. 4: 546–66.

Arregui, J. and R. Thomson. 2009. "States' Bargaining Success in the European Union." *Journal of European Public Policy* 16, no. 5: 655–76.

Auel, K. and T. Christiansen. 2015. "After Lisbon: National Parliaments in the European Union." *West European Politics* 38, no. 2: 261–81.

Auel, K. and O. Höing. 2014. "Parliaments in the Euro Crisis: Can the Losers of Integration Still Fight Back?" *Journal of Common Market Studies* 52, no. 6: 1184–93.

Auel, K. and O. Höing. 2015. "National Parliaments and the Eurozone Crisis: Taking Ownership in Difficult Times?" *West European Politics* 38, no. 2: 375–95.

Bailer, S. 2004. "Bargaining Success in the European Union." *European Union Politics* 5, no. 1: 99–123.

Bailer, S. 2011. "Structural, Domestic, and Strategic Interests in the European Union: Negotiation Positions in the Council of Ministers." *Negotiation Journal* 27, no. 4: 447–75.

Bailer, S., M. Mattila, and G. Schneider. 2015. "Money Makes the EU Go Round: The Objective Foundations of Conflict in the Council of Ministers." *Journal of Common Market Studies* 53, no. 3: 437–56.

Beramendi, P. and D. Stegmueller. 2017. *The Political Geography of the Eurocrisis*. Durham: Duke University Press.

Bernhard, W.T. and D. Leblang. 2016. "Sovereign Debt, Migration Pressure, and Governmental Survival." *Comparative Political Studies* 49, no. 7: 907–38.

Brunnermeier, M.K., H. James, and J.-P Landau. 2016. *The Euro and the Battle of Ideas*. Princeton: Princeton University Press.

Copelovitch, M., J. Frieden, and S. Walter. 2016. "The Political Economy of the Euro Crisis." *Comparative Political Studies* 49, no. 7: 811–40.

Cramme, O. and S. Hobolt. 2015. *European Union under Stress*. Oxford: Oxford University Press.

Cross, J.P. 2013. "Everyone's a Winner (almost): Bargaining Success in the Council of Ministers of the European Union." *European Union Politics* 14, no. 1: 70–94.

Csehi, R. and U. Puetter. 2017. "Problematizing the Notion of Preference Formation in Research About the Euro Crisis." *EMU Choices Working Paper*.

Degner, H. and D. Leuffen, D. 2019. "Franco-German Cooperation and the Rescuing of the Eurozone." *European Union Politics* 20, no. 1: 89–108.

Dür, A., P. Bernhagen, and D. Marshall. 2015. "Interest Group Success in the European Union: When (and Why) Does Business Lose?" *Comparative Political Studies* 48, no. 8: 951–83.

Dür, A. and G. Mateo. 2013. "Gaining Access or Going Public? Interest Group Strategies in Five European Countries." *European Journal of Political Research* 52, no. 5: 660–86.

Finke, D. and S. Bailer. 2019. "Crisis Bargaining in the European Union: Formal Rules or Market Pressure?" *European Union Politics* 20, no. 1: 109–33.

Frieden, J. 1999. "Actors and Preferences in International Relations." In *Strategic Choice and International Relations*, edited by D.A. Lake and R. Powell. Princeton: Princeton University Press.

Frieden, J. and S. Walter. 2017. "Understanding the political economy of the Eurozone Crisis." *Annual Review of Political Science* 20: 371–90.

Gelpi, C., J. Reifler, and P. Feaver. 2007. "Iraq the Vote: Retrospective and Prospective Foreign Policy Judgments on Candidate Choice and Casualty Tolerance." *Political Behavior* 29, no. 2: 151–74.

Golub, J. 2012. "How the European Union Does Not Work: National Bargaining Success in the Council of Ministers." *Journal of European Public Policy* 19, no. 9: 1294–315.

Hagemann, S., S. Bailer, and A. Herzog. 2019. "Signals to Their Parliaments? Governments' Use of Votes and Policy Statements in the EU Council." *Journal of Common Market Studies* 57, no. 3: 634–50.

Hagemann, S., S.B. Hobolt, and C. Wratil. 2017. "Government Responsiveness in the European Union: Evidence from Council Voting." *Comparative Political Studies* 50, no. 6: 850–76.

Hagemann, S. and B. Hoyland. 2008. "Parties in the Council?" *Journal of European Public Policy* 15, no. 8: 1205–21.

Hernandez, E. and H. Kriesi. 2016. "The Electoral Consequences of the Financial and Economic Crisis in Europe." *European Journal of Political Research* 55, no. 2: 203–24.

Hix, S. 1999. *The Political System of the European Union.* Basingstoke: Macmillan.

Hobolt, S. and C. Wratil. 2020. "Contestation and Responsiveness in EU Council Deliberations." *Journal of European Public Policy* 27, no. 3: 362–381.

Hobolt, S.B. and C. Wratil. 2015. "Public Opinion and the Crisis: The Dynamics of Support for the Euro." *Journal of European Public Policy* 22, no. 2: 238–56.

Hooghe, L., G. Marks, and C.J. Wilson. 2002. "Does Left/Right Structure Party Positions on European Integration?" *Comparative Political Studies* 35, no. 8: 965–89.

Iyengar, S., M.D. Peters, and D.R. Kinder. 1982. "Experimental Demonstrations of the 'Not-So-Minimal' Consequences of Television News Programs." *American Political Science Review* 76, no. 4: 848–58.

Iyengar, S. and A. Simon. 1993. "News Coverage of the Gulf Crisis and Public Opinion: A Study of Agenda-setting, Priming, and Framing." *Communication Research* 20, no. 3: 365–83.

Jacobs, L.R. and B.I. Page. 2005. "Who Influences US Foreign Policy?" *American Political Science Review* 99, no. 1: 107–23.

Klüver, H. 2009. "Measuring Interest Group Influence Using Quantitative Text Analysis." *European Union Politics* 10, no. 4: 1–15.

Klüver, H. 2013. *Lobbying in the European Union: Interest Groups, Lobbying Coalitions, and Policy Change.* Oxford: Oxford University Press.

Kudrna, Z., S. Bailer, S. Târlea, and F. Wasserfallen. 2019. "Worlds of Domestic Preference Formation in EMU Politics." *Unpublished paper.*

Lehner, T. and F. Wasserfallen. 2019. "Political Conflict in the Reform of the Eurozone." *European Union Politics* 20, no. 1: 45–64.

Lelieveldt, H. and S. Princen. 2015. *The Politics of the European Union.* Cambridge: Cambridge University Press.

Lundgren, M., S. Bailer, L.M. Dellmuth, J. Tallberg, and S. Târlea. 2019. "Bargaining Success in the Reform of the Eurozone." *European Union Politics* 20, no. 1: 65–88.

Lundgren, M., J. Tallberg, and F. Wasserfallen. 2020. "Supranational Influence in the European Union: The Differentiated Impact of the European Commission." *Unpublished paper.*

Marks, G. and M. Steenbergen. 2002. "Understanding Political Contestation in the European Union." *Comparative Political Studies* 35, no. 8: 879–92.

Mearsheimer, J. J. and S.M. Walt. 2006. "The Israel Lobby and US Foreign Policy." *Middle East Policy* 13, no. 3: 29–87.

Miklin, E. 2009. "Government Positions on the EU Services Directive in the Council: National Interests or Individual Ideological Preferences." *West European Politics* 32, no. 5: 943–62.

Moravcsik, A. 1993. "Preferences and Power in the European Community: A Liberal Intergovernmentalist Approach." *Journal of Common Market Studies* 31, no. 4: 473–524.

Moravcsik, A. 1997. "Taking Preferences Seriously: A Liberal Theory of International Politics." *International Organization* 51, no. 4: 513–53.

Moravcsik, A. 1999. "A New Statecraft? Supranational Entrepreneurship and International Cooperation." *International Organization* 53, no. 2: 267–306.

Moravcsik, A. 2018. "Preferences, Power and Institutions in 21st-century Europe." *Journal of Common Market Studies* 56, no. 7: 1648–74.

Nugent, N. and M. Rhinard. 2016. "Is the European Commission Really in Decline?" *Journal of Common Market Studies* 54, no. 5: 1199–215.

Puntscher Riekmann, S. and D. Wydra. 2013. "Representation in the European State of Emergency: Parliaments against Governments?" *Journal of European Integration* 35, no. 5: 565–82.

Sandholtz, W. and A. Stone Sweet. 1998. *European Integration and Supranational Governance.* Oxford: Oxford University Press.

Schlipphak, B. and O. Treib. 2017. "Playing the Blame Game on Brussels: The Domestic Political Effects of EU Interventions Against Democratic Backsliding." *Journal of European Public Policy* 24, no. 3: 352–65.

Schneider, G. and K. Baltz. 2003. "The Power of Specialization: How Interest Groups Influence EU Legislation." *Rivista di Politica Economica* 93, no. 1: 253–83.

Schneider, G. and K. Baltz. 2005. "Domesticated Eurocrats: Bureaucratic Discretion in the Legislative Pre-Negotiations of the European Union." *Acta Politica* 40, no 1: 1–27.

Schneider, G., D. Finke, and K. Baltz. 2007. "With a Little Help From the State: Interest Intermediation in the Domestic Pre-negotiations of EU Legislation." *Journal of European Public Policy* 14, no. 3: 444–59.

Tallberg, J. 2002. "Delegation to Supranational Institutions: Why, How, and with What Consequences?" *West European Politics* 25, no. 1: 23–46.

Târlea, S. and S. Bailer. 2020. "Technocratic Cabinets in European Negotiations." In *The Technocratic Challenge to Democracy,* edited by E. Bertsou and D. Caramani. Milton Park and New York: Routledge.

Târlea, S., S. Bailer, H. Degner, L.M. Dellmuth, D. Leuffen, M. Lundgren, J. Tallberg, and F. Wasserfallen. 2019. "Explaining Governmental Preferences on Economic and Monetary Union Reform." *European Union Politics* 20, no. 1: 24–44.

Wasserfallen, F. 2014. "Political and Economic Integration in the EU: The Case of Failed Tax Harmonization." *Journal of Common Market Studies* 52, no. 2: 420–35.

Wasserfallen, F., D. Leuffen, Z. Kudrna, and H. Degner. 2019. "Analysing European Union Decision-Making During the Eurozone Crisis with New Data." *European Union Politics* 20, no. 1: 3–23.

Winzen, T. 2012. "National Parliamentary Control of European Union Affairs: A Cross-national and Longitudinal Comparison." *West European Politics* 35, no. 3: 657–72.

Winzen, T., R. de Ruiter, and J. Rocabert. 2018. "Is Parliamentary Attention to the EU Strongest When it is Needed the Most? National Parliaments and the Selective Debate of EU Policies." *European Union Politics* 19, no. 3: 481–501.

Chapter 3

Preference Formation During the Eurozone Crisis

A Cross-National Comparison

Sabine Saurugger, Thomas Warren, Hussein Kassim, Shaun P. Hargreaves Heap, and Scott James

3.1 INTRODUCTION

How political actors develop their preferences is one of the central questions in politics. In the EU policy process, preferences are considered the main element that explains the direction, scope and tempo of integration. The 2010–2015 Eurozone Crisis put these processes under extreme duress. Starting from a broad political science understanding of 'preferences' and 'preference formation', this chapter first considers a range of conceptual approaches. While liberal intergovernmentalism (LI) conceptualises national preference formation as an independent first step in the integration process, other theoretical frameworks have developed more integrated explanations. These approaches have made it possible to treat preference formation as a complex pluridimensional process, whether in the EU or other contemporary political systems, be they centralised or federalist.

Nonetheless, even scholars who use the LI terminology are critical of how it theorises the process of preference formation and how it conceptualises preferences, and especially how preferences are linked to positions. In other words, although the value of 'preferences' and 'preference formation' as concepts is widely recognised, there are often deep reservations about how they are defined and deployed by LI (Kassim, Saurugger and Puetter, 2020). The aim of this chapter is to reflect critically on the usefulness of 'preferences' and 'preference formation' for understanding how actors aggregate views in EU decision-making. Rather than using the definitions offered by LI as a starting point, this introduction undertakes a broader review of, in particular, how preference formation has been conceptualised and theorised.

Empirically, the chapter uses the experience of preference formation in three member states – France, the UK and Germany – to question the compartmentalised understanding of preference formation, which, according to LI, takes place within a strictly domestic context. It draws on the *EMU Choices* dataset, composed of responses obtained in semi-structured interviews conducted with high-level civil servants in the then twenty-seven member states. The comparison, moreover, draws on preference formation in four areas: the initial Greek rescue; the capitalisation of the European Stability Mechanism; the legal nature of the debt brake enshrined with the Treaty on Stability, Coordination and Governance (TSCG); and reverse qualified majority voting. The value of the comparison is that it compares four different types of policy at different phases of the crisis, which not only provides a broader empirical basis but reduces the risk of extrapolating generalisations on the basis of a single atypical case.

3.2 THEORETICAL APPROACHES TO PREFERENCE FORMATION

Preference and preference formation are central aspects of politics: how and why actors establish what they want, and how to pursue what they want, is crucial in understanding how political and social systems function. Political science sub-disciplines, including international relations, political economy and public policies, address these questions from diverse epistemological perspectives.

Preference Formation in Rational Choice Approaches

Rational choice approaches in international relations and foreign policy-making equate state preferences with 'interests' and consider them as fixed. Political outcomes result from the pursuit by relevant actors of their material interests defined more or less directly in terms of the economic benefits that will ensue from cooperation (Frieden and Rogowski 1998; Rogowski 1989). The main value of this approach is it highlights the material interests that underpin many political outcomes.

As with other conceptual frameworks, rational choice approaches are not uniform. In the literature on foreign economic policymaking, some scholars argue that national preferences largely reflect either the country's major economic interests (Rogowski 1989 ; Frieden 1991; Moravcsik 1993, 1998), while others emphasise the policy preferences of central decision makers (e.g., Krasner 1978; Gilpin 1981). Realism goes further and claims that state preferences may not reflect domestic preferences at all. Here, the state is seen as an autonomous actor, which often pursues an independent goal of promoting the general wellbeing of society as a whole.

LI differentiates itself by its insistence that state preferences are not fixed. For analytical clarity, this chapter will take LI's stylised interpretation of preference formation as per Moravcsik (1993, 1998) as a starting point and will also discuss the revised version, in which LI is considerably broadened in response to the in-depth critiques made of the approach since its initial appearance (Moravcsik and Schimmelfennig 2019, 66–7). It contends that state preferences are derived from domestic and transnational social pressures (Moravcsik 1993, 1998, 2018; Schimmelfennig 2014, 2015). National preferences, according to Moravcsik (1998, 24), are an 'ordered and weighted set of values placed on future substantive outcomes' driven by geopolitical and economic interests in relation to European integration. Preferences are 'not simply a particular set of policy goals but a set of underlying national objectives independent of any particular international negotiation' (Moravcsik 1998, 20).

This definition is important in two ways. First, it asserts that preference formation is a domestic process that is independent of any specific interaction at the EU level, and thus implies a temporal sequencing. Second, the definition allows for an analytical differentiation between 'preference formation' and 'position taking' (see also Degner and Leuffen 2017, 3). The latter occurs during intergovernmental exchanges and may be the result of compromises, side payments or the formation of alternative coalitions (Moravcsik 1998, 64–6). LI assumes that preferences are enduring. This allows for cases where preferences and government positions differ, even at the cost of tension with LI's more general claim that preferences are socially constructed. The analytical distinction is rooted in the conviction that domestic preference formation is more fundamental than, and prior to, position taking.

According to LI, national decision makers, elites and economic interest groups are central to national preference formation, and preferences are the basis for negotiation in interstate bargaining. The preferences of socio-economic actors in particular affect those of political actors, and vice versa, in forming domestic preferences in interstate bargaining. These interactions introduce an institutional aspect (Milner 1997). Due to their electoral interests, the policy preferences of political actors can be affected by interest groups, or socio-economic actors' policy preferences might be influenced by those of political actors, because of the latter's agenda-setting power and advantages in accessing primary information (Kim 2016, 293).

Criticisms of these approaches are based on the context in which national preference formation took place during the EMU crisis. This chapter argues that the core conceptualisation of preference formation as state-based, unidirectional and unchanged by the regime (Moravscik 1993, 1995) is erroneous. Preference formation takes place in a multi-level, interdependent system, such as the European Union, which does not allow for the insulation of domestic processes that LI stipulates, the sequencing between preference formation and intergovernmental bargaining it proposes, or the separation of preferences and positions on which it insists. Traditional understandings of preference formation as a domestic process of interest aggregation and competition, independently of external pressures and influences, therefore, require revision (Csehi and Puetter 2017).

The release of 'preferences' and 'preference formation' from their moorings in LI makes it possible to address a broader series of questions when analysing state preference formation in the EU: Do institutional constraints at the domestic level lead to different types of preference formation? Is preference formation a strictly domestic process or do other debates in other member states – beyond those that concern globalisation (Moravcsik and Schimmelfennig 2019, 67) – also influence national preference formation? And, finally, how do feedback loops and the empowering and disempowering of certain actor groups influence preference formation in the EU?

Institutionalist Approaches

While intergovernmentalism in its broadest sense understands actors defining state preferences in particular as political elites, experts, economic interest groups and even parties, *institutionalists* define these domestic variables in a much broader sense. In an older tradition, the institutions in question refer to the formal legal structure of political systems, particularly the 'public laws that concern formal governmental organisations' (Eckstein 1979, 2), as well 'the ideas embedded in them' (see Rhodes 2011, 142, 145). In this approach, practised by, among others, Duverger, Finer and Eckstein, 'legal rules and procedures are the basic independent variable, and the functioning and fate of democracies, the dependent variable' (Rhodes 2011, 145). Moreover, these 'rules are prescriptions; that is, behaviour occurs because of a particular rule. For example, local authorities limit local spending and taxes because they know the central government . . . can impose a legal ceiling or even directly run the local authority' (Rhodes 2011, 145). Furthermore, the old institutionalism is comparative, historical and inductive (Rhodes 2011, 146).

While the old institutionalism focuses on formal institutions and their interaction in political systems, the new institutionalism has a quite different understanding of 'institutions' and a very different research programme.

Whether or not the new institutionalism in its main variants is interpreted as a reaction to behaviouralism (March and Olsen 1984, Hall and Taylor 1996, Adcock et al. 2006), its exponents criticise 'old institutionalism' as 'atheoretical' (Thelen and Steinmo 1992, 2). Though the various new institutionalisms adopt different methodological approaches, they share what Rhodes (2011, 144) describes as a 'modernist-empiricist epistemology', where 'institutions such as legislatures, constitutions and civil services are treated as discrete objects that can be compared, measured and classified'.

How does consideration of the differences between the old and new institutionalisms relate to preferences and preference formation? For the older tradition, examination of the respective powers and responsibilities of political institutions would be the starting point for understanding national preferences or positions. Variants of the new institutionalism have different starting points. Rational choice institutionalism takes individual preferences for optimising material advantage as a given and holds that self-interest can explain the selection, persistence and decline of particular institutions. Historial, sociological as well as discursive institutionalisms consider preferences as socially constructed and argue that they are open to change (Hall 1993; Berman 1998; Blyth 2002; Schmidt 2013; Carstensen and Schmidt 2015). Preferences are based not only on expected or feared consequences but also on what actors perceive as contextually appropriate behaviour (March and Olsen 1989; Finnemore 1993).

Turning to preference formation, institutionalist approaches would not argue that it is the rational interests of actors aiming for economic benefits that contribute to national preference formation, but that domestic structures crucially determine how preferences are shaped. Domestic institutions structure standard operating procedures that are nationally specific. Hence, whereas LI assumes that pluralist processes of interest mobilisation take place in national settings that are broadly similar or interchangeable, this chapter argues that national political systems differ in ways that are consequential to the formation of preferences. Institutions are nation- or state-specific. Even on minimal Schattschneiderian grounds, cross-national differences in the arrangement of institutions that constitute the political system will inevitably affect preference formation, since institutions mobilise bias in different ways. This institutionalist insight fundamentally challenges the pluralist premises of the LI model, which assumes that interests mobilise spontaneously and compete against each other, and that institutions have no influence in either process.

Although not usually considered an institutionalist approach, the *new intergovernmentalism* (NI) (Bickerton et al. 2015; Puetter 2014) directly addresses the notion of preference formation in ways that are important for institutionalists. NI's core argument that member states are reluctant to empower supranational institutions, notably the Commission, along the lines of the classic community method, but instead pursue further integration by delegating decision-making authority to intergovernmental bodies, is compatible with the institutionalist notion of preference formation as an embedded process. NI also highlights member state preferences for a particular institutional form of EU-level decision-making, such as the European Council and the Eurogroup, where member governments themselves take collective executive decisions on the most sensitive political issues, including bailouts or corrective prescriptions for domestic economic policy. In the absence of legislative decision-making, unanimity among member governments becomes the main decision-making rule and consensus seeking, the guiding norm. Policy deliberation takes place between executive actors who undertake simultaneously all key policy functions: formulation, adoption and implementation. The institutional configurations at EU level are aligned with member state administrations – politicians and top civil servants – in a transnational policymaking environment.

Moreover, for NI, preference formation has become an inherently transnational process involving governmental elites. The administrative underpinnings of this deliberative intergovernmentalism (Puetter 2012) contradict the assertion that preferences are forged in a domestic setting independently of and prior to their advancement at the EU level. Rather, it implies an amalgamation. NI also assumes that frictions in representative democracy and changes to the role of specific societal actors, such as trade union and organised business, are key sources of the relative autonomy of governments determining their own preferences on EU integration. Although this autonomy comes with the caveat that governments constantly worry about their legitimation, governments are able to make standalone inputs in EU politics (Bickerton et al. 2015, 714).

The implications for preference formation in the EU as a multi-level system are significant. The possibility, discussed above, that the preferences presented and defended by member governments at the EU level are shaped in some measure by EU institutional norms is an insight consistent with the new institutionalism. But there are also others. Institutionalist perspectives can inform a better understanding of the range of domestic factors that influence preference formation. Although front and centre in discussion of the national coordination of EU policy (Kassim et al. 2000, 2001), where the central question is what position governments adopt and defend in policy negotiations at the EU level, domestic institutions rarely feature in explanations of preference formation. They are notably absent – or appear only in the most abstract form – in the liberal intergovernmentalist framework. Yet the respective roles played by governments and legislatures, by national and sub-national authorities, and by central banks are not only likely to be relevant to how a state positions itself in EU discussions but as a key variable in accounting for cross-national differences. In this context, the old institutionalism may, in the absence from LI of a convincing account of interest mobilisation, interest aggregation or theory of the state, provide important insights into how, within the domestic setting, governmental institutions arrive at a decision on what position to defend at the EU level (Dimitrakopoulos and Kassim 2004). This leads to the chapter's first argument: that the *domestic institutional framework* in which preference formation occurs is a key factor in preference formation and that institutional frameworks vary cross-nationally.

More broadly, conceiving the EU as a multi-level system rather than a forum for 'hard bargaining' between governments, as LI proposes, creates the possibility that pressure for what counts as 'appropriate behaviour' may derive from a wide range of sources. They include other member state governments, or even public opinion in other member states – *horizontal factors* – within the EU setting. Expertise, ideology and technical knowledge may also be important. In this context, McNamara (1998) shows that fundamental developments in economic theory played a key role in shifting the preferences of EU member states towards EMU. Paradigms or appropriate behaviour can be understood as beliefs about cause-and-effect relationships, which are central to establishing fundamental preferences over specific courses of action: 'Causal beliefs are rooted in theories about how the world works, but the credibility of those theories turns on our experience of using them. As experience shifts, so do our causal beliefs' (Hall 2005, 152).

Finally, the *circular or feedback dimension* of preference formation also needs to be taken into account. Rather than the outcome of a distinctively government-centric process, preferences are likely to be formed by different political actors at different levels of the EU's multi-level polity who relate to each other in different ways. As Marks et al. (1996) reminded us more than two decades ago, governments are only one among many political actors, albeit the most powerful. Studies of preference formation need also to pay attention to associated problems. The scholarly literature on EU governance distinguishes between input, output and throughput legitimacy (Schmidt 2013), for example, but there are also cases where political actors or societal interests do not form or articulate a particular preference on a particular issue. In addition, although broader scepticism towards or approval of EU integration in itself does not amount to a clearly articulated preference for a particular policy option, it, nevertheless, may become an input in preference formation of other actors, as NI flags (see also Schirm 2018). Research on preference formation, therefore, needs to place a premium on detailed process tracing and avoid broad generalisations about patterns of preference aggregation that have not been submitted to the empirical test.

3.3 NATIONAL PREFERENCE CONSTRUCTION IN THREE MEMBER STATES

A comparison between France, the UK and Germany illustrates the importance of these three factors for understanding national preference formation. The *domestic institutional setting*, the *horizontal* and the *circular dimension* of preference formation explain to what extent, when and why member state preferences change during negotiations.

Domestic Institutional Setting

The domestic institutional setting is, as pointed out by LI, a factor of stability. In France, economic governance is dominated by a small number of civil servants and representatives of the banking sector, who form tight policy networks. These networks draw together officials from parts of the French administration responsible for European economic governance (the head of the Treasury and the economic advisers of the French presidency) and the chairs of the six largest banks (Crédit Agricole, BNP Paribas, Société Générale, Crédit Mutuel, Caisse d'épargne and Banque Populaire). The governor of the Banque de France and the finance minister are also involved in the network. The members of these networks come from similar social backgrounds and may have been beneficiaries of the revolving doors between high-level French administration and private banks (Fontan and Saurugger 2020).

This cultural and professional homogeneity has been a powerful asset for French governments, making it possible to bridge the public and private sectors (Jabko and Massoc 2012). Indeed, some scholars argue that French economic governance is *post-dirigiste* precisely because these networks align the interests of private banks and the state (Clift 2012; Clift and Woll 2012). Hence, French economic policymaking is characterised by close cooperation between banks and government, which fits well with LI, because interests between state and non-state interests are not confrontational (Schelkle 2012; Grossman and Woll 2014).

The interviews undertaken as part of *EMU Choices* show that these tightly drawn French networks were crucial in reducing the uncertainty caused by the crisis. Two sets of players were central in the formation of French preferences during the negotiations on the first Greek bailout (February–June 2010): the top civil servants at the Treasury and the French President's cabinet. French civil servants made a deal with French banks, based on the Vienna initiative template[1], as early as February 2010. While the banks committed to keeping Greek debt on their balance-sheets in order to stabilise its value, the French government affirmed that Greek debt would not be restructured and that it would provide liquidity to the Greek government to ensure payment of coupons to its creditors (interview 2). In parallel, the president's cabinet persuaded Nicolas Sarkozy that a common rescue fund was needed to stabilise the French banking system and alleviate systemic risks within the Eurozone (interview 2). Furthermore, members of the Treasury attend meetings of the Eurogroup and, even more importantly, its preparatory councils, the Economic and Financial Committee (EFC) and the Eurogroup Working Group subcommittee. As a result of their participation in these meetings, officials from the Treasury were able to collect information about the crisis before other French civil servants, giving it strong leverage in interministerial interactions.

In short, the first Greek rescue was aligned with French preferences (financial assistance without debt restructuring). Insider reports underline that French officials were at the forefront of the resistance against the option of debt restructuring because of French bank exposure during the Spring 2010 meetings, involving agents from the International Monetary Fund (IMF), the Commission, the European Central Bank and European member state governments (Blustein 2015, 9–11).

By contrast, German officials were divided between competing poles: a Conservative CDU minister of finance and liberal FDP minister of economy. On the question of financial assistance to Greece, Chancellor Angela Merkel strongly emphasised on European stability, but the FDP preferred to see Greece go bankrupt. Indeed, a grassroots movement within the party forced an internal referendum to let party members decide its position, which weakened FDP influence within the coalition (Zimmerman 2014). The issue became salient when the legislature clashed with the executive. As in France, decisions on EMU issues were mainly driven by the executive, but in Germany, parliament fought for a greater say, which the German Federal Constitutional Court granted to it, even if the parliament then failed to translate its powers into action. At the same time, a number of CDU and FDP MPs tried for their own political purposes to mobilise public opinion against support for Greece.

Debate on other issues was less intense. The debt brake was not controversial as it had been envisaged by the German constitution. On ESM lending capacity, all sides wanted to keep the German contribution small. And, on the issue of reverse qualified majority voting, internal debate was limited as the government was in favour and saw it as a tool for making other member states more compliant.

Preference formation in Germany was largely driven by the executive, but other actors also tried to exert influence. In the case of the Greek bailout, Germany's largest tabloid, *Bild,* ran a campaign to push Greece out of the euro. Also, although only three complaints were filed (Saurugger and

Fontan 2019), the German Federal Constitutional Court loomed as a potential veto player and was invoked by various actors to pressure for certain policies.

The UK government's autonomy, not only from domestic interests but also from shared norms or a solidarity with its European partners, was evident throughout the Eurozone Crisis. London's prime concern when the crisis broke was that the UK should not be financially liable for what it believed was 'the Eurozone's business' (interview 11), associated with a 'flawed project' (interview 10). Limiting the 'contagion' was also a concern.

In the case of the first Greek bailout, the UK was opposed, but conceded reluctantly, under intense US pressure, to a Commission-administered bailout. The UK would, in any case, have been outvoted (Darling 2011, 301).[2] The decision was made within a small circle of actors – essentially, Alasdair Darling, chancellor of the outgoing Labour government, who had consulted George Osborne, his Conservative successor. At this point, there was only limited awareness among politicians or the public about the issue.

Two future crisis episodes confirm the importance of the domestic institutional setting for UK government preference formation. By the time the European Council announced the ESM in October 2010, backbench opposition had become more vocal. Prime Minister Cameron's focus was on securing a quid pro quo in exchange for the political risk he was taking in supporting a stabilisation fund for the Eurozone. However, attempts by the UK government to secure EU budget reform or use the proposed treaty amendment to transfer powers to the member states gained no traction (interview 10). Holding firm until late in the negotiations, Cameron managed to secure an understanding that once the ESM was in place, the EFSM would no longer be used for bailouts of Eurozone member states.

The following year, when Germany demanded a treaty change to adopt what became known as the 'Fiscal Compact', the UK again saw an opportunity to redefine the UK's relationship with the EU. Under pressure from an increasingly hostile parliament, the actions that followed were decided in No 10, in secret (Miller 2012). At the December 2011 European Council, Cameron tried to secure a veto over future financial regulation to protect the City of London. When this was rejected, Cameron used the UK veto over treaty reform, forcing other EU leaders along a path which led to agreement on the Fiscal Compact in the form of an intergovernmental treaty.

Horizontal Dimension of Preference Formation

According to the LI framework, the formation of national preferences is independent from international bargaining. However, findings from *EMU Choices* strongly challenge this assumption. National preferences in relation to the Eurozone do not emerge from a domestic setting prior to or in isolation from other member states or the wider EU system.

In the case of France, preferences are influenced by the Eurozone's institutional structure, even before the process of intergovernmental bargaining begins. French officials internalise Germany's red lines in evolving their own policy preferences. Moreover, the iterative nested games that characterise the policy process in the Eurozone present 'windows of opportunity' to French negotiators to advance their positions or protect their red lines.

French preference formation is historically intertwined with German preferences, even if scholars disagree on the respective influence exerted by the two countries and their impact on policy. Some scholars argue that Germany is a 'reluctant hegemon', which played a 'waiting game' during the crisis (Bulmer 2014; Matthijs 2016). From this perspective, France is merely another Eurozone country affected by German strategies, without any influence on them (Clift and Ryner 2014; Lux 2018). Others claim that Germany's preferences coincided with those of France (Rothacher 2015; Degner and Leuffen 2017; Schild 2013), and that the policies of the post-crisis Eurozone were shaped mainly by Paris, which managed to 'invert the rules of the Maastricht Treaty' (Rothacher 2015). A third group of scholars suggests that post-crisis policies stem from a compromise between the two largest Eurozone countries, whose preferences gradually converged (Schmidt and Crespy 2014; Van Esch 2014).

Our results show that while French policy space was constrained by German preferences, Eurozone reform outcomes did not contradict French red lines. When Eurozone countries set up the ESM, French negotiators would have preferred a higher capitalisation than the €500 billion agreed, but did not request it because German negotiators would not agree. In the words of one Treasury official: 'French negotiators internalise German preferences when building their policy positions. We would not propose a policy blueprint that would go against German red lines' (interview 3).

French negotiators are constantly updated on the evolution of German red lines via constant telephone contact with their German counterparts (interviews 1, 2, 4). The openness of the contact is the result of frequent meetings and a shared willingness to strike policy compromises, within parameters set by red lines laid down in Berlin and Paris. According to an official at Franrep, 'these channels of communication are open in order to find a proper balance between the logic of conditionality and debt mutualisation' (interview 4). These findings are consistent with the main tenets of NI, which emphasise that a transnational policymaking environment increases consensus-seeking behaviour, but challenge LI's insistence on the insulation of domestic preference formation.

Second, even though the relationship with Germany constrains its policy options, France remains a key player in Eurozone negotiations.

Luxembourgish, Dutch and Belgian EFC members argue that the Eurozone policy space is shaped by three groups: Germany and other ordo-liberal countries (Finland, the Netherlands), France and Southern Europe countries (Spain, Italy) and the supranational institutions (European Commission, European Central Bank). Other countries follow the positions defined by one of the nodal points or try to build bridges between them (interviews 5, 6, 7), either because they do not have the same levels of expertise or the structural power to define their policy positions autonomously.

France also relies on iterative nested games within the Eurozone to ensure that policy compromises do not drift too far from its preferences. French negotiators underlined, for example, that the capitalisation of the ESM was less important than its use, which, following French pressure, was enlarged to cover bank bailouts (interviews 2 and 3). Similarly, France was able to agree to the 'debt brake' in the Treaty on Stability, Coordination and Governance in the Economic and Monetary Union (TSCG), first because French negotiators did not breach their red lines. The government wanted to avoid a constitutional change. Instead, France built an alliance with Italy to push forward the idea that the implementation of an organic law was sufficient commitment (interview 2).

Second, French negotiators received something in exchange. The TSCG was part of a Franco–German compromise in which Germany accepted the creation of a Banking Union, while France agreed on stricter fiscal rules (interview 3). According to one EFC member, the ECB was also part of the compromise:

> The decisive moment was the ECB measures. When the ECB announced its long-term refinancing operations in late 2011, the implicit counterpart for these measures was the implementation of the TSCG. This is how it has been "sold" to French Members of the Parliament.
>
> (interview 2)

Even when a decision runs counter to the preferences of Paris, French negotiators have been able to ensure that the final agreement includes appropriate caveats. France was able to agree the RQMV reform[3], for example, once it was convinced that it was vague enough to avoid automatic sanctions and that the European Commission would not have enough political power to initiate procedures (interviews 1 and 2).

In summary, French domestic preferences are formed in a multi-level and iterative nested game. Germany and France form an asymmetrical relationship in which French negotiators 'internalise' German preferences, although the opposite might not be true. However, France is sufficiently powerful to exploit the policy spaces offered by the iterative nested games in the

Eurozone and manages to strike policy compromises that do not transgress its red lines. Open lines of communication and high levels of trust between EFC members help member states to formulate initial positions that are sufficiently close to allow policy compromise.

The German government is also influenced by horizontal debates outside its borders, if to a lesser extent. When, after the euro crisis outbreak in February 2010, Germany and the UK initially resisted the French proposal of a joint European rescue mechanism for Greece (Wasserfallen et al. 2017) in response to pressure by domestic elites (Degner and Leuffen, 2020), the German government finally coordinated with France on a regular basis in order to contain the divergence in preferences (Degner 2019). Chancellor Merkel justified her government's consent to a fiscal emergency mechanism, which de facto circumvented the 'no-bailout clause' of the EU treaties (Art. 125.1 TFEU), on the grounds that any other political strategy, especially 'Eurobonds', would be extremely costly. In the face of public opposition to financial aid (Bechtel et al. 2014), Merkel's government tried to make aid conditional on EMU reforms aiming at stronger economic coordination, ratification and compliance with the Fiscal Compact, and sanctions for euro members in breach of fiscal rules (Bulmer 2014, 1254). The French government, in turn, tried to cushion the German demand for fiscal rigidity with its concept of a *gouvernement économique*, which was popular among French political elites across the political spectrum (Howarth 2007). However, domestic pressures in Germany were stronger than horizontal and transnational institutional framing (Degner and Leuffen, 2020). Hence, one of the main reasons for abandoning opposition to the Greek rescue plan was the effect a Greek bankruptcy would have on the German as well as French banks (interview 1).

While preference formation in France was strongly influenced by the dynamics of multi-level EU negotiations, and in Germany less so, UK preferences emerged in the UK domestic setting largely independently of the EU negotiating forum in which they were presented and defended. On the first Greek bailout, Eurozone members, notably France, Germany and Spain, favoured a coordinated European response. In contrast, the UK, in alliance with Sweden, another non-Eurozone member, wanted the IMF to channel financial support to Greece, arguing that only the Fund had the necessary technical expertise (*Financial Times* 2010).

Some scholars contend that EU member states were moved by a common European interest to save the euro (Schimmelfennig 2015). However, no shared interest or norm was evident in UK decision-making, which was more strongly shaped by the domestic institutional and political context. During EU-level negotiations on the creation of the ESM, the UK government resorted to bilateral action after a series of impact assessments carried out by the Treasury revealed the exposure of UK banks to Eurozone sovereign debt: 'We were worried that fire from the burning house would spread to the UK', one senior official noted (interview 11). UK prime minister Cameron tried to persuade Chancellor Merkel and the President of the ECB, Jean-Claude Trichet, to take more decisive action to allow member states to borrow at more attractive rates, but he was left frustrated when both parties were reluctant to listen. Similarly, the following year when Cameron wielded the now infamous UK veto, the UK was left isolated and adrift in Europe (interview 7). In sharp contrast to France and Germany, preferences in the UK government were not modified by EU-level negotiations. The open communication that defined the relations of other member states were absent in the UK case, and there was no attempt to craft a compromise solution with other member states or to manage divergence.

The UK example offers, at best, mixed support for an LI reading. While consistent with LI to the extent that the preference formation took place in the domestic setting, distinct from the intergovernmental bargaining phase, the UK experience provides no evidence to support the pluralist model of preference formation at the heart of LI. The UK's position was determined by the PM and the chancellor, independently of mobilised societal interests. At the same time, the UK case challenges the consensus among critics of LI that preferences are explained by shared norms or orientations in the EU institutional context. Deliberative intergovernmentalism, NI and discursive institutionalism (Carstensen and Schmidt 2015) 'emphasise the central role of intergovernmental decision-making forums' and argue that deliberation and discourse are the mechanisms through which Europe exerts its effects. Yet the UK appears not to have been influenced by the interaction or shared norms.

It could be argued that empirical support for the approaches that emphasise shared norms and consensus-building arises out of selection bias due to their exclusive focus on Eurozone members. If shared norms are an effect of Eurozone membership, that could account for France's internalisation of German preferences. The UK's increasing exclusion from key intergovernmental decision-making forums during the crisis, including the monthly informal meetings between euro-area finance ministers, the Commission and the European Central Bank that had a key role in deliberating on the technical design of new post-crisis policy mechanisms and instruments (Puetter 2013) would be further evidence. Indeed, key reports on fiscal, banking, financial and political union over the long-term excluded the UK. The UK's exclusion certainly fuelled concerns in London about the consequences of differentiated integration, how Eurozone reforms would affect the single market, especially in financial services, and the status of Eurozone 'outs'.

There was also little evidence of shared values among Eurozone outsiders. Although Denmark, Sweden and Poland shared some of the UK's concerns about the peripheralisation of non-Eurozone members, the UK took a more extreme position, as Cameron's veto on the Fiscal Compact testifies. Other non-Eurozone members, some of whom saw themselves as possibly joining at some point in the future, were more concerned to maintain close relations with the Eurozone core (Adler-Nissen 2014).

Circular Dimension of Preference Formation

The circular dimension of preference formation, or the 'public backlash', has been forefronted in post-functionalist approaches (Hooghe and Marks 2009). Popular mobilisation on EU issues opens the door to electoral contestation. Crises are especially salient for citizens, leading to public demands for action, which create incentives for governments to align their positions with public opinion in order to avoid sanctioning at the polls. Public opinion is, therefore, a further pressure on member state preferences.

Findings from *EMU Choices*, however, show in France, but not Germany or the Netherlands, that neither domestic politics nor electoral outcomes has affected preference formation in any of the four policy issues under discussion.[4] The government has a high level of autonomy in EU matters, which was further extended in 2002 when the French political system became unambiguously presidential. In addition, the time pressures exerted by financial markets at times of crisis limit the number of actors involved.

These factors explain why French negotiators worked in isolation from political parties and other parts of the administration during the crisis management phase. In the weekend preceding the set-up of a €125 billion rescue fund to recapitalise the Spanish banking system in 2012, for example, two members of the Treasury were able to confirm France's financial commitment over the telephone to their EFC partners, without consulting other domestic players (interviews 1 and 2). In fact, French interviewees took the view that the Treasury and the President's office were the key players – indeed, the only players – and that other institutions, including parliament, and political actors, both the governing and opposition parties, played no part at this stage of the crisis (interviews 1, 2, 3, and 4). As well as the pressure to act quickly, they had the relevant specialist expertise.

Data from *EMU Choices* also shows the involvement of a small number of actors in countries such as France or the UK. The position of French officials, in particular, contrasted sharply with their counterparts in other countries, including Germany and the Netherlands, where EFC participants had to obtain a negotiation mandate from their parliaments and to report on the final agreements. These hearings were sometimes broadcast on national

TV (interview 5). In fact, though perhaps counter-intuitively, these controls gave leverage to Dutch and German EFC representatives. Tying their own hands proved to be a winning strategy during the Eurozone negotiations since it narrowed the set of feasible options in their favour (Putnam 1988). One French EFC member noted that some policy options, including Eurobonds, were not discussed in early 2010 because a German counterpart reported he did not have the negotiating mandate allowing him to participate in such talks (interview 2). When a French finance minister asked the *Assemblée Nationale* to convene ex-post hearings after the negotiations, however, members of parliaments declined the offer on the grounds that they did not have the time or technical skills (interview 4).

As the TSCG was the most politicised issue, it might be expected that feedback loops would be important. The 2012 French presidential election campaign suggested that this might be the case, as European issues were at the centre of the two main political parties' manifestos and speeches (Grossman and Sauger 2014; Crespy and Schmidt 2014). Francois Hollande pledged, for example, that, if he was elected, he would renegotiate the TSCG and put more emphasis on growth. Interviews conducted as part of *EMU Choices* show, however, that the Treasury played an important role in 'reminding [the newly elected French President of] previous French engagements [made under Sarkozy's presidency] to its EU partners' (interview 1). Despite intense pressure from his own party, which eventually led to the secession of a group of MPs (*Les frondeurs*[5]), President Hollande reneged on his campaign promise. One interviewee drew the conclusion that: 'On Eurozone issues, the Treasury matters more than the Socialist party' (interview 1). However, other factors were also at play, most notably the refusal of Germany to reopen negotiations on the issue (interview 3).

In Germany, findings from *EMU Choices* show that citizens and parliaments mattered in national preference formation on the Fiscal Compact and the ESM (Degner and Leuffen, 2020). In November 2011, shortly before Eurozone member states agreed upon the final versions of the ESM treaty and the Fiscal Compact Treaty, a poll found that 79 per cent of the German population rejected Eurobonds, with only 15 in favour. Similarly, 80 per cent of the population supported a special tax on banks in March 2010, and 58 per cent a FTT in January 2012. The interests of German business interests did not always align on these issues. In July 2011, for instance, the BDI reiterated its demand for a combined debt-restructuring and investment programme for Greece, which was unpopular measure among the German population (Degner and Leuffen, 2020).

The influence of public opinion and interest groups on the formation of UK preferences varied between stages of the crisis. During the early phase, the decision about whether the UK should support a Commission proposal to support Greece in May 2010 was taken by a small coterie of individuals. Other ministers were not aware of the issue, parliament had shown little interest, and domestic interests had not mobilised (interviews 8, 9). In this instance, the prime minister and chancellor acted on their judgement on what course of action would best serve the UK's economic interests. At other times, the government acted with a specific constituency in mind. This was most clearly the case where the UK sought to defend the interests of the City of London over the threat of the euro-area caucusing; although, it was also reflected in the constructive role played by the UK in the design of the Banking Union.

More generally, the opinion of parliament became increasingly important over this period. In particular, backbench Conservative MPs and Eurosceptic newspapers, such as the *Daily Mail*, *Daily Telegraph* and *The Sun*, opposed the use of UK taxpayers' money to support the Eurozone. The transition in May 2010 from a Labour government led by Gordon Brown, with Alastair Darling as chancellor, that had met the financial and economic crisis with reflationary and expansionist policies to a Conservative–Liberal Democrat coalition, headed by David Cameron, with George Osborne in Number 11, that took the view that the UK had successfully responded to the crisis and that championed austerity, was an important factor, but might have been more pronounced had it happened at a later stage of the Eurozone Crisis. Earlier on, short-term political calculations were at the forefront in driving the formation of UK preferences.

Summarising, LI has largely neglected the role of public opinion in European integration (Hobolt and Wratil 2015). Evidence has been provided here that the politicisation of the Eurozone Crisis across member states often created pressure on the preferences of member states; although, public opinion did not directly influence positions at the negotiating table. Another question is to what extent the positions of member states influenced the domestic public opinion in return. Of course, the continued influence of economic interest group positions on national preferences is entirely consistent with LI's baseline model. However, the above analysis has revealed the importance of domestic institutional context and horizontal forces on member state preferences during the Eurozone Crisis.

3.4 CONCLUSION

This chapter has considered how preference formation has been conceptualised and theorised by the main analytical approaches. The financial and economic crisis only reaffirmed the fundamental importance to EU studies of understanding how preferences are formed, and it has prompted an intense debate on how they are best explained (Csehi and Puetter 2017).

Although the LI framework remains the 'baseline' for many scholars, its account of preference formation is hotly contested by critics from a range of theoretical perspectives, even though the process remains at the centre of their enquiries.

Drawing on data from *EMU Choices*, this chapter has explored preference formation in three key member states – France, Germany and the UK – in relation to four policy issues during the Eurozone Crisis, chosen from different phases, since the crisis was a process not an event. The comparative strategy has been highly instructive. The findings challenge the traditional LI understanding of preference formation, as a pluralistic process of interest mobilisation, aggregation and competition that takes place in an exclusively domestic setting, prior to and independently of EU-level negotiations and developments in other member states.

In reporting the involvement of very different actors, influences and processes in each of the three country cases, the chapters demonstrate the importance of three important variables that are absent from the LI account: domestic institutional frames that privilege some institutions and actors, while limiting the access of others; horizontal factors, arising from member states interdependence within the EU; and circular feedback mechanisms, which are significant in some countries on some issues. It also, thereby, underscores the very different national conditions under which preference formation takes place, repudiating the assumption that domestic political space is somehow homogeneous across the EU. This is an important finding that opens up many possible avenues for future enquiry. It makes also clear that member states, despite defending their national preferences loudly at the European level as their own, have already been influenced by other member states even before bargaining begins at the EU level.

However, member states do not share norms in all cases. Hence, the limited purchase of shared norms, which the comparative analysis also reveals, has implications for future research. While critics of LI have converged on explanations that emphasise shared norms and suggest that the latter arise from interaction within a particular institutional setting, the UK seems to have been resistant to these pressures or effects. This suggest that the conditions under which norms are communicated and inculcated need to be carefully specified and submitted to the empirical test.

NOTES

1. The Vienna initiative is a private–public framework where large banks and supranational institutions coordinate to maintain bank exposure in East, Central and Southeast Europe.

2. The meeting took place following Labour's defeat in the 2010 elections, but before the Conservative–Liberal Democratic coalition took office. Alasdair Darling consulted the incoming Chancellor, George Osborne, warning him that the UK could not mobilise a blocking coalition.

3. The RQMV proposal was put forward by the Benelux countries to avoid breaches of the Stability and Growth Pact by large member states, as it occurred in 2005 (interviews 5, 6, 7). It is not part of a specific Franco–German deal.

4. For a different view, see Rothacher 2015, Crespy and Schmidt 2014.

5. *Les frondeurs* did not leave the Socialist Party or the parliamentary group, but their opposition to Hollande was reported widely in the media (Clift and McDaniel 2017, 408).

REFERENCES

Adcock, R., M. Bevir, and S.C. Stimson. 2007. "Historicizing New Institutionalism." In *Modern Political Science: Anglo-American Exchanges Since 1880*, edited by R. Adcock, M. Bevir, and S. C. Stimson, 259–89. Princeton: Oxford University Press.

Adler-Nissen, R. 2014. *Opting Out of the European Union: Diplomacy, Sovereignty and European Integration*. Cambridge: Cambridge University Press.

Bickerton, C. J., D. Hodson, and U. Puetter. 2015. *The New Intergovernmentalism: States and Supranational Actors in the Post-Maastricht Era*. Oxford: Oxford University Press.

Blustein, P. 2015. "Laid Low: The IMF, the Euro Zone and the First Rescue of Greece." *CIGI Papers Series* 61, April: 1–21.

Blyth, M. 2002. *Great Transformations: Economic Ideas and Institutional Change in the Twentieth Century*. Cambridge: Cambridge University Press.

Bulmer, S. 2014. "Germany and the Eurozone Crisis: Between Hegemony and Domestic Politics." *West European Politics* 37, no. 6: 1244–63.

Carstensen, M. B. and V.A. Schmidt. 2016. "Power Through, Over and In Ideas: Conceptualizing Ideational Power in Discursive Institutionalism." *Journal of European Public Policy* 23, no. 3: 318–37.

Clift, B. 2012. "Comparative Capitalisms, Ideational Political Economy and French Post-dirigiste Responses to the Global Financial Crisis." *New Political Economy* 17, no. 5: 565–90.

Clift, B. 2013. "Le Changement? French Socialism, the 2012 Presidential Election and the Politics of Economic Credibility Amidst the Eurozone Crisis." *Parliamentary affairs* 66, no. 1: 106–23.

Clift, B. and S. McDaniel. 2017. "Is this Crisis of French Socialism Different? Hollande, the Rise of Macron, and the Reconfiguration of the Left in the 2017 Presidential and Parliamentary Elections." *Modern and Contemporary France* 25, no. 4: 403–15.

Clift, B. and C. Woll. 2012. "Economic Patriotism: Reinventing Control Over Open Markets." *Journal of European Public Policy* 19, no. 3: 307–23.

Clift, B. and M. Ryner. 2014. "Joined at the Hip, But Pulling apart? Franco-German Relations, the Eurozone Crisis and the Politics of Austerity." *French Politics* 12, no. 2: 136–63.

Crespy, A. and V. Schmidt. 2014. "The Clash of Titans: France, Germany and the Discursive Double Game of EMU Reform." *Journal of European Public Policy* 21, no. 8: 1085–101.

Csehi, R. and U. Puetter. 2017. "Problematizing the Notion of Preference Formation in Research About the Euro Crisis." *EMU Choices Working Paper*, December, 2017. https://emuchoices.eu/wp-content/uploads/2017/12/2017_Working-Paper-Csehi-Puetter_Problematizing-the-notion-of-preference-formation-in-research-about-the-euro-crisis-.pdf.

Degner, H. 2016. "European Integration in Response to the 'Euro Crisis' 2010-2013." In *Crisis and Institutional Change in Regional Integration*, edited by S. Saurugger and F. Terpan, 23–40. London: Routledge.

Degner, H. 2018. "Crisis and Integration. Explaining Regional Integration in Europe in Response to Transboundary Crises 1993-2015." PhD diss., University of Konstanz.

Degner, H. 2019. "Public Attention, Governmental Bargaining, and Supranational Activism: Explaining European Integration in Response to Crises." *Journal of Common Market Studies* 57, no. 2: 242–59.

Degner, H. and D. Leuffen. 2017. "Powerful Engine or Quantité Negligeable? The Role of the Franco-German Couple during the Euro Crisis." *EMU Choices Working Paper*, November, 2017. https://emuchoices.eu/2017/11/06/degner-h-and-leuffen-d-2017-powerful-engine-or-quantite-negligeable-the-role-of-the-franco-german-couple-during-the-euro-crisis-emu-choices-working-paper-2017/.

Degner, H., & Leuffen, D. (2020). Crises and responsiveness: Analysing German preference formation during the Eurozone crisis. *Political Studies Review, 18*, no 4: 491-506.

Dimitrakopoulos, D. G. and H. Kassim. 2004. "Deciding the Future of the European Union: Preference Formation and Treaty Reform." *Comparative European Politics* 2, no. 3: 241–60.

Eckstein, H. 1979. "On the 'Science' of the State." *Daedalus* 108, no. 4: 1–20.

Finnemore, M. 1993. "International Organizations as Teachers of Norms: The United Nations Educational, Scientific, and Cultural Organization and Science Policy." *International organization* 47, no. 4: 565–97.

Fontan, C. 2013. "Frankenstein in Europe. The impact of the European Central Bank on the Management of the Eurozone Crisis." *Politique européenne* 42, no. 4: 22–45.

Fontan, C. and S. Saurugger. 2020. "Between a rock and a hard place: Preference formation in France during the Eurozone Crisis." *Political Studies Review, 18*, no 4: 507–524.

Frieden, J. A. 1991. "Invested Interests: The Politics of National Economic Policies in a World of Global Finance." *International Organization* 45, no. 4: 425–51.

Frieden, J. A. and R. Rogowski. 1996. "The Impact of the International Economy on National Policies: An Analytical Overview." In *Internationalization and domestic politics*, edited by R. O. Keohane, 25–47. Cambridge: Cambridge University Press.

Gilpin, R. 1981. *War and Change in World Politics*. Cambridge: Cambridge University Press.

Grossman, E. and N. Sauger. 2014. "'Un Président Normal'? Presidential (in-) Action and Unpopularity in the Wake of the Great Recession." *French Politics* 12, no. 2: 86–103.

Grossman, E. and C. Woll. 2014. "Saving the Banks: The Political Economy of Bailouts." *Comparative Political Studies* 47, no. 4: 574–600.

Hall, P. A. 1993. "Policy Paradigms, Social Learning, and the State: The Case of Economic Policymaking in Britain." *Comparative Politics* 25, no. 3: 275–96.

Hall, P. A. 2005. "Preference Formation as a Political Process: The Case of Monetary Union in Europe." In *Preferences and Situations,* edited by I. Katznelson and B.R. Weingast, 129–60. New York: Russell Sage Foundation.

Hall, P. A. 2012. "The Economics and Politics of the Euro Crisis." *German Politics* 21, no. 4: 355–71.

Hall, P.A. and R.C. Taylor. 1996. "Political Science and the Three New Institutionalisms." *Political Studies* 44, no. 5: 936–57.

Hooghe, L. and G. Marks. 2009. "A Postfunctionalist Theory of European Integration: From Permissive Consensus to Constraining Dissensus." *British Journal of Political Science* 39, no. 1: 1–23.

Howarth, D. J. 2007. "Making and Breaking the Rules: French Policy on EU 'Gouvernement Économique'." *Journal of European Public Policy* 14, no. 7: 1061–78.

Jabko, N., and E. Massoc. 2012. "French Capitalism Under Stress: How Nicolas Sarkozy Rescued the Banks." *Review of International Political Economy* 19, no. 4: 562–85.

Kassim, H., S. James, T. Warren, and S. Hargreaves Heap. (2020). "Preferences, Preference Formation and Position Taking in q Eurozone Out: Lessons from the United Kingdom." *Political Studies Review 18*, no. 4: 525–541.

Kassim, H., Saurugger, S., & Puetter, U. (2020). The Study of National Preference Formation in Times of the Euro Crisis and Beyond. *Political Studies Review, 18*, no. 4: 463–474.

Kassim, H., A. Menon, B.G. Peters, and V. Wright. 2000. *The National Coordination of EU Policy*. 2 Volumes. Oxford: Oxford University Press.

Kim, Min-hyung. 2016. "Theorizing National Preference Formation." *Cambridge Review of International Affairs* 29, no. 1: 290–308.

Krasner, S.D. 1978. *Defending the National Interest Raw Materials Investments and U.S. Foreign Policy*. Princeton: Princeton University Press.

Lux, J. 2018. "Disciplining Large Member States During the Crisis: Analyzing the Discursive Strategies of the EU and German Actors on France." *Critical Policy Studies* 12, no. 1: 44–60.

March J. G. and J.P. Olsen. 1989. *Rediscovering Institutions: The Organizational Basis of Politics*. New York: The Free Press.

March J. G. and J.P. Olsen. 1984. "The New Institutionalism: Organisational Factors in Political Life." *American Political Science Review* 78: 738–49.

Marks, G., L. Hooghe, and K. Blank. 1996. "European Integration from the 1980s: State-Centric v. Multi-level Governance." *Journal of Common Market Studies* 34, no. 3: 340–78.

Matthijs, M. 2016. "Powerful Rules Governing the Euro: The Perverse Logic of German Ideas." *Journal of European Public Policy* 23, no. 3: 375–91.

McNamara, K.R. 1998. *The Currency of Ideas: Monetary Politics in the European Union*. Ithaca, New York: Cornell University Press.

Milner, H.V. 1997. *Interests, Institutions, and Information: Domestic Politics and International Relations*. Princeton: Princeton University Press.

Moravcsik, A. 1998. *The Choice for Europe. Social Purpose and State Power from Messina to Maastricht*. Ithaca, New York: Cornell University Press.

Moravcsik, A. 1993. "Preferences and Power in the European Community: A Liberal Intergovernmentalist Approach." *Journal of Common Market Studies* 31, no. 4: 473–524.

Moravcsik, A. 1997. "Taking Preferences Seriously. A liberal Theory of International Politics." *International Organizations* 51, no. 4: 513–53.

Moravcsik, A. 2018. "Preferences, Power and Institutions in 21st-century Europe." *Journal of Common Market Studies* 56, no. 7: 1648–74.

Olender, M. 2012. "Germany's Euro Crisis: Preferences, Management, and Contingencies." *Review of European and Russian Affairs* 7, no. 2: 1–17.

Puetter, U. 2012. "Europe's Deliberative Intergovernmentalism - The Role of the Council and European Council in EU Economic Governance." *Journal of European Public Policy* 19, no. 2: 161–78.

Puetter, U. 2014. *The European Council and the Council. New Intergovernmentalism and Institutional Change*. Oxford: Oxford University Press.

Putnam, R. D. 1988. "Diplomacy and Domestic Politics: The Logic of Two-Level Games." *International Organisation* 42, no. 3: 427–60.

Höpner, M. and A. Schäfer. 2015. "Integration Among Unequals: How the Heterogeneity of European Varieties of Capitalism Shapes the Social and Democratic Potential of the EU." In *Routledge Handbook of European Politics*, edited by J.M. Magone, 725–45. London: Routledge.

Rhodes, R.A. 2011. "Old Institutionalisms." In *The Oxford Handbook of Political Institutions*, edited by S.A. Binder, R.A. Rhodes, and B.A. Rockman. Oxford: Oxford University Press.

Rogowski, R. 1989. *Commerce and Coalitions: How Trade Affects Domestic Political Alignments*. Princeton, Princeton University Press.

Rothacher, J. U. 2015. "How Domestic Politics Shaped the French Government's Position During the Euro Crisis." *European Politics and Society* 16, no. 2: 256–79.

Saurugger, S. and C. Fontan. 2019. "The Judicialization of EMU Politics: Resistances to the EU's New Economic Governance Mechanisms at the Domestic Level." *European Journal of Political Research* 58, no. 4: 1066–87.

Schelkle, Waltraud. 2012. "Policymaking in Hard Times: French and German Responses to Economic Crisis in the Euro Area." In *Coping With Crisis: Government Reactions to the Great Recession*, edited by J. Pontusson and N. Bermeo, 130–62. New York: Russell Sage Foundation.

Schimmelfennig, F. 2014. "European Integration in the Euro Crisis: The Limits of Postfunctionalism." *Journal of European Integration* 36, no. 3: 321–37.

Schimmelfennig, F. 2015. "Liberal Intergovernmentalism and the Euro Area Crisis." *Journal of European Public Policy* 22, no. 2: 177–95.

Schirm, S.A. 2018. "Societal Foundations of Governmental Preference Formation in the Eurozone Crisis." *European Politics and Society* 19, no. 1: 63–78.

Schmidt, V.A. 2013. "Democracy and Legitimacy in the European Union Revisited: Input, Output and 'Throughput'." *Political Studies* 61, no. 1: 2–22.

Thelen, K. and S. Steinmo. 1992. "Introduction." In *Structuring Politics: Historical Institutionalism in Comparative Analysis*, editedy by S. Steinmo, K. Thelen, K. and F. Longstreth. Cambridge: Cambridge University Press.

Van Esch, F. A. 2014. "Exploring the Keynesian–Ordoliberal Divide. Flexibility and Convergence in French and German Leaders' Economic Ideas During the Euro-Crisis." *Journal of Contemporary European Studies* 22, no. 3: 288–302.

Wasserfallen, F., D. Leuffen, Z. Kudrna, and H. Degner. 2019. "Analysing European Union Decision-Making During the Eurozone Crisis with New Data." *European Union Politics* 20, no. 1: 3–23.

Zimmermann, H. 2014. "A Grand Coalition for the Euro: The Second Merkel Cabinet, the Euro crisis and the Elections of 2013." *German Politics* 23, no. 4: 322–36.

List of Interviews Quoted in the Chapter

Interview 1, French Treasury/EFC member, Paris, October 2017
Interview 2, French Treasury/EFC member, Paris, October 2017
Interview 3, French Treasury, Paris, November 2017
Interview 4, French Permanent Representation, Brussels, December 2017
Interview 5, Dutch Ministry of Finance/EFC member, Brussels, November 2017
Interview 6, Belgiam Ministry of Finance/EFC member, Brussels, November 2017
Interview 7, Luxembourgish Treasury/EFC member, Luxembourg, October 2017
Interview 8, former UK Treasury official, Brussels, November 2016
Interview 9, former UK Treasury official, London, November 2016
Interview 10, former UK minister, London, February 2017
Interview 11, former official, UK Permanent Representative, October 2017

Chapter 4

Southern Europe and the Eurozone Crisis Negotiations

Preference Formation and Contested Issues

Leonardo Morlino and Cecilia Emma Sottilotta

4.1 INTRODUCTION

With the exception of Malta, South European countries were severely hit by the Great Recession, that is, the financial and economic crisis that started in 2008 and brought about profound consequences such as the emergence of protest parties (Morlino and Raniolo 2017), the growth of Euroscepticism (Verney 2017), unprecedented levels of political instability (Bosco and Verney 2016), a shrinking of the welfare state (e.g. Wulfgramm, Bieber, and Leibfried 2016) and higher socio-economic inequality (Dolvik and Martin 2015). A number of measures, including financial assistance schemes and a strengthening of the Stability and Growth Pact (SGP) rules, were introduced at the EU level in response to the crisis during the 2011–2013 period, after being negotiated and approved in a relatively short time. Although they imposed budget constraints bound to seriously impair their ability to respond to voters' demands, South European governments voted in favour of those reforms. In the most debt-ridden countries, citizen dissatisfaction contributed to a delegitimisation of traditional leaders and parties and paved the way for the emergence of new actors who were successfully mobilised by new political entrepreneurs exploiting the potential of protest spread across society (Morlino and Raniolo 2017, 58). In sum, constraints to government responsiveness in Southern Europe created a favourable environment for populist movements and parties to flourish (Morlino 2011, 211).

The question arising from these circumstances is: what were the determinants of preference formation for South European countries during the Eurozone Crisis negotiations? More specifically, why did those governments decide to be unresponsive to their public opinion while other Eurozone governments were much more responsive (on this point, see for instance The Economist 2012; Degner and Leuffen 2019)?

In order to answer this question, we focus on two contested issues that emerged during the negotiations: the introduction and lending capacity of the European Stability Mechanism (ESM) and the constitutionalisation of a balanced budget as requested by the Treaty on Stability, Coordination and Governance in the Economic and Monetary Union (TSCG) also referred to as the 'Fiscal Compact'. Although these are not the only issues to surface during the negotiations, they are, nonetheless, among the most salient ones as they epitomise the member states' preferences on fundamental questions which are still debated today. While comparative analyses of the crisis in the sub-region usually focus on the largest South European countries only (see, e.g., Hassel 2014; Matthijs 2014; Morlino and Raniolo 2017), this chapter also includes Malta and Cyprus, therefore providing a complete and more nuanced picture of the responses to the crisis.

Section 4.2 illustrates the theoretical framework and data used to tackle our research question. Section 4.3 contains a synthetic account of the unfolding of the crisis in the countries considered. Section 4.4 shows that, with the exception of Malta, decision-making in South European countries was mostly characterised by a low level of involvement of the parliaments and, consequently, the decisions were made by a limited number of individuals with a very low level of parliamentary opposition engagement. Sections 4.5 and 4.6 discuss national preference formation in the countries considered vis-à-vis two relevant issues emerged during the negotiations. Section 4.7 concludes, highlighting convergences and divergences in preference formation across South European member states.

4.2 DATA AND THEORETICAL FRAMEWORK

Liberal intergovernmentalism (LI), especially in its most recent reformulation (see Moravcsik and Schimmelfennig 2019) has been widely applied to answer questions relating to preference formation in the process of European integration. At the same time, it should be noted that in its original formulation Moravcsik (1998, 18) envisaged European integration as

> a series of rational choices made by national leaders. Choices responded to constraints and opportunities stemming from the issue of specific societal (largely economic) interests of powerful domestic constituents, the relative power of states stemming from asymmetrical interdependence and the role of institutions in bolstering the credibility of interstate commitments.

Moreover, it should also be considered that limitations of LI are defined by the assumption of a decision-making context, in which information is rich, transaction costs are low, the substantive consequences of integration choices are relatively intense and predictable. Moreover, LI explains policymaking best in issue areas where social preferences are relatively certain and well defined (Moravcsik and Schimmelfennig 2019, 82). Such limitations are indeed evident when it comes to explaining preference formation in South European countries during the Eurozone Crisis. In fact, as further illustrated in the chapter, in five out of the six cases analysed (the exception being Malta), our data show that the 'substantive consequences of integration choices' and especially the long-term implications of those choices in terms of (further) constraints on domestic budgets were not fully appreciated nor thoroughly debated by parliaments, nor did public opinion play a significant role as a constraint on the decision-makers. This ties in with the arguments put forward by Puetter (2014) and Csehi and Puetter (2017): during the crisis, member states' preferences were inherently connected to their EU-level interactions rather than being the result of a purely domestic deliberation process. In the context of the Eurozone Crisis negotiations, South European decision-makers committed to policies that would inevitably constrain their future ability to respond to citizens' demands. To explain this choice, this chapter engages with LIs, combining it with cues derived from the literature on responsiveness (on the relevance of connecting these two literatures, see Degner and Leuffen 2019).

The crisis exposed the gap between 'responsive' and 'responsible' government, which has become wider and more difficult to handle for EU member states' policymakers due to fundamental changes in the context in which they operate: rather than responding to just one principal, that is the electorate, they are influenced and constrained by a number of supranational players, including European institutions. If we define responsiveness as a government's ability to satisfy the demands of the electorate in terms of policies, services and distribution of material as well as symbolic goods (Eulau and Karps 1977), it is evident that the sheer amount of resources available to satisfy those demands represents a key constraint for the government itself. In other words, pursuing fiscal discipline, especially at a time of economic crisis, inevitably affects a government's ability to meet the needs of its populace, engendering a loss of autonomy that conjures the idea of a 'democracy without choice' (Ruiz-Rufino and Alonso 2017). The question nonetheless is: to what extent, in the context of the Eurozone Crisis negotiations, was the gap between responsiveness and responsibility due to a perceived lack of viable alternatives? Is it possible, for instance, to exclude any genuine commitment to neoliberal policies by South European governments, considering that the role played by different ideological stances has been used to explain differences in the introduction of reforms under austerity in Southern Europe (Perez and Rhodes 2015; Picot and Tassinari 2017)? After all, to mention just one case, during the negotiation of the Maastricht Treaty, Italian policymakers believed that the only way to carry through meaningful reforms was to anchor Italy to the process of economic and monetary integration by accepting an external constraint on domestic policymaking, the *vincolo esterno* (Dyson and Featherstone 1999; Quaglia 2004; Sottilotta 2019). In that case, committing to external obligation was a way to break the vicious circle of clientelism that had characterised Italy's post-war political economy and push forward much-needed structural reforms. Of course, although Southern Europe is often presented as a relatively homogeneous group of debt-ridden countries (Hall 2012; Schild 2013; Schimmelfennig 2015; Copelovitch et al. 2016), decision-makers from each and every country cannot be expected to have assessed the situation in the exact same way, hence the relevance of a cross-country comparison. To shed light on how South European incumbent governments interpreted each situation, official documents were relied on as well as research conducted in the framework of the Horizon 2020 Project 'The Choice for Europe since Maastricht' (*EMU Choices*)[1], based on thirty-four in-depth elite interviews with former negotiators and policymakers such as ministers of finance, high-ranking officials from ministries of finance, central bank governors, members of parliament and former European and/or foreign affairs ministers from the countries considered. The names and exact positions of the interviewees are subject to strict confidentiality as stipulated in the Data Management Policy and Ethics Clearance of the *EMU Choices* project.

The interviews used for this study are a subset of a larger dataset, EMU Formation (EMUf), created by the *EMU Choices* research consortium and relying on 141 structured interviews conducted in the 28 EU member states between May 2016 and March 2017. The dataset includes influence scores for twenty-three different domestic and external actors that were potentially involved in the formation of national preferences vis-à-vis reforms in fiscal and economic governance of the EMU that were debated between 2010 and 2015. The codes used for citing interviews in this chapter (e.g. 'ITA1') are a simplified version of those used by the EMU Formation dataset created by the *EMU Choices* consortium.[2]

4.3 THE UNFOLDING OF THE CRISIS: SIX DIFFERENT STORIES

To better illustrate the background against which the decisions under scrutiny were made, it is useful to recall how the crisis unfolded in each of the countries considered. Figure 4.1 provides a visual representation of the different evolutions of the crisis in Southern Europe as reflected in the spread between Germany's ten-year government bonds' yields and those of the countries considered, highlighting the dramatic reaction of financial markets to economic and political developments in all South European countries, again with the exception of Malta. Table 4.1 provides a synthetic overview of the most immediate causes for the crisis in each country, emphasising each country's key vulnerabilities, while table 4.2 summarises the changes of government, including information on whether the new cabinet was the result of a general election, a snap election or a government reshuffle.

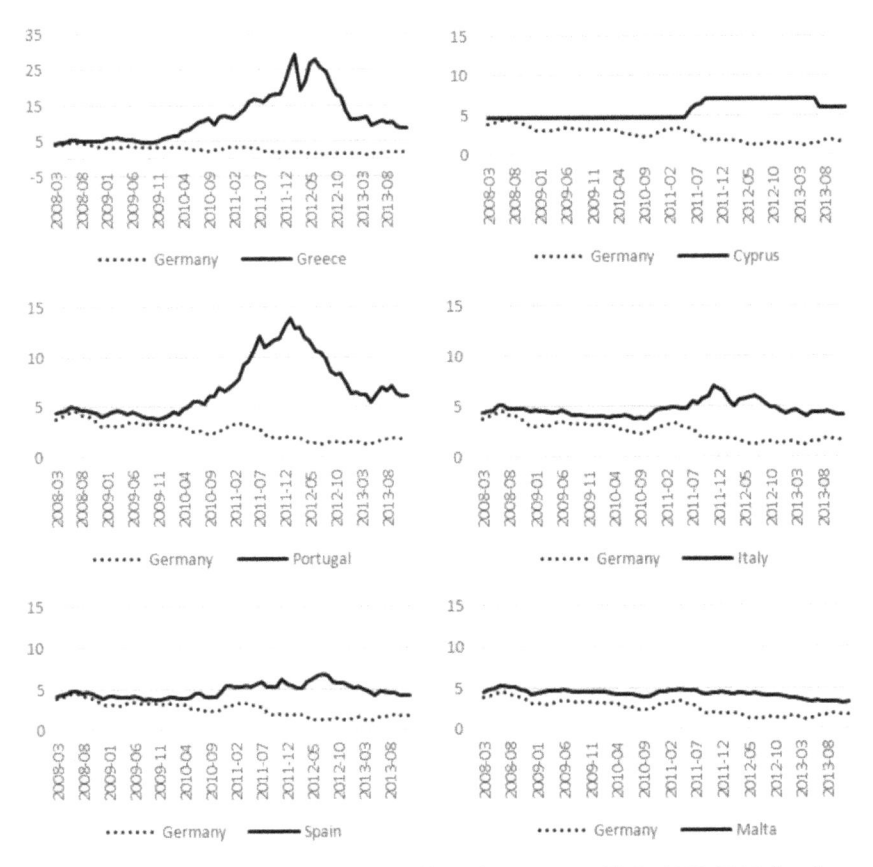

Figure 4.1 Long-Term Interest Rates (%) on Government Debt 2008–2013. Southern Europe vs. Germany. Note: There is a difference in scale in the representation of the spread between Greek and German sovereign bonds vis-à-vis the other five South European countries. Source: Authors' elaboration based on data by the OECD and the European Central Bank (2018).

Table 4.1 A Comparative Overview of the Causes of the Crisis in Southern Europe

Country	Vulnerability
Greece	Loose budgetary policy
	Excessive borrowing
	Poor accounting practices
Portugal	Economic stagnation
	Low productivity in the decade prior to the crisis
Spain	Construction bubble fed by easy credit and subsequent shock
	Inadequate banking sector regulation
Italy	Economic stagnation
	High public debt
	Low productivity in the decade prior to the crisis
	Poor quality of regulation
Cyprus	Sluggish growth since 2008
	High levels of government spending since 2008
	Hypertrophic banking sector
	Overexposure of the banking system to Greek financial institutions

As for Greece, a tradition of poor accounting practices combined with excessive government borrowing created the conditions for the 'perfect debt storm' to happen in the second half of 2009, once the financial crisis started in the United States spread to European markets. Accordingly, the Greek one is the only crisis genuinely linked to budgetary policy (Stein 2011).[3] Facing bankruptcy and the risk of a forced 'Grexit', as reflected in skyrocketing government bonds' yields (see figure 4.1), the centre-left government, led by George Papandreou, sought and obtained a first bailout worth €110 billion in May 2010; a new short-lived cabinet led by technocrat Lucas Papademos took over in November 2011 and finalised the negotiation of a second bailout package in February 2012; political instability led to new elections in May and June 2012, resulting in a coalition government led by centre-right leader Antonis Samaras. In spite of their divergences in ideological orientation, all Greek cabinets proved to be willing to commit the country to painful structural reforms to avert the risk of an imminent exit from the Eurozone.

After Greece and Ireland, Portugal became the third Eurozone country to apply for a bailout. In the face of increasing pressure from financial markets and the looming risk of a default, in September 2010 the Portuguese government announced the introduction of austerity measures, including a freeze on state pensions, cuts in public sector wages and a rise in value-added tax (Wise 2010). On 23 March 2011, the Portuguese parliament rejected a further government-sponsored austerity package, a move that triggered the resignation of the prime minister and paved the way for a snap election the following June. Amid political turbulence and after losing access to financial markets, in April

Table 4.2 Changes of Government in Southern Europe (2008–2015)

Country	2008	2009	2010	2011	2012	2013	2014	2015
Cyprus	Christofias, AKEL, Feb.24 (presidential election)			DISY, May 22 (general election)		Anastasiades, DISY,		
Greece	(Karamanlis, ND, since March 2004)			Papademos, independ, Nov.11 (government reshuffle)	Pikrammenos independ, May 16 (snap election) Samaras, ND, June 20 (constitutionally dictated snap election)			Tsipras, Syriza, Jan.26 (snap election)
Italy	Berlusconi, PdL, May 8 (general election)			Monti, independ, Nov. 16 (government reshuffle)		Letta, PD, April 28 (general election)	Renzi, PD, Feb. 22	
Malta	Gonzi, NP, March 10 (general election)					Muscat, LP, March 11 (general election)		
Spain	(Zapatero, PSOE, since April 2004)			Rajoy, PP, Dec. 21 (snap election)				

2011 Portugal applied for a bailout. In May, a memorandum of understanding (MoU) listing the conditions for disbursement of financial support was signed by the Portuguese government and the 'Troika' (the European Commission, the European Central Bank and the International Monetary Fund). The need to minimise the risk of a forced withdrawal from the Eurozone prompted the Portuguese executive to completely align with the Troika's requests in terms of policies of structural adjustment (POR5, POR6), to the point of appearing 'more German than the Germans' (Lisi and Ramalhete 2019).

Also, for Spain, the enabling conditions for the crisis cannot be directly found in the lack of fiscal discipline. Unlike Greece and Italy, in the years before 2008, Spain did not engage in excessive borrowing. Moreover, unlike Portugal, its GDP growth rate in the five years before the crisis hit was between 3 and 4 per cent, and consequently the public debt was on a negative trend (World Bank 2015). The distinctive feature of the Spanish case is the construction bubble fed by easy credit. When the bubble burst in 2011, the shock spread to the rest of the economy through virtually all existing channels: tightening financial conditions slowed down demand for housing, which pushed down house prices and had a negative impact on employment and on the banking sector (especially the regional *cajas*). These circumstances led to the June 2012 decision by the Spanish government, led by Mariano Rajoy, to accept (up to) €100 billion as a 'loan' from the ESM to recapitalise the country's ailing banks. A formal MoU was avoided; nonetheless, in order to receive financial support and contain the risk of a financial meltdown, the Spanish government accepted harsh conditions, with nationalised banks, cutting jobs and imposing losses on their creditor bondholders.

Italy's situation when the crisis erupted was yet different from that of the other South European countries. For most of its recent history, Italy has been characterised by high public debt. Nonetheless, the country has also always had a good reputation in terms of debt management. Italy's Achilles heel was (and to a large extent still is) to be found in the poor quality of regulation, a business climate that discourages foreign and domestic investment, low labour productivity, corruption, all factors that account for 'two lost decades' of economic growth in the country, as the IMF recently put it (Miglierini 2016).

Just as in Greece, the crisis resulted in political fallout and governmental instability. As fear of contagion – epitomised by skyrocketing ten-year-bonds' yields – soared at the end of 2011[4], Silvio Berlusconi's government was replaced by a technocratic cabinet led by former EU commissioner Mario Monti. Italy is the only country which managed to avoid any direct Troika involvement; although, this can be explained as the effect of an 'internalisation' of a 'Troika-type' oversight via the installation of Monti's technocratic cabinet (Sacchi 2015; Moschella 2017; Morlino and Sottilotta 2017). The perceived risk of a possible default and a humiliating 'Italexit' from the 'euro club' produced a substantial alignment of all domestic actors in supporting government-sponsored austerity measures whose possible long-term fallout in terms of unresponsiveness was essentially overlooked by decision-makers.

While, until 2007, Cyprus' fiscal position was quite sound, by May 2011, the country's situation had dramatically changed. The roots of Cyprus' financial difficulties can be found in sluggish growth since the beginning of the financial crisis in 2008 and increases in government spending after the Cypriot Communist party took over in the same year, complemented by the overexposure of the Cypriot banking system to Greek financial institutions. On 26 October 2011, the European Council agreed to

> a significantly higher capital ratio of nine per cent of the highest quality capital and after accounting for market valuation of sovereign debt exposures, both as of 30 September 2011, to create a temporary buffer . . . to be attained by 30 June 2012.
>
> (European Council 2011)

At that point, a feedback loop in Cyprus was unavoidable: while it was extremely hard for Cypriot banks to raise the necessary capital, it would have been equally difficult if not impossible for the government to bail out the banks. On June 30, 2011, Cyprus lost access to international financial markets. As seen in figure 4.1, the curve becomes flat as a result of capital controls.

Unwilling to initiate a structural adjustment programme under the aegis of the Troika, in the second half of 2011, the Cypriot government bought itself some time by securing a €2.5 billion emergency loan from Russia, which was, nonetheless, only meant to offer support for the country's budget deficit and excluded any recapitalisation of the country's banking sector (Katsourides 2014, 52). In June 2012, a downgrade of the Cypriot sovereign by all of the 'Big Three' credit rating agencies made government debt not eligible as collateral for borrowing from the euro system. As the risk of exiting the Eurozone materialised, the government finally asked for assistance for its banking system (The Economist 2013). In March 2013, the newly elected conservative president agreed to a bailout deal worth €10 billion and envisaging a haircut to bank deposits under the threat that the ECB would stop providing liquidity to the Cypriot banking system (The Economist 2013). A MoU between Cyprus and the Troika was finally signed in April 2013. The Cypriot government eventually acknowledged that the cost of exiting the Eurozone would be much higher than that of adopting harsh austerity measures (Katsourides 2019).

Unlike the other five South European countries, Malta was virtually untouched by the sovereign debt crisis in the Eurozone. In spite of the relevant role played by financial services in the Maltese economy, due to generally good levels of capitalisation, the relatively low level of external exposure of domestic banks (Azzopardi 2009, 105) and overall economic stability, in the 2013 Maltese general elections, the issues of competence and credibility of the rival parties dominated and there was the success of the Labour Party led by Joseph Muscat (Fenech 2013).

Unsurprisingly, as summarised in table 4.2, in those five countries, the structural adjustment measures required as a result of negotiations with supranational institutions interfered with the domestic electoral cycle, with the sole exception of Cyprus, which has a fixed-term parliament. Greece, Spain and Portugal all held snap elections in the 2009 to 2012 period, while Italy experienced a government reshuffle.

4.4 SOUTH EUROPEAN CHOICES: WHO WERE THE DECISION-MAKERS?

In light of the rapid unfolding of events during the most acute phase of the crisis (2010 to 2013) and the limited financial resources available to the EU, it is not surprising that, in general, the member states' governments played a central role even after the activation of EU mechanisms. Indeed, especially at the height of the crisis, an intergovernmental logic prevailed, with member states pursuing their national interest through bargaining and deliberation within the Council of the EU (Bickerton et al. 2015) while the Commission and the European Parliament were effectively marginalised (see, e.g., Fabbrini 2013).

As illustrated in the next section, the South European countries reacted differently to the contested issues that emerged during the Eurozone Crisis negotiations, but one common aspect was the concentration of decision-making in the hands of the executive, typically the prime minister and the minister of finance.

For our purposes, it is important to consider the relative influence exerted by domestic actors involved in the processes of deliberation and national preference formation. The case of Greece is once again emblematic. Since its inception (1974), the Third Greek Republic has typically been characterised by a dominant role of the prime minister, which can be ascribed to institutional factors such as the strong agenda-setting power of the government and the fact that the ratification of the budget follows a procedure whereby MPs are not allowed to propose amendments (Alexopoulos 2015). In this vein, as stressed by Sotiropolous (2015), the poor record of the Greek Parliamentary Committee on European Affairs is one of the factors explaining the lack of elaborated positions on policy issues arising in the EU public sphere. It is, therefore, unsurprising that the parliament's involvement in the formation of preferences during the Eurozone Crisis negotiations was marginal, to the point that crucial policy documents, such as the May 2010 MoU, were 'presented to the Greek Parliament as a piece of information rather than an issue to be debated in the Parliament's plenum' (Sotiropoulos 2019).

Matters of institutional architecture also explain a similar pattern of executive dominance in Portugal, where a process of governmentalisation of mainstream parties took place whereby the ministerial selection of experts and non-partisan members of the professional elites reinforced leaders' power over the cabinet (Lisi 2015, 59–60). Such asymmetry is all the more evident when it comes to parliamentary control over the government on European issues. In particular, in the context of the implementation of Portugal's MoU, after the June 2011 general election, the centrality of the government was underpinned by new Prime Minister Passos Coelho's decision to appoint technocratic, non-partisan ministers in key austerity-stricken portfolios, namely economy, healthcare and education. This move was dictated by Passos Coelho's preference for ministers displaying ideological proximity with him and substantial alignment with the preferences expressed by Germany on EU matters (Moury and Standring 2017), and de facto enhanced the new ministers' accountability vis-à-vis the prime minister (Lisi and Ramalhete 2019).

For Spain, a high level of centralisation in decision-making could also be observed, and in parallel, the number of actors involved in the process was strikingly small. This is epitomised, for instance, by the fact that the constitutionalising of the debt brake, which required the amendment of Article 135 of the Spanish Constitution, was not publicly debated, but rather agreed upon behind closed doors by the ruling PSOE and the main opposition party, the PP, and then submitted to the parliament, resorting to a swift procedure and without confirmatory referendum (Gutiérrez Calvo and Muñoz 2011). A low level of involvement of the parliament and other relevant social and political actors also characterised the negotiation by the PP-led government of the MoU for the financial support Spain received, albeit avoiding a formal bailout supervised by the Troika. In fact, the Spanish MoU was kept secret until its existence was disclosed by the Dutch Ministry of Economics in the context of a parliamentary debate on the Spanish bailout (Navarro 2012). This secrecy engendered strong criticism of the Spanish government when it became clear that financial support was indeed conditional to relevant reforms in the Spanish banking system (Coller Porta and Ramírez de Luis 2019).

Italy is another case in which the parliament was essentially marginalised throughout the Eurozone Crisis negotiations. On the one hand, in the period considered, Italy was struggling to regain credibility in the eyes of international markets and of the other EU countries, Germany in particular. Such a 'national emergency' explains why, as mentioned above, there was very little debate and virtually no opposition to the constitutionalisation of the debt brake, while austerity measures, such as a reform of the pension system promoted by Monti's technocratic government, were approved by the parliament with a comfortable majority (Pogliotti and Rota Porta 2012). On the other hand, it should also be noticed that, as one interviewee put it, 'the engagement of the parliament . . . [was] very much dependent on the level of competence of MPs, which was not necessarily high, especially considering the technical nature of the issues discussed during the negotiations' (ITA.00). Unsurprisingly, the flow of information between government and parliament before the relevant meetings at the EU level was also typically poor.

As the crisis unfolded, doubts began to surface in Malta as to whether the crisis could eventually engulf the Maltese economy and whether joining the EMU had been a 'wise step' (Pace 2019, 109). The pattern of decision-making was very different there, with a long and intense debate taking place in the parliament throughout the Eurozone Crisis. Such parliamentary involvement is epitomised by the fact that debate on the Fiscal Compact lasted more than nine sittings over two legislatures, thanks to the role played by the opposition, which insisted that parliament retain control and have the final word on every measure adopted during the negotiations.

Issues of national sovereignty were key also to Cyprus, which shares with Malta the small state status and the British colonial legacy (Faustmann 2008). Nevertheless, compared to Malta, the management of the Eurozone Crisis negotiations was much more concentrated in the hands of the executive. While this concentration of power is partially due to institutional factors, considering the country's presidential system, the capability of the parliament to scrutinise the activity of the government was due to the lack of resources and know-how on both EU-related and budgetary issues (Katsourides 2019). This resonates with the thesis that the Cypriot elites' failure to foresee possible negative developments for Cyprus and the overexposed banking system was symptomatic of the dominance of local politics over sound economic policymaking in response to the crisis (Orphanides 2014, 15).

In sum, it is possible to conclude that Eurozone Crisis decision-making in Southern Europe was crucially influenced by governmental elites, which is in line with the results obtained by other researchers working on similar issues. Based on the EMU Positions (EMUp) dataset developed by the *EMU Choices* consortium (see Wasserfallen et al. 2018),[5] Tarlea et al. (2019) conducted a quantitative analysis of a larger number of contested issues, including those analysed here. In explaining preference formation during the Eurozone Crisis negotiations, they emphasise the lack of correlation between public opinion and governments' negotiating positions and, therefore, confirm that decisions were actually made by a relatively small group of individuals, as suggested above; moreover, they show that governmental preferences were mainly influenced by the conditions of the domestic financial sector: in the presence of a highly exposed financial sector, the government was more willing to accept expansions in the prerogatives of European institutions. As already mentioned, it is important to keep in mind that, in broader terms, none of the governments of the six South European members states had intented to leave the monetary union. It is well known that the status quo was largely preferred to any 'exit' scenario as the Eurozone was recognised as a necessary shield against market speculations.

The prospect of a systemic crisis engendered by the uncontrolled default of one of the larger South European member states was perceived as a serious threat even in the case of Malta, whose membership in the Eurozone was not directly at stake. This preference for the status quo, complemented by the fear of markets' punishment, also implied that no leader could openly express benign interest in the problems that were afflicting other South European countries. This explains why a Southern coalition never materialised, and any leader's initiatives in that sense were bound to be dismissed by other leaders. The lesson learnt by Italian Prime Minister Romano Prodi, who in September 1996 unsuccessfully tried to convince Spanish Prime Minister Aznar to coalesce with him to soften the Maastricht parameters for admission into the Eurozone, stands as the last attempt to create a South European coalition on these issues. In order to further explore preference formation in the countries considered, it is necessary to look at some of the contested issues that emerged during the Eurozone Crisis negotiations and unpack the positions adopted by the countries considered. This required a focus on the introduction and the lending capacity of the ESM and the constitutionalising of a balanced budget as requested by the Fiscal Compact.

4.5 THE CREATION AND SIZE OF THE ESM

A key measure negotiated during the crisis was the introduction of a permanent facility devoted to financial stability, the ESM, to replace the pre-existing temporary schemes (see table 4.3). During the negotiations, an important issue emerged with regard to the possibility to endow the ESM with firepower greater than €500 billion, a figure that was considered adequate by some member states, such as Germany, Austria and Finland. Looking at the preferences expressed by the South European countries, it is possible once again to notice that while (although with different nuances) there was an overall preference for the ESM to be larger, the six South European member states did not coalesce and eventually accepted the €500 billion figure. The European Council decided to establish the ESM in March 2011.

Greece: Although the Greek government would have preferred a larger ESM, at that point, Greece was already under the yoke of the first MoU,

Table 4.3 Preferences of South European Member States on Creation and Size of the ESM

Member State	National Preference
Cyprus	The government was in favour of the creation of the ESM with as big firepower as possible (CYP04, CYP05).
Greece	The government wanted the ESM to be larger than 500 billion euro (HEL1, HEL2, HEL4).
Italy	The government wanted the ESM to be larger than 500 billion euro (ITA1).
Malta	The government wanted the ESM to be as large as necessary (MLT4, MLT5).
	The government wanted the ESM to be as large as possible, but knew that a size greater than 500 billion euros would be difficult to achieve (POR2, POR4, POR5).

which meant it was relegated to a role of policymaker, and it had no other option than to support the establishment of a new institution which, in the future, would be at the disposal of Eurozone countries facing major economic difficulties (Sotiropoulos 2019).

Spain: The socialist government led by José Luis Rodríguez Zapatero was very much in favour of the introduction of an ESM whose lending capacity be as large as possible, based on the belief that the introduction of a European mechanism would be a first step in the direction of fixing the incomplete architecture of the Eurozone. It should also be recalled that the financial situation of Spain was quickly deteriorating; therefore, the Spanish government participated in the ESM negotiation knowing it could possibly need to resort to it in the near future.

Portugal: The government maintained a low profile on this issue. In fact, it preferred the ESM to have a higher amount available for lending, the more, the better (Lisi and Ramalhete 2018). Nonetheless, the Socialist cabinet in power never expressed this preference openly, for fear of creating the perception of an imminent default among the financial markets and the other EU member states. This is essentially one of the reasons why most countries, especially those in a vulnerable situation, ended up bandwagoning with the larger EU member states instead of promoting the creation of a 'peripheral' coalition to advance an alternative agenda.

Italy: The issue of ESM size was not discussed publicly. However, all of the institutional actors involved, including the Bank of Italy, would have preferred a larger lending capacity, being well aware that €500 billion would have been perhaps enough to bail out a smaller member state but was certainly an inadequate amount to rescue larger member states, such as Italy and Spain. As for Portugal, what shaped the Italian government's position was the risk of creating the perception of an imminent default. The medium-to-long-term costs of the ESM were overlooked in the face of the short-term need to reassure the markets of Italy's creditworthiness.

Malta and Cyprus: As already stressed, Malta was not experiencing financial turbulences at the time of the ESM negotiations. Therefore, unsurprisingly, the domestic debate hinged on the necessity to provide the EU with a powerful tool to settle uncertainty and calm financial markets. The introduction of the ESM was essentially perceived by all political actors as a 'nasty medicine which you would have to swallow', as a former Maltese policymaker put it (MLT3), to mitigate systemic risks. There was virtually no domestic debate in Cyprus, where the government immediately lent its support for the creation of the ESM with the highest possible lending capacity: this measure was perceived as an indispensable tool to support Greece and other troubled EU member states (Katsourides 2019).

What emerges from the data is that the key priority informing the preferences expressed by the six countries considered was the need to reduce uncertainty and restore market stability. The apparently more neutral position of Portugal is also revealing insomuch as it lends further support to the explanation of why a Southern coalition did not emerge. As stated above, the government's top priority in that case was to avoid being seen in a situation of imminent financial default.

4.6 CONSTITUTIONALISING THE DEBT BRAKE

Another important issue that emerged during the negotiation of the Fiscal Compact was whether and how to institutionalise the commitment of member states to budget discipline by incorporating a debt brake into the domestic legal systems (see table 4.4). In the first two drafts of the treaty, reference was made to 'national binding provisions of a constitutional or equivalent nature', a vision that embodied the German preference while the final text (approved on 2 March 2012) included a 'softened' version of the original formula, referring to 'provisions of binding force and permanent character, preferably constitutional, that are guaranteed to be respected throughout the national budgetary processes' (Kreilinger 2012, 4). This issue was particularly sensitive not only because of its symbolic value but also because procedures of constitutional reform varied greatly across EU countries.

Greece: The Greek constitution is rigid, and a complex and lengthy procedure has to be set in motion to amend it. Moreover, enshrining the balanced budget rule into the constitution would have meant giving it high visibility at a time of social conflict and high political risk for the government. At the same time, due to its predicament, it was virtually impossible for Greece not

Table 4.4 Preferences of South European Member States on Constitutionalisation of the 'Debt Brake'

Member State	National Preference
Cyprus	The government opposed the constitutionalisation of the 'debt brake' and it was introduced via ordinary legislation (CYP2).
Greece	The government's position was constrained by constitutional impediments which did not allow it to pass anything more than an ordinary law (HEL1, HEL2, HEL3, HEL4). A constitutional reform would have also been politically difficult to achieve (HEL5).
Italy	The government strongly supported the constitutionalisation of the 'debt brake' as a way to show commitment vis-à-vis austerity (ITA0, ITA4).
Malta	The government was in favour of binding legislation but not necessarily constitutional in nature (MLT1, MLT3, MLT4, MLT5).
	The government was in favour of binding legislation but not necessarily constitutional in nature (POR1, POR3, POR4).
Spain	The government strongly supported the constitutionalisation of the 'debt brake' as a way to calm down financial markets (ESP1, ESP5).

to commit to the balanced budget rule, and the choice for the government was, once again, whether to secure immediate gains in continued financial support or a 'Grexit'. For these reasons, and also to preserve its sovereignty in matters of fiscal policy, Greece quickly ratified the treaty on 10 May 2012, but opted for an ordinary law without amending its constitution.

Spain: The positions adopted by Spain and Italy in this issue instead were quite similar and went in the direction of a swift incorporation of the balanced budgets rule in their constitutions. Both countries were in a very delicate situation as they desperately needed to reassure financial markets of their creditworthiness. In Spain, the incorporation of the debt brake rule into the constitution was decided within a week, without extensive debate and with the sole opposition of Socialist party leader Alfredo Pérez Rubalcaba (Coller Porta and Ramírez de Luis 2018).

Italy: The technocratic cabinet led by Mario Monti had been voted in office in November 2011 with the precise intent to reestablish Italy's credibility and avoid direct intervention by the Troika (Morlino and Sottilotta 2017). Therefore, and ironically for a country which before joining the monetary union had typically relied upon high deficits and competitive devaluations, in Italy there was virtually no opposition to the constitutionalising of the debt brake, except for two small opposition parties, that is, the Northern League and Italia dei Valori (see, e.g., Camera dei Deputati 2012). The debt brake was incorporated in the constitution in an exceptionally short time,[6] with the last vote taking place on 17 April 2012. Moreover, constitutional law 1/2012 containing the provision was passed swiftly by both chambers of the parliament with a two-thirds majority, which avoided the possibility of a confirmative referendum.

Portugal: In this case, the situation was more complex. Social Democratic Prime Minister Passos Coelho was clearly in favour of the constitutionalisation of the debt brake, a position strongly supported also by the minister of finance. Nonetheless, contrary positions were expressed by members of the Socialist Party. Eventually, on the eve of the European Council meeting that approved the final text of the Fiscal Compact, the government realised it would be impossible to achieve the two-third majority needed to enact the constitutional reform for incorporating the debt brake. This resulted in a compromise solution that is the incorporation of such a rule on 20 December 2012, via the amendment of the Budgetary Framework Law, which is a law of reinforced value vis-à-vis ordinary legislation.

Malta and Cyprus: As had happened for the other reforms, the Fiscal Compact was subject to intense debate in Malta. The treaty was submitted to Parliament on 5 March 2012, and approved fifteen months later – when it had already come into effect following its ratification by twelve Eurozone member states. As one interviewee noticed, the distinctive feature of that debate was that Malta's government and MPs conducted it assuming that whatever was decided would one day apply to Malta. On the contrary, in Cyprus, the debate over the Fiscal Compact took place mostly with reference to Greece, while little if any attention was given to the hypothesis that Cyprus may find itself in a difficult position. The treaty was ratified on 26 July 2012, and the debt brake rule was introduced via ordinary legislation (Katsourides 2019).

Decision-makers in Spain and Italy showed a strong preference for the preservation of the status quo, which was under threat, while the implications of reforms in terms of constraints to responsiveness were essentially not problematised. Consequently, the strategy adopted was an immediate constitutionalising of the fiscal brake.

In the other four countries, the same assessment was constrained by domestic factors and produced a cautious avoidance of deeper internal conflicts. Consequently, the debt brake was approved through ordinary legislation (Greece, Cyprus, Malta) or a law of reinforced value (Portugal).

4.7 CONCLUSION

The positions of South European countries during the Eurozone Crisis negotiations did not reflect the long-term preferences of the wider public. In other words, the austerity-orientated decisions made by South European countries against the backdrop of the Eurozone Crisis were essentially unresponsive. As stressed in the literature on the effects of the crisis on Southern Europe (see, e.g., Bosco and Verney 2016; Morlino and Raniolo 2017), low levels of government responsiveness contributed to exacerbating a democratic malaise whose consequences for the future stability of democracy in the region are indeed unforeseeable. To explain why and how those decisions were made, a theoretically informed analysis was conducted of the determinants of domestic preference formation during the Eurozone Crisis negotiations in Cyprus, Greece, Italy, Malta, Portugal and Spain.

Keeping in mind the results of complementary research (see Tarlea et al. 2019), table 4.5 summarises the main factors shaping the way in which the decisions under scrutiny were made. According to LIs, domestic deliberation, mediated by decision-makers' electoral concerns, should be relevant in determining South European member state's positions during the analysed negotiations. Contrary to these expectations, in all cases, including Malta, decisions were essentially taken by small governmental elites with little deliberation and in the absence of domestic debate on the long-term consequences of the Eurozone reforms. What emerges from the empirical analysis is that, within a framework of uncertainty and urgency generated by the crisis, in the countries considered, there was a low level of parliamentary involvement, with the sole exception of Malta.

Within such a framework, committing to structural reforms was the only alternative perceived as viable by South European decision-makers. This option was underpinned by incumbent governments' underlying preference for the status quo, despite the likely electoral punishment that would ensue. There was no evidence found to suggest that ideological commitment to neoliberal policies played a substantial role in the preference formation process. Instead, although with different nuances, South European decision-makers were found to have assessed the situation in terms of emergency. Hence, their willingness to commit to neoliberal policies to avert the imminent risk of a forced exit from the Eurozone or generalised financial mayhem. It is possible to conclude that the unresponsive decisions made by governmental elites across Southern Europe

Table 4.5 The Determinants of Preference Formation on Eurozone Crisis Decisions: Southern Europe

Contested Issue	Determinants of Preferences
Creation and size of the ESM	• Expected immediate gain vis-à-vis market stability

were due to a complex mix of loss aversion, anticipated short-term gains in market stability as well as domestic specificities linked to potential conflict. Moreover, it is important to notice that the implications of the lack of responsiveness in the decision-making process are relevant both from a theoretical standpoint and in terms of future preference formation. From the point of view of theory, the results resonate with Schimmelfennig's claim that while LIs provides a convincing account of the bargaining process at the height of the crisis, it accounts only partially for national preference formation (2018). In particular, domestic parliaments were not able to balance the intergovernmental logic that dominated the Eurozone Crisis negotiations (Fabbrini 2013). The lack of public debate surrounding austerity measures and poor responsiveness by decision-makers in general unsurprisingly paved the way for the rise of widespread Eurosceptic sentiment even in countries which had traditionally been firmly 'pro-European', such as Greece, Italy and Spain. This, in turn, means that any future steps towards deepening the fiscal and monetary union will likely become extremely contested within domestic political arenas, as epitomised, for instance, by the heated debate that took place in December 2019 in Italy concerning the reform of the ESM (Fortuna 2019).

NOTES

1. The grant agreement (European Union's Horizon 2020 research and innovation programme) is no. 649532 . This chapter is partly based on Morlino, L. and Sottilotta, C.E. (2019) "Southern Europe and the Eurozone Crisis Negotiations. Preference Formation and Contested Issues", *South European Society and Politics*, 24:1, 1–28.

2. In the original dataset, the coding was slightly different, eg. ITA01.ITA, where the first part of the code 'ITA' refers to the country, the number that is, '01', identifies the interviewee, and the final part of the code, that is, '.ITA', refers to the research team which carried out the interviews. To maximise readability, we maintained the first and the second part of the code. The *EMU Choices* project datasets and codebooks are available at www.EMUchoices.eu/data

3. It can be recalled that in 2004, Greece had already received a warning from the European Commission for under-reporting budget deficit data (Saragosa 2004).

4. As shown in figure 4.1, in November 2011, the Italian ten-year government bond yields almost reached 7 per cent, with a spread of over 5 per cent vis-à-vis the German Bund.

5. While the EMUf dataset used for this chapter focuses on preference formation and is based on in-depth structured interviews with former policymakers, the EMUp dataset covers member states' preferences on contested policy issues related to EMU reforms between 2010 and 2015, mapping forty-seven issues related to EFSF, ESM, Six/Two Packs, Fiscal Compact and the Banking Union legislation.

6. The first draft of the constitutional law had been approved on 30 November 2011 (Il Sole 24 Ore 2012).

REFERENCES

Alexopoulos, A. 2015. "Greece: Government as the Dominant Player". In *The Role of Governments in Legislative Agenda Setting*, edited by B.E. Rasch and G. Tsebelis, 145–63. Abingdon: Routledge.

Andretta, M. 2018. "Protest in Italy in Times of Crisis: A Cross-Government Comparison." *South European Society and Politics* 23, no. 1: 97–114.

Azzopardi, R.M. 2009. "Malta's Open Economy: Weathering the Recessional Storm?" *South European Society and Politics* 14, no. 1: 103–20.

Bickerton, C.J., D. Hodson, and U. Puetter. 2015. "The New Intergovernmentalism: European Integration in the Post-Maastricht Era." *Journal of Common Market Studies* 53, no. 4: 703–22.

Bosco, A. and S. Verney. 2012. "Electoral Epidemic: The Political Cost of Economic Crisis in Southern Europe, 2010–11." *South European Society and Politics* 17, no. 2: 129–54.

Bosco, A. and S. Verney. 2016. "From Electoral Epidemic to Government Epidemic: The Next Level of the Crisis in Southern Europe." *South European Society and Politics* 21, no. 4: 383–406.

Camera dei Deputati. 2012. "Resoconto Sommario." *Seduta del 12 Gennaio 2012*, no. 569. http://www.camera.it/_dati/leg16/lavori/stenografici/sed569/pdfsomm.pdf.

Coller Porta, X. and F. Ramírez de Luis. 2019. "Unstable Preferences and Policy Changes: Spain". In *The Politics of the Eurozone Crisis in Southern Europe: A Comparative Reappraisal*, edited by L. Morlino and C.E. Sottilotta, 133–72. London: Palgrave Macmillan.

Copelovitch, M., J. Frieden, and S. Walter. 2016. "The Political Economy of the Euro Crisis." *Comparative Political Studies* 49, no. 7: 811–40.

Csehi, R. and U. Puetter. 2017. "Problematizing the Notion of Preference Formation in Research About the Euro Crisis." *EMU Choices Working Paper*, December, 2017. https://emuchoices.eu/wp-content/uploads/2017/12/2017_Working-Paper-Csehi-Puetter_Problematizing-the-notion-of-preference-formation-in-research-about-the-euro-crisis-.pdf.

Degner, H. and D. Leuffen. 2019. "Crises and Responsiveness: Analysing German Preference Formation during the Eurozone Crisis." *Political Studies Review* 2019: 1–16.

Dolvik, J.E. and A. Martin. 2015. *European Social Models from Crisis to Crisis. Employment and Inequality in the Era of Monetary Integration.* Oxford: Oxford University Press.

Dyson, K. and K. Featherstone. 1999. *The Road to Maastricht: Negotiating Economic and Monetary Union*. Oxford: Oxford University Press.

Eulau, H. and P. Karps. 1977. "The Puzzle of Representation: Specifying Components of Responsiveness." *Legislative Studies Quarterly* 2, no. 3: 233–54.

European Council. 2011. "Statement by the Euro Area Heads of State or Government." *European Council*, December 11, 2011. https://www.consilium.europa.eu/uedocs/cms_data/docs/pressdata/en/ec/126658.pdf .

Fabbrini, S. 2013. "Intergovernmentalism and Its Limits: The Implications of the Euro Crisis on the European Union." *Comparative Political Studies* 46, no. 9: 1003–29.

Faustmann, H. 2008. "Aspects of Political Culture in Cyprus." In *The Government and Politics of Cyprus*, edited by J. Ker-Lindsay and H. Faustmann, 17–44. Oxford: Peter Lang.

Fenech, D. 2013. "The 2013 Maltese General Election: Unplugging the Blockage." *West European Politics* 36, no. 5: 1088–94.

Fortuna, G. 2019. "Italy's Conte Rebukes Opposition as Debate Over ESM Reform Heats Up." Euractive, December 3, 2019. https://www.euractiv.com/section/economy-jobs/news/italys-conte-rebukes-opposition-as-debate-over-esm-reform-heats-up/.

Gutiérrez Calvo, V. and R. Muñoz. 2011. "Reforma exprés y sin referéndum." *El País*, August 23, 2011. https://politica.elpais.com/politica/2011/08/23/actualidad/1314128715_080054.html.

Hall, P.A. 2012. "The Economics and Politics of the Euro Crisis." *German Politics* 21, no.4: 355–71.

Hassel, A. 2014. "Adjustments in the Eurozone: Varieties of Capitalism and the Crisis in Southern Europe." *LSE 'Europe in Question' Discussion Paper Series*, no. 76. http://www.lse.ac.uk/europeanInstitute/LEQS%20Discussion%20Paper%20Series/LEQSPaper76.pdf.

Hill, C. 2003. *The Changing Politics of Foreign Policy*. London: Palgrave.

Jervis, R. 1976/2017. *Perception and Misperception in International Politics.* Princeton: Princeton University Press.

Katsourides, Y. 2014. "The Comeback of the Right in Crisis-Ridden Cyprus: The 2013 Presidential Elections." *South European Society and Politics* 19, no. 1: 51–70.

Katsourides, Y. 2019. "Institutional Inertia, Ignorance and Short-Circuit: Cyprus." In *The Politics of the Eurozone Crisis in Southern Europe: A Comparative Reappraisal*, edited by L. Morlino and C.E. Sottilotta, 27–56. London: Palgrave Macmillan.

Kydd, A.H. 2008. "Methodological Individualism and Rational Choice." In *The Oxford Handbook of International Relations*, edited by C. Reus-Smit and D. Snidal, 425–43. Oxford: Oxford University Press.

Kreilinger, V. 2012. "The Making of a New Treaty: Six Rounds of Political Bargaining." *Policy Brief Notre Europe*, no. 32. http://www.institutdelors.eu/media/newtreaty_v.kreilinger_ne_feb2012.pdf?pdf=ok.

Lisi, M. 2015. *Party Change, Recent Democracies and Portugal. Comparative Perspectives*. Lanham, MD: Lexington.

Lisi, M. and V. Ramalhete. 2019. "Challenges and Opportunities Under Conditionality: Portugal." In *The Politics of the Eurozone Crisis in Southern Europe: A Comparative Reappraisal*, edited by L. Morlino and C.E. Sottilotta, 173–201. London: Palgrave Macmillan.

Matthijs, M. 2014. "Mediterranean Blues: The Crisis in Southern Europe." *Journal of Democracy* 25, no. 1: 101–15.
Miglierini, J. 2016. "Italy Economy: IMF Says Country Has 'Two Lost Decades' of Growth." *BBC News*, July 12, 2016. http://www.bbc.com/news/business-36770311.
Moravcsik, A. 1998. *The Choice for Europe. Social Purpose and State Power from Messina to Maastricht*. Ithaca: Cornell University Press.
Moravcsik, A. and F. Schimmelfennig. 2019. "Liberal Intergovernmentalism." In *European Integration Theory*, edited by A. Wiener, T.A. Börzel, and T. Risse, chapter 4. Oxford: Oxford University Press.
Morlino, L. 2011. *Changes for Democracy: Actors, Structures, Processes*. Oxford: Oxford University Press.
Morlino, L. and F. Raniolo. 2017. *The Impact of the Economic Crisis on South European Democracies*. London: Palgrave Macmillan.
Morlino, L. and C.E. Sottilotta. 2017. "Circumventing Constraints by Internalizing Troika Oversight? Italy and the Euro Crisis Negotiations." *EMU Choices Working Paper*, October, 2017. https://emuchoices.eu/2017/10/10/morlino-l-and-sottilotta-c-2017-circumventing-constraints-by-internalizing-troika-oversight-italy-and-the-euro-crisis-negotiations-emu-choices-working-paper-2017/.
Morlino, L. and C.E. Sottilotta. 2019. *The Politics of the Eurozone Crisis in Southern Europe: A Comparative Reappraisal*. London: Palgrave Macmillan.
Mosca, L. and M. Quaranta. 2017. "Voting for Movement Parties in Southern Europe: The Role of Protest and Digital Information." *South European Society and Politics* 22, no. 4: 427–46.
Moschella, M. 2017. "Italy and the Fiscal Compact: Why Does a Country Commit to Permanent Austerity." *Italian Political Science Review* 47, no. 2: 205–25.
Moury, C. and A. Standring. 2017. "'Going Beyond the Troika': Power and Discourse in Portuguese Austerity Politics." *European Journal of Political Research* 56, no. 3: 660–79.
Navarro, B. 2012. "Holanda publica los documentos del rescate bancario español que el Gobierno oculta." *La Vanguardia*, July 12, 2012. http://www.lavanguardia.com/economia/20120712/54324841036/holanda-publica-documentos-rescate-bancario-espanol-que-gobierno-oculta.html.
Ngai, V. 2012. "Stability and Growth Pact and Fiscal Discipline in the Eurozone." *Wharton Financial Institutions Center Working Paper*, the University of Pennsylvania. https://fic.wharton.upenn.edu/wp-content/uploads/2016/11/12-10.pdf.
OECD. 2018. "Long-term interest rates (indicator)." Organisation for Economic Cooperation and Development iLibrary. doi:10.1787/662d712c-en.
Orphanides, A. 2014. "The Euro Area Crisis: Politics Over Economics." *Atlantic Economic Journal* 42, no. 3: 243–63.
Ortega, E. and J. Peñalosa. 2012. "The Spanish Economic Crisis: Key Factors and Growth Challenges in the Euro Area." *Banco de España Occasional Paper*, no. 1201. https://papers.ssrn.com/sol3/papers.cfm?abstract_id=2016027.
Otero-Iglesias, M., S. Royo, and F. Steinberg. 2016. "The Spanish Financial Crisis: Lessons for the European Banking Union." *Real Instituto Elcano Informe 20*, March 2016. http://www.realinstitutoelcano.org/wps/wcm/connect/990df1804

c31d6e0b752bf07355a34ad/Informe-Elcano-20-Spanish-financial-crisis-Lessons-European-Banking-Union.pdf?MOD=AJPERES&CACHEID=990df1804c31d6e0b752bf07355a34ad.

Pace, R. 2019. "Dissecting the Exceptional Case: Malta." In *The Politics of the Eurozone Crisis in Southern Europe: A Comparative Reappraisal*, edited by L. Morlino and C.E. Sottilotta, 109–32. London: Palgrave Macmillan

Perez, S. and M. Rhodes. 2015. "The Evolution and Crises of the Social Models in Italy and Spain." In *European Social Models From Crisis to Crisis: Employment and Inequality in the Era of Monetary Integration*, edited by J.E. Dølvik and A. Martin, 177–213. Oxford: Oxford University Press.

Picot, G. and A. Tassinari. 2017. "All of One Kind? Labour Market Reforms Under Austerity in Italy and Spain." *Socio-Economic Review* 15, no. 2: 461–82.

Pogliotti, G. and A. Rota Porta. 2012. "La riforma Fornero è legge. Il ministro: il lavoro non è un diritto." *Il Sole 24 Ore*, June 27, 2012. http://www.ilsole24ore.com/art/notizie/2012-06-27/fornero-riforma-lavoro-buona-104438.shtml?uuid=AbvmwsyF.

Puetter, U. 2014. *The European Council and the Council - New Intergovernmentalism and Institutional Change*. Oxford: Oxford University Press.

Quaglia, L. 2004. "Italy's Policy Towards European Monetary Integration: Bringing Ideas Back In?" *Journal of European Public Policy* 11, no. 6: 1096–111.

Reis, R. 2015. "Looking for a Success in the Euro Crisis Adjustment Programs: The Case of Portugal." *Brookings Papers on Economic Activity*, Fall 2015: 433–58. https://www.brookings.edu/wp-content/uploads/2016/07/PDFReisTextFallBPEA.pdf.

Ruiz-Rufino, R. and S. Alonso. 2017. "Democracy Without Choice: Citizens' Perceptions of Government Autonomy during the Eurozone Crisis." *European Journal of Political Research* 56, no. 2: 320–45.

Sacchi, S. 2015. "Conditionality by Other Means: EU Involvement in Italy's Structural Reforms in the Sovereign Debt Crisis." *Comparative European Politics* 13, no. 1: 77–92.

Saragosa, M. 2004. "Greece Warned on False Euro Data." *BBC News*, December 1, 2004. http://news.bbc.co.uk/2/hi/business/4058327.stm.

Schild, J. 2013. "Leadership in Hard Times: Germany, France, and the management of the Eurozone Crisis." *German Politics and Society* 31, no. 1: 24–47.

Schimmelfennig, F. 2015. "Liberal Intergovernmentalism and the Euro Area Crisis." *Journal of European Public Policy* 22, no. 2: 177–95.

Schimmelfennig, F. 2018. "Liberal Intergovernmentalism and the Crises of the European Union." *JCMS: Journal of Common Market Studies* 56, no. 7: 1578–94.

Schuknecht, L., P. Moutot, P. Rother, and J. Stark. 2011. "The Stability and Growth Pact: Crisis and Reform." *CESifo DICE Report,* March, 2011. https://core.ac.uk/download/pdf/6692918.pdf.

Sotiropoulos, D.A. 2015. "The Greek Parliament and the European Union after the Lisbon Treaty: A Missed Opportunity to Empower Parliament." In *The Palgrave Handbook of National Parliaments and the European Union*, edited by C. Hefftler, C. Neuhold, O. Rozenberg, and J. Smith, 335–47. London: Palgrave Macmillan.

Sotiropoulos, D.A. 2019. "In the Eye of the Hurricane: Greece." In *The Politics of the Eurozone Crisis in Southern Europe: A Comparative Reappraisal*, edited by L. Morlino and C.E. Sottilotta, 57–83. London: Palgrave Macmillan.

Sottilotta, C.E. 2019. "'Vincolo Esterno' or Muddling Through? Italy." In *The Politics of the Eurozone Crisis in Southern Europe: A Comparative Reappraisal*, edited by L. Morlino and C.E. Sottilotta, 85–107. London: Palgrave Macmillan.

Stein, J.L. 2011. "The Diversity of Debt Crises in Europe." *CESifo Forum, April, 2011.* https://www.cesifogroup.de/portal/page/portal/B85E3F45A41D1112E04400144FAFB1DA.

Tarlea S., S. Bailer, H. Degner, L.M. Dellmuth, D. Leuffen, M. Lundgren, J. Tallberg, and F. Wasserfallen. 2019. "Explaining Governmental Preferences on Economic and Monetary Reform Union." *European Union Politics* 20, no. 1: 24–44.

The Economist. 2012. "Slow, But Popular – Germany and the Euro Crisis." *The Economist*, December, 8. https://www.economist.com/europe/2012/12/08/slow-but-popular.

The Economist. 2013. "What Happened in Cyprus." *The Economist*, March 28, 2013. http://www.economist.com/blogs/freeexchange/2013/03/interview-athanasios-orphanides.

Verney, S. 2017. "Losing Loyalty. The Rise of polity Euroscepticism in Southern Europe." In *The Routledge Handbook of Euroscepticism*, edited by B. Leruth, N. Startin, and S. Usherwood, 168–85. London: Routledge.

Wasserfallen, F., D. Leuffen, Z. Kudrna, and H. Degner. 2018. "Analysing European Union Decision-Making During the Eurozone Crisis with New Data." *European Union Politics* 20, no. 1: 3–23.

Wise, P. 2010. "Portugal Announces Austerity Package." *Financial Times*, September 29, 2010. https://www.ft.com/content/36f5b1c6-cbfe-11df-bd28-00144feab49a?mhq5j=e2.

World Bank. 2015. "World Development Indicators." *The World Bank Data Catalog*. http://data.worldbank.org/data-catalog/world-development-indicators.

Wulfgramm M., T. Bieber, and S. Leibfried. 2016. *Welfare State Tranformations and Inequality in OECD Countries*. London: Palgrave-MacMillan.

Chapter 5

National Constitutional Law as Manifold Steeplechase for Fiscal Integration

Elisabeth Lentsch

5.1 INTRODUCTION

The European Economic and Monetary Union (EMU), as defined in the Maastricht Treaty, conceptualises monetary and fiscal policy as two sides of the same coin. However, only the former was communitarised. Thus, in principle, member states kept their sovereignty for economic and fiscal policies, and national governments can decide how to raise and use their public revenues, including taxation, debts and public spending. The common concern on the EU level is limited to economic policy, supplemented by supervising national fiscal discipline. The latter is a rule-based framework including the Stability and Growth Pact (SGP), which should guarantee member states' sound public finances and the sustainability of the balance of payments. However, over time, these provisions could not prevent rising national fiscal deficits and debts and the resulting economic and financial crisis revealed the weaknesses of the original architecture of EMU.

During and after the crisis, the call for a genuine EMU, including further development of common fiscal rules towards a fiscal union to safeguard the integrity of the Eurozone, "became louder" (European Commission 2012, 2017a, 2017b; Junker et al. 2015; Van Rompuy 2012; Van Rompuy et al. 2012). Several measures introduced to combat the crisis may be considered as the fiscal union's rudiments (Thirion 2017), but their deepening is impeded by the fact the EU is not a federal state.[1] It does not dispose of powerful fiscal capacity, such as a right to raise taxes, which would allow for any fiscal distributional policy or to address macroeconomic instability by counter-cyclical policies (Leino-Sandberg and Saarenheimo 2018). According to Article 311 TFEU, 'the Union shall provide itself with the means necessary to attain its objectives and carry through its policies.' However, the EU budget is – with approximately only 2 per cent of the total of public expenditures – extremely limited. The substance of economic and fiscal policies, including financial 'firepower' remains in the hands of the member states.

Debates about the increase of contributions as well as the introduction of new possible resources are ongoing (Maduro 2012; Monti et al. 2016), but they are constrained by the legal requirement of a unanimous Council decision and ratification by all member states.[2] The progress towards fiscal union is, thus, limited to very modest proposals that cannot, on their own, improve the resilience of the Eurozone as a whole. There is a discussion about the common fiscal stance that should enhance collective responsibility and guide member states' fiscal decisions for the Eurozone as a single entity (European, Commission 2016a, 2017a).[3] Similarly, the European Fiscal Board strives to increase the cooperation with and among national fiscal boards to enhance compliance with the fiscal rules (European Commission 2016b).

More far-reaching initiatives suggest the establishment of a central fiscal stabiliser for counter-steering asymmetric shocks in the EU.[4] EU institutions advocated a gradual development of an autonomous fiscal capacity for the Eurozone (Van Rompuy 2012) that would provide an incentive – in the form of financial support – to member states in financial difficulties to adopt necessary structural reforms as recommended within the European Semester (Van Rompuy 2012, 5; Monti et al. 2016; European Commission 2017c, 10). Institutionally, the Eurozone Treasury and a Eurozone finance minister could support such mechanism, but the Commission included only the latter initiative in its communication "on related reforms" (European Commission 2017d).

The second layer of a substantive Fiscal Union would have to consist of integrating the "European Stability Mechanism" (ESM) into the EU legal framework. Generally speaking, it is a mechanism safeguarding the stability of the Eurozone as a whole, including financial assistance for member states in difficulties, 'subject to strict conditionality'.[5] A possible third layer would be the development of a fully fledged system of fiscal federalism that includes a division of competences for taxation and expenditure, which normally would include explicit elements of redistribution and solidarity (Blöchliger and Vammalle 2012; Woźniakowski 2018).

These fiscal integration proposals touch on the sensitive sphere of fiscal and budgetary policies that form a core of national constitutional frameworks. One hurdle relates to the constitutional obstacles set out by the EU Treaties. Comprehensive EMU reform will not be legally feasible without respective EU Treaty changes (Lentsch 2018). What will be needed for further transfer of EMU competences to the supranational level are adequate EU Treaty bases, sufficient financing tools for the envisaged mechanisms and the guarantee of democratic legitimacy. Such treaty revisions, including the adaption of EMU competences, require political consensus and ratification in all member states, which may not be easily achieved. Still, for completing the EMU and creating a further integrated fiscal union, these hurdles are to be overcome.

5.2 SUBSTANTIVE CONSTITUTIONAL HURDLES FOR EU CRISIS MANAGEMENT

National constitutional pre-conditions for further transfer of competences to the supranational level also shape the development of a genuine Fiscal Union – in addition to the required EU Treaty changes and related political hurdles. Member states are not ready to sacrifice their constitutional principles for EU membership. However, experience indicates they are ready to accept certain modifications in transferring powers to the Union.

Further fiscal integration bears on the core prerogative of the nation-state: budgetary power. Any international or supranational initiatives and agreements raise concerns about the interference with national sovereignty and identity. However, the recent adoption of crisis management measures and respective findings of constitutional courts and review bodies support the need for discussion of the constitutional feasibility of EMU reform.

A predominant feature of the adopted crisis measures was to advance national fiscal discipline by supranational and intergovernmental law. The member states agreed to stronger fiscal rules on supervision, coordination and possible sanctions. At the same time, to safeguard the stability of the Eurozone as a whole, they introduced bailout mechanisms for the benefit of financially distressed member states.

All reforms, such as the SGP upgrade, the adoption of the intergovernmental agreement on the Treaty on Stability, Coordination and Governance (TSCG) and the financial assistance mechanisms for emergency cases, as well as the Banking Union, changed the EMU system (Lentsch 2017). The impact both at the EU and national level was significant and triggered legal controversies. Most legal turmoil caused the EMU-related measures to be adopted as intergovernmental agreements instead of EU legal measures, in particular, the TSCG and the European Stabilisation Mechanism (ESM) and its predecessors. The use of intergovernmental legal instruments raised contestation and contention over their compatibility with EU Treaties and national constitutions. The measures adopted outside the EU framework might be more visible in the resulting tension vis-à-vis constitutional limits and challenges. These intergovernmental agreements are not protected by the constitutional EU membership clauses, which provide, to a certain extent, a shield against constitutional challenges, given that the main ambition is opening up the national legal orders for EU law (Griller et al. 2021).

These controversies can be observed in constitutional reviews and provide information on the constitutional limits imposed on fiscal integration. The national constitutional bodies were challenged to provide judgements concerning the delimitation of national identity and the ultra vires doctrine of the internationally adopted measures. The latter may become of importance considering past national challenges, such as the – first-ever – preliminary ruling procedures opened by the German Constitutional Court in the Gauweiler and Weiss cases (Gauweiler 2015; Weiss 2017). Integrating the TSCG and/or the ESM into the EU legal order and creating a genuine Fiscal Union triggers exactly this type of controversy. Therefore, the constitutional debate about the TSCG and the ESM will inform future conversations about amending the Treaties.

5.2.1 Treaty on Stability, Coordination and Governance

In 2012, the intergovernmental TSCG conclusion reached by all EU member states (except the UK and the Czech Republic) was closely connected to the EMU system. It aims to foster budgetary discipline by imposing stricter supranational budgetary limitations than those covered under the EU Six-Pack legislation. Most importantly, it lowers the 0.5 per cent limit of the annual structural deficit of the GDP at market prices (Regulation 1466/1997, Article 2a). It included an obligation to implement those limits 'through provisions of binding force and permanent character, preferably constitutional, or otherwise guaranteed to be fully respected and adhered to throughout the national budgetary processes' (TSCG, Article 3(2)). All participating member states implemented this agreement, but, for partly political, partly constitutional reasons, only a few member states (Germany, Spain, Italy and Slovenia (see table 5.1)) included the balanced budget rule as a 'golden rule' in the preferred constitutional rank to give it higher legal validity (European Commission 2017f). Only Ireland amended its constitution to fulfil the TSCG obligations. Others, such as Austria, Belgium, Estonia, Finland, Lithuania, Latvia and Portugal, provided for a higher hierarchical status than ordinary law (European Commission 2017g).

Table 5.1 TSCG, Balanced Budget Rule Implementation

Constitutional Amendment		Ordinary Law	
Ratified	Amended	Higher status law	Budgetary law
Spain, Germany, Italy, Slovenia	Ireland	Austria, Belgium, Estonia, Finland, Lithuania, Latvia, Portugal	Bulgaria, Cyprus, Denmark, France, Greece, Luxembourg, Malta, Netherlands, Romania, Slovakia

The ratification and implementation of the TSCG, in particular the balanced budget rule, raised controversies, mostly on its compatibility with the national constitutions. The main argument concerned restricting national parliaments' fiscal room for manoeuvre, arguably curtailing their budgetary sovereignty as guaranteed in the constitutions.

These contestations became evident by several motions for constitutional review (see table 5.2) before national review bodies (Saurugger and Fontan

Table 5.2 Court Cases – Balanced Budget Rule Implementation

State	Cases	Outcome
AT	VfSlg. 19.809/2013	Application held partly inadmissible, partly unfounded. The Constitution leaves a considerable scope for securing the macroeconomic balance and their striving for sustainable and sound finances.
BE	Constitutional Court judgement no 62/2016	The Treaty obligations are constitutional, but 'national identity is to be preserved'.
ES	Constitutional Court ECLI:ES:TC:2012:9A	The complaint was declared inadmissible. The political participation rights in the debate and the applied procedure was not interfered with.
FI	Constitutional Law Committee Opinions 37/2012, 34/2011 and minutes 49/2012	The curtailed budgetary powers are not significantly limiting the constitutionally protected budgetary powers of parliament.
FR	Constitutional Council decision n° 2012-653 DC	The adoption as organic law is constitutional does not cross the constitutional boundaries.
DE	BVerfG:2011:rs20110907.2bvr098710, BVerfG:2012:rs20120912.2bvr139012, BVerfG:2014:rs20140318.2bvr139012.	The budgetary autonomy is not interfered with, but rather preserved.

2017). In Ireland, a referendum was held to authorise the Irish ratification of the TSCG and allow it to be inserted as new Article 29.4.10° in the constitution (Barrett 2020).

Spain amended Article 135 of its constitution, but did so in September 2011, before the signature and ratification of the TSCG. This constitutional amendment was challenged before the Constitutional Court, claiming the right to political participation was breached because the parliamentary debate had been curtailed and the wrong amendment procedure was applied. The Constitutional Court declared the complaint inadmissible but still tackled the defendants' arguments (Constitutional Court of Spain 2012). Accordingly, it outlined the proposal that affected the contents of Article 135 SC on budgetary stability, and thus, the general procedure of Article 167 SC was correct (Constitutional Court of Spain 2012, para 2).[6] In this context, it also found options for urgent procedures; the limitation of the debate to the Plenary and the reduction of time for submitting amendments are all available for constitutional amendments (Constitutional Court of Spain 2012, para 13,14).

In France, the contention was that any changes to both parliament's and government's prerogatives in adopting budget laws require a revision of Articles 34 and 47 of the Constitution, specifying the respective division of powers. The Constitutional Council, by contrast, considered a 'soft' implementation of Article 3(2) TSCG by organic law as the viable legal form. This adoption as organic law was constitutional because it went as far as possible towards implementing a new budgetary 'discipline' but without crossing the constitutional boundaries. The principle of annuality of the budget and the discretion of government and parliament with regard to the content of budget and social security finance laws was respected (Décision n° 2012-653 DC du 9 août 2012).

In Austria, the TSCG had been adopted as ordinary legislation. After ratification, the debt brake was inserted into the new stability pact – being a state treaty between the Federation and its provinces. Accordingly, the Federal Budget Law, which deals with the general framework of federal budgeting, was amended. The Constitutional Court was called upon to decide whether the TSCG should have been treated as a constitutional amendment. It was contended that the TSCG debt brake was a restriction of the budgetary sovereignty of the National Council because the voting procedure under Article 7 TSCG[7] constrained the voting of the Austrian representative in the Council.[8] The legal basis of the parliament's assent was challenged as well.[9] The court declared the application partly inadmissible, partly unfounded. It avoided questions on 'budgetary sovereignty' but emphasised that Article 13 para 2 B-VG left 'considerable scope for securing the macroeconomic balance and striving for sustainable and sound finances' (Constitutional Court of Austria 2013).

In Belgium, the TSCG allegedly violated Article 34 of the national constitution, which states 'specific powers can be assigned by a treaty or by a law to institutions of public international law'. The Constitutional Court approved the treaty but affirmed, at the same time, that Article 34 preserves the national identity (Constitutional Court of Belgium 2016). The judgement can be read as a form of identity review with implications for further E(M)U integration (Gérard and Verrijdt 2017).

In Germany, the Constitutional Court did not see any infringement on budgetary responsibility. It felt the TSCG preserved budgetary autonomy rather than limited it (BVerfG 2011, para 104; BVerfG 2012, para 120), given that it echoes the terms and concepts of both the Six-Pack and the German Constitution (BVerfG 2014, para 243; BVerfG 2012, para 198f). The court also concluded that TSCG does not empower the Commission to set up binding parameters for the German budget (BVerfG 2014, para 244), thus, the Bundestag's budgetary responsibility remains untouched (Korioth and Marx 2020).

In contrast, the Finnish Constitutional Law Committee of the national parliament, which provides an ex-ante constitutional review, announced that the Fiscal Compact curtails parliament's budgetary powers. However, it also emphasised that this does not amount to a significant limitation.[10]

All in all, the alleged violations of national constitutions were not upheld by constitutional review bodies. The claims were partly dismissed or proved unfounded, partly ruled as compatible with national constitutions.

5.2.2 Financial Assistance Mechanisms

Financial market turbulence and the following hike in national debts of some member states arguably put the stability of the Eurozone at risk. What followed was a wave of financial solidarity measures for member states with solvency and liquidity problems (European Council 2010a) adopted both at the EU and intergovernmental level. It all started with coordinated bilateral loans to Greece that other Eurozone member states provided jointly with the International Monetary Fund (Eurozone governments 2010). Financial stability facilities, open also to other member states, followed: the European Financial Stability Mechanism (EFSM), the European Financial Stability Facility (EFSF) and, finally, the European Stability Mechanism (ESM) (European Council 2010b; Council of the European Union 2010; EFSF Framework Agreement 2010; ESM Treaty 2012).[11]

These measures invited even more controversy about their legality, both at EU and national level. Again, constitutional review bodies were called to decide on the constitutionality of the adopted solidarity mechanisms (see table 5.3). The most disputed issue was the compatibility with the budgetary norms and principles of national frameworks.

National laws allowing for bilateral loans to Greece as well as the EFSF were challenged before the German Constitutional Court (GCC). This court

Table 5.3 Court Cases – Financial Assistance Mechanisms

State	Cases	Outcome
AT	Constitutional Court judgement VfSlg 19.750/2013 on ESM agreement	The ESM participation is constitutional. The parliament decides on a wide range of general political and complex financial, monetary and economic policy assessments and considerations. Thus, related political questions may not to be answered by the Constitutional Court.
BE	Constitutional Council judgement no. 156/2012 on ESM agreement	Inadmissible.
DE	GCC ECLI:DE:BVerfG:2011:rs201 10907.2bvr098710 on Greece support and on agreement	Claims are inadmissible. The Bundestag has a margin of evaluation on decisions on expenditures and guarantees regarding EMU measures. Limits are only unforeseeable burdens or the undermining of the principle of permanent budget autonomy.
DE	GCC ECLI:DE:BVerfG:2014: rs20140318.2bvr139012 on ESM agreement	The ESM is constitutional. It must be guaranteed that the Bundestag keeps its decisive influence over the granting of financial aid, it must not lose its de-facto veto position and does not forfeit its voting rights in the board of governors of the ESM.
EE	Supreme Court decision 3-4-1-6-12 on ESM agreement	The claim was dismissed. The international treaty in the sphere of EU law and the limitation of parliamentary control in the emergency voting procedure of the ESM was accepted because of its aim and ability to support the stability of the euro area.
FI	Constitutional Law Committee Opinion 14/2011 on agreement	Constitutionality is given as all major decisions in the EFSF affecting MS' guarantee liabilities require unanimity and parliament's budgetary power is guaranteed. The Grand Committee of Parliament has effective right to decide on the position by Finland's representative in the Board of Directors. Also the domestic implementing enactment included a provision, which obliges the government to seek parliament's authorisation for every guarantee given under the Agreement.
FI	Constitutional Law Committee several checks Opinion 13/2012 on ESM agreement	Constitutionality is given as unanimous decision on stability support provided by ESM provides a veto power and thus the parliament holds both de jure and de-facto influence on the government's voting position. Constitutional limits: the parliament's constitutional prerogatives have to be preserved, such as the rights of information and participation in domestic decision-making pertaining to EU affairs.
IE	High Court of Ireland, Pringle [2012] IEHC 296 (2012 3772P) on ESM agreement	Even though the budgetary, fiscal and economic sovereignty of Ireland is diminished, the delegation of sovereignty was constitutional.
NL	Council of State Opinion of 1 March 2012 on ESM agreement	The Treaty is democratically legitimised, but enormous financial obligations require the involvement of the States General in the decision-making of the ESM institutions.

Source: Author.

has a reputation for being the most prominent and explicit in its reviews of ultra vires and identity cases related to EU integration to guarantee democratically legitimate decisions on behalf of German citizens. The court accepted the representation of citizens via the European Parliament and via the national governments within the European Council as sufficient democratic legitimation for the European Union. However, the only institution democratically legitimated by the German citizens is the Bundestag, which must ensure that democratic representation and accountability is guaranteed for the German people. That includes ensuring any transfer of powers does not undermine its own powers to the point that it no longer controls the powers executed over the citizen, known as *Integrationsverantwortung* (BVerfG 2009).

In the EFSF case and bilateral loans to Greece, the German court found the submitted claims inadmissible, emphasising the legislature's 'latitude of assessment, which the Federal Constitutional Court must respect' (BVerfG 2011, para 132). The GCC considered the laws related to the Bundestag's budgetary responsibility to ensure they do not result in unforeseeable burdens or undermine the principle of permanent budget autonomy (BVerfG 2011, para 135).

The most heated controversy was triggered by the treaty on the establishment of the ESM. The GCC ruled that despite Germany's capital contributions to the ESM, 'the budgetary autonomy of the German Bundestag is sufficiently safeguarded'. However, arrangements under budgetary law must be made to ensure that possible capital calls pursuant to the ESM Treaty can be met fully and in time within the agreed-upon upper limits so that a suspension of Germany's voting rights in the ESM bodies is reliably excluded' (BVerfG Press Release 2014). The principle of democracy is to be ensured as long as the Bundestag remains in control of fundamental budgetary decisions. The court argued that the principle of democracy would only be violated if Germany became liable 'to such an extent that budgetary autonomy would not only be constrained but would, in fact, cease to exist, at least for a considerable period of time' (BVerfG Press Release 2012). Germany cannot lose its de-facto veto position and must make sure it does not forfeit its voting rights on the ESM board of governors (BVerG 2014, para 191, 199).

This jurisprudence advanced the doctrine of the Bundestag's 'overall budgetary responsibility'. Accordingly, 'the principle of democracy requires that the German Bundestag remains the place where autonomous decisions on revenue and expenditure are made, including those concerning international and European liabilities.' The GCC specified that fundamental fiscal decisions about public revenue and public expenditure – motivated, inter alia, by social policy considerations – must remain the responsibility of the Bundestag (BVerfG 2014, para 162). However, such doctrine should not be misunderstood as an absolute limit to further integration. Instead, it emphasises that budgetary choices should be made by parliament and 'the larger the financial amount of the liability commitments . . . , the more effectively structured the German Bundestag's rights to approve and to refuse and its right to monitor must be' (BVerfG 2014, para 163). While the court also mentioned financial and time-related limits on such decisions, they remain undefined and make a violation of constitutional rules improbable, if not impossible (Korioth and Marx 2019).

In Ireland, public attention focused on the Thomas Pringle v Ireland case, which was brought before the Court of Justice of the European Union (CJEU) for a preliminary ruling on the ESM's compatibility with the EU Treaties (CJEU 2012). Ultimately, the Irish Court held that the ESM Treaty did not constitute an unconstitutional delegation of sovereignty in the sense of *Crotty v An Taoiseach*, which would diminish budgetary, fiscal or economic sovereignty of Ireland and would have required a positive referendum (High Court of Ireland 2012).

In its constitution, Austria introduced new provisions to deal with the participation of the National Council in ESM decision taking.[12] The provisions provide for information rights and create an obligation for the Austrian representative on the ESM board to agree to any ESM decision granting stability aid upon the National Council's authorisation only. However, due to Austria's comparably small share in the ESM, the country may be overruled in an emergency vote requiring an 85 per cent majority in the ESM (calculated on the percentage of shares). The Constitutional Court was also called upon to rule on, among other claims, the constitutionality of Austria's participation in the ESM.[13] The court declared, against the background of the already-enacted constitutional provision mentioned above, that the participation in the ESM was merely a political question. Austrian economic and fiscal constitutional rules only marginally restrict politics (Constitutional Court of Austria 2013, para 13). Furthermore, the transfer of sovereign rights to the ESM does, according to the Constitutional Court, not exceed the limits (Constitutional Court of Austria 2013).[14]

In Finland, the Constitutional Law Committee examined the ESM several times against the budgetary power of parliament and Finland's sovereignty. According to the committee's – not legally binding, but politically authoritative – opinion, in all major decisions affecting the financial liability under the ESM, Finland must have a veto power to safeguard Finland's sovereignty and its parliament's fiscal power. Accordingly, those decisions must be taken by mutual agreement, that is, unanimously, by the Board of Governors. As for the ESM emergency procedure, Finland demanded that the ESM draft be amended to leave outside the emergency procedure decisions affecting the liability of members. This was implemented during further treaty negotiations, thus removing the conflict with the constitution. The Committee also stressed parliament's right to information on decision-making under the ESM Treaty (Constitutional Law Committee 2012; Leino and Salminen 2013). The final version of the ESM Treaty, according to the verdict of the Constitutional Law Committee, does not include any transfer of authority 'of significance' for Finland's sovereignty within the meaning of Section 94 of the Constitution on international obligations (Constitutional Law Committee 2012).

The Estonian Supreme Court dismissed the claim that substantial budgetary decisions, which would violate the constitutional principle of parliamentary democracy and the budgetary powers of the parliament and, thus, the principles of a democratic state, could be made under the emergency voting procedure without involving the Estonian parliament (Supreme Court of Estonia 2012). The court accepted the limitation of parliamentary control as legitimate and proportionate. Even though the emergency procedure under Article 4(4) TESM requiring 85 per cent of the votes cast interferes with the constitution, it was found justified as a protection of the economic and financial sustainability of the Eurozone, which is seen as contained in Estonia constitutional values.

In the Netherlands, the Council of State, a constitutionally established advisory body, issued an opinion on the approval of the ESM Treaty. It considered that financial obligations under an international treaty have to be democratically legitimised. Depending on the weight of financial obligations, preliminary approval of the treaty alone might be insufficient. Should those obligations be too great, the national parliament may need to be involved in the ESM institutions' decision-making (Council of State of the Netherlands 2012, 5). The respectively adopted Information Protocol stipulates that the Dutch Minister on the ESM Board of Governors should not consent to any decision on ESM aid before discussing the matter with the Lower House (Dijsselbloem 2014). Even if this is a mere political arrangement, a working group of the Standing Committee of the Lower House opined that it effectively creates a veto power for the Lower House (de Vries 2014).

In Portugal, the EMU governance measures did not directly impact the constitutional framework but led to a number of judicial cases challenging Portuguese austerity measures that were justified by its EMU membership. Several measures were invalidated arguably because they went beyond international (including ESM) obligations and, thereby, violated Portuguese fundamental values, especially social rights (Martins and de Sousa Loureiro 2020). Finally, the Belgian Constitutional Court was unique in rejecting the appeals solely on admissibility issues (Constitutional Court of Belgium 2012).

Overall, this review indicates that substantive legal constraints on further fiscal integration are considerable, even though no constitutional infringements have been ascertained to date. In essence, what was at stake in each case was 'national identity' – more specifically, the alleged violation of national parliaments' budgetary decision-making autonomy and budgetary responsibility. Yet, decisions of constitutional review bodies to date can be summarised as concluding that, while the national constitutions guarantee such autonomy, the restrictions imposed by both the TSCG and the ESM did render the resulting obligations unconstitutional.

The most important fiscal aspect of the TSCG, the balanced budget rule, was transposed into the domestic legal order of all member states as well as Bulgaria, Denmark and Romania. In some member states, constitutional review procedures took place. Partly they challenged the way treaty obligations were implemented, partly they challenged substantive legal matters. As far as the constitutional review bodies found the complaints admissible and entered into substantive scrutiny, they avoided any verdict of a violation of the constitution.[15] The impression might arise that several review decisions were strongly motivated by teleologically reducing the significance of the TSCG's impact on the room of manoeuvre for national budgets. There was clearly no doubt there was a determination to strengthen budgetary discipline throughout the Eurozone. There was no ruling that could have caused additional turbulence on the financial markets and consequent problems for the member states.

Admittedly, the sheer number of legal proceedings is no proof for the legal weight of the argument. What might be said, though, is that the legality of the path taken was and still is not beyond doubt, even retrospectively. It is only that the constitutional courts (and review bodies) exerted their peace-preserving function in ending the legal challenges.

For the financial support mechanisms, again, the review bodies partly denied the admissibility of the complaints and confirmed the respect of constitutional limitations, partly specifying potential limits, in particular on parliamentary budgetary autonomy. The Austrian Constitutional Court emphasised the large margin of political discretion when it comes to complex financial, monetary and economic policy assessments. The Estonian Supreme Court accepted the limitation of parliamentary control for the sake of Eurozone stability and thus the stability of Estonia. The Irish Constitutional Court (after the CJEU Pringle Judgement), the Finnish Constitutional Law Committee, the GCC and the Dutch Council of State held that the financial assistance mechanisms remained within the limits of the constitutional safeguards of parliamentary powers.

The German and Finnish review bodies were more explicit on the limits for the financial solidarity measures. They considered unforeseeable or sizeable financial burden as absolute obstacles and, thus, not constitutional. Furthermore, they felt any adoption of the financial support must not lead to permanent limitation on budgetary autonomy. Thus, the adoption procedure should ensure a de-facto veto position guaranteed by the unanimity voting rule for the national parliaments. In other member states, review bodies required parliaments to be provided with information on all major decisions with financial consequences. Until this point, the existing case law on financial stability mechanisms did not offer any concrete definitions on absolute and ultimate limits that can be imposed on the budgetary autonomy of parliaments.

As in the case of TSCG, the courts were generous in giving priority to the stability of the Eurozone, which was seen as endangered during the period. As a consequence, it seems fair to conclude that these issues would remain of relevance for future reform scenarios. The findings of the courts and constitutional committees impose constraints on adopting the existing proposals, including integration of the ESM to EU law or the European Monetary Fund (European Commission 2017e). The adoption of essential modification of the unanimity rule in the decision-making procedure will be difficult. Any further measures aiming for a common Fiscal Union, which involves fiscal solidarity functions in a permanent way, will be challenged for their compatibility with national constitutional safeguards (see Griller and Lentsch 2021).

5.3 PROCEDURAL CONSTITUTIONAL HURDLES

Analysis of the jurisprudence of constitutional review bodies provides backward-looking information on substantive legal constraints that may shape the course of further fiscal integration. This can be complemented by a forward-looking analysis of procedural hurdles imposed on the adoption of EU Treaty change and the amendment of a national constitution. Any deepening of the Fiscal Union will require EU Treaty amendments that need to pass through a ratification process.[16] Moreover, if such EMU reform imposes significant limitations on parliaments' budgetary autonomy, it is also likely to require constitutional amendments in some member states where existing rules preclude a further shift of fiscal competences to the EU level. The European Commission tries to argue that such reform initiatives can be done on the basis of the existing treaty provisions (Commission 2017b, 2017c, 2017d, 2017e, 2017f) while respecting all legal constraints imposed by national constitutions, but experience with the crisis measures demonstrates that reform proposals are likely to be contested in the EU and national courts.

The *EMU Choices* project compiled comparative data on national requirements imposed on the EU Treaty ratification and EMU-induced constitutional amendments. The *EMU Legal Index* dataset provides data on seven types of procedural requirements (see table 5.4) that may become – under plausible circumstances – relevant veto points in the process of treaty adoption

Table 5.4 Potential Veto Points

Code	The Definition of the Potential Veto Point
PRF	Parliamentary formations: How many parliamentary formations must decide on the adoption of EMU-induced constitutional amendment? Ballots: How many ballots are the relevant parliamentary formations required to cast for the adoption of EMU-induced constitutional amendment? Majorities: What are the majorities required for the adoption of EMU-induced constitutional amendment?
SIG	Head of State: Is the signature of the head of state required for the EMU-induced constitutional amendment?
REF	Referendum: Is any referendum possible or mandatory for the adoption of EMU-induced constitutional amendment? Ex-ante constitutional review: Is ex-ante constitutional review required for the EMU-induced constitutional amendment? Ex-post constitutional review: Is ex-post constitutional review required for the EMU-induced constitutional amendment?

or EMU-induced constitutional amendment. While these seven procedural requirements cannot cover the full variety of the respective procedures in all twenty-eight member states (see Kudrna and Lentsch 2019), they serve as a reminder of prevailing legal constraints imposed on EMU reforms.

Table 5.5 presents the coding table developed to capture some variation in the procedural requirements associated with each veto point. It combines the analysis of formal procedures in twenty-eight EU member states with expert judgement on the potential use of these requirements in the light of the prevailing legal culture and past experience. While the first four components can be coded on the basis of formal rules, the latter three require a degree of judgement by country experts.

Figure 5.1 summarises procedural requirements for the adoption of treaty change in EU countries. Furthermore, in case EMU reform triggers a constitutional amendment procedure at the national level, the procedural hurdles in the given member state are indicated in figure 5.2. These figures simply sum up numerical codes assigned to each option listed in table 5.5.

Both indices indicate that EU countries share broadly similar combinations of parliamentary formation, ballot and majority requirements for treaty adoption and constitutional amendment. The variation in both processes stems primarily from the role of the referendum as well as the difference in the estimated use of the ex-ante or ex-post constitutional review. While aggregation by summing ordinal codes requires very strong methodological assumptions for interpretation, both indices provide more granular information than similar proxies elaborated so far for national legal constraints (see Kudrna and Lentsch 2019). The *EMU Legal Index* data is the most comprehensive

Table 5.5 Coding Procedural Requirements

Code	Procedure	Options
PRF	Parliamentary formations	1 one parliamentary chamber 2 two or joint parliamentary chamber(s) 3 more than two/joint parliamentary formations, including newly elected parliament
	Ballots	1 one vote in any of the relevant parliamentary formations 2 two votes in any of the relevant parliamentary formations 3 more than two votes in any of the relevant parliamentary formations
	Majorities	1 only simple majorities required 2 both simple and constitutional majorities required 3 only constitutional majorities required
SIG	Head of State	0 no signature required or legal obligation to sign 1 signature required, but its absence can be surmounted by other constitutional actor(s) 2 signature required and can veto ratification
REF	Referendum	0 no referendum foreseen 1 consultative (legally non-binding) referendum possible 2 consultative (legally non-binding) referendum mandatory 3 legally binding referendum possible 4 legally binding referendum mandatory
	Ex-ante constitutional review	0 no ex-ante review possible 1 procedurally difficult to invoke, outcome legally non-binding 2 procedurally difficult to invoke, outcome legally binding 3 procedurally easy to invoke, outcome legally non-binding 4 procedurally easy to invoke, outcome legally binding 5 mandatory review, outcome legally non-binding 6 mandatory review, outcome legally binding

for EU states and veto points, and the most up-to-date indicator of procedural requirements available for quantitatively orientated research on EU decision-making.

The relevance of procedural constraints for any national or EU decision can be analysed only on case-by-case basis. When all potential veto stakeholders agree unanimously on the desirability of the treaty change or constitutional amendment, then the change will pass, even under the most rigid procedural requirements (Tsebelis 1999). However, when there is a political disagreement, procedural rules captured by the two legal indices matter much more. The

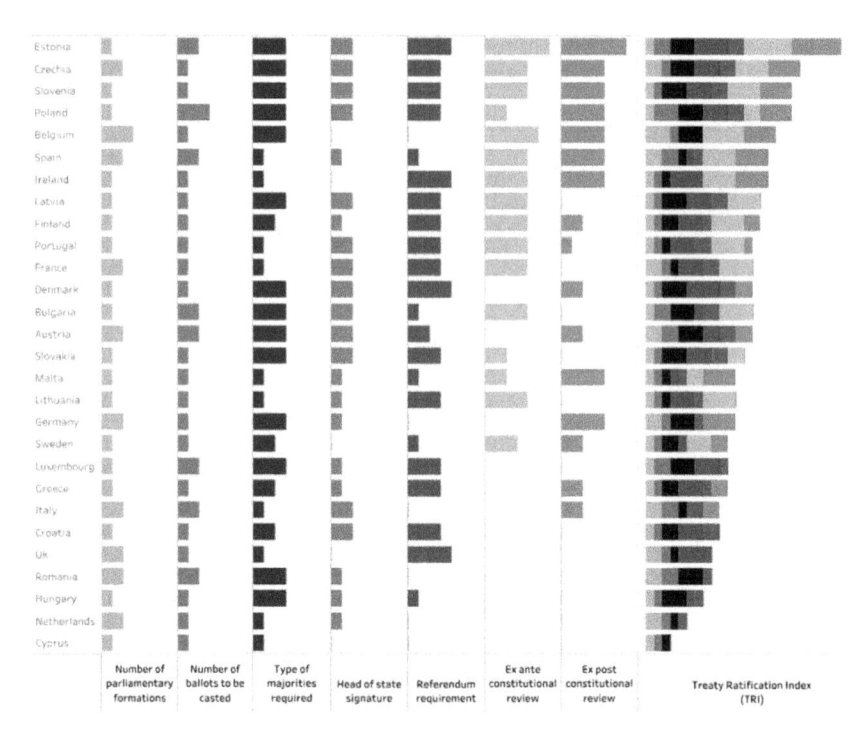

Figure 5.1 EU Treaty Ratification in EU Member States – Procedural Requirements.
Source: EMU Legal index.

procedural requirements will structure the political process and co-determine the outcome as the more demanding requirements generally provide the opponents of change with more opportunities to block the change at one of the veto points. Therefore, a systematic comparison of cross-country differences in existing procedural hurdles can support the analysis of forward-looking scenarios.

5.4 CONCLUSION

Creating a genuine European Fiscal Union could provoke a steeplechase of national legal requirements, and manifold hurdles will have to be overcome to reach the finish line. The EU Treaties provide only for limited competences in the field of fiscal and economic policies. Further comprehensive steps would most likely need EU Treaty reform, which requires unanimity among the member states expressed through the various ratification procedures.

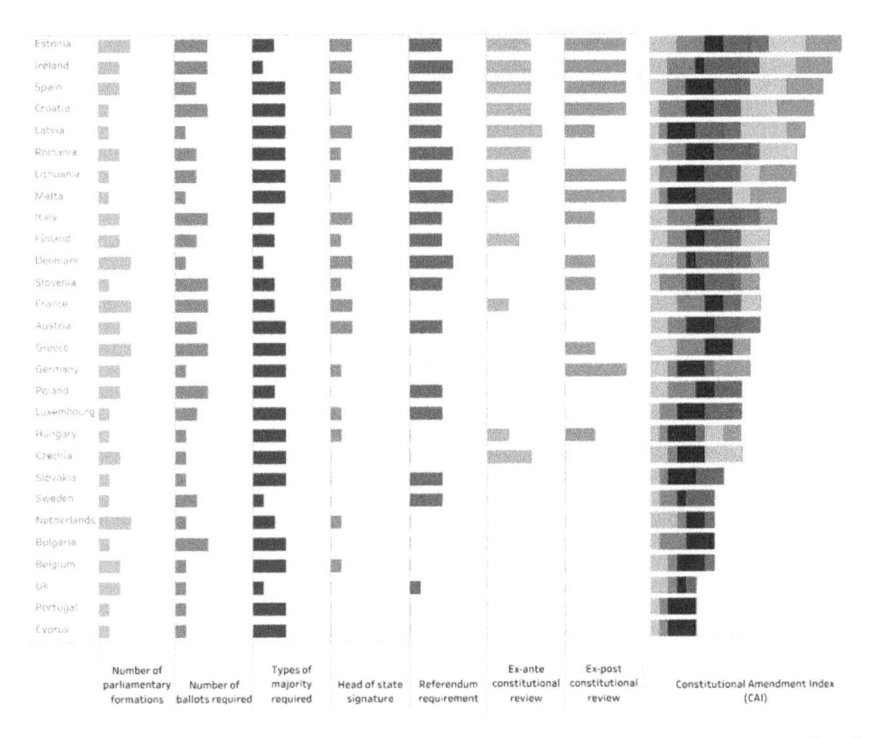

Figure 5.2 Constitutional Amendment in EU Member States – Procedural Requirements. Source: EMU Legal index.

The transfer of fiscal competences to the supranational or international level touches on the sensitive field of national sovereignty. The safeguarding of national identity and core competences, including parliamentary budgetary autonomy, which were considered by several national constitutional review bodies, may become pertinent in the EMU reform debate. The more future changes that affect protected elements such as national tradition, the more challenging it will be to achieve political consensus. Even if it is worthwhile stressing that none of the past reforms have activated legally unsurmountable hurdles in terms of 'sufficient autonomy', we have yet to point out that the sheer number of challenges and the weight of the arguments indicate such hurdles are not out of the question.

The jurisprudence on the intergovernmentally adopted EMU fiscal rules and fiscal solidarity tools demonstrates that, so far, no concrete definitions on absolute and ultimate limits to the budgetary autonomy of parliaments have emerged. However, it seems fair to conclude that these issues would remain of relevance for any future reform scenarios, which curtail the budgetary sovereignty to a more advanced degree. As evidenced in the past, related issues might become pertinent before national constitutional bodies.

The aim must be to ensure full legality of any future EMU reforms and avoid constitutional clashes, which the courts might detect ex post on a case-by-case basis.

NOTES

1. Even if there is a case in calling the EU a federal system. However, regarding economic policy, it is embryonic, at best.

2. Article 311(3) TFEU; Article 2 Decision 2014/335/EU, Euratom of 26 May 2014 on the system of own resources of the European Union, OJ L 168/105.

3. In general, a fiscal stance shall give orientation to fiscal policy by governments' discretionary decisions on tax and expenditure.

4. This formed part of the debate at the very beginning of the discussions on the monetary integration Werner report 1970, MacDougall Report 1977.

5. To use the words of article 136 para 3 TFEU, and on the basis of the assumption that there is, currently, no way back to the strict reading of Article 125 TFEU that would at least allow if not require to abstain from such EU measures. In terms of proposals, COM (2017e) 827 final, 6.12 2017, proposing a Council regulation on the establishment of the European Monetary Fund has to be taken into account.

While it is possible to conceptualise a 'fiscal union' as encompassing extra EU measures, this would mean ignoring the argument that developing a fiscal union for the Eurozone should, first and foremost, be done within the EU, and was only done outside not for conceptual but for legal and political reasons. In the recent debate, creating an EMF has been kept separate from the idea of a fiscal union.

6. The defendants argued that, given the connection of the constitutional amendment proposal with the Preliminary Title and fundamental rights, the aggravated procedure of Article 168 SC should have been followed.

7. According to Art 7 TSCG Eurozone countries commit, except in the case of qualified majority opposition, to support the Commission's recommendations at all stages of the Excessive Deficit Procedure.

8. Art 69 para 1 B-VG: As a minister is a highest executive authority, he or she cannot get instructions. In this regard, the application argued that the Art 7 TSCG is a kind of instruction and therefore an infringement of Art 69 para 1 B-VG.

9. Art 9 para 2 B-VG.

10. Opinions 37/2012, 34/2011 and minutes 49/2012 of the Constitutional Law Committee.

11. The Treaty Establishing the European Stability Mechanism (ESM Treaty) was finally concluded on 2 February 2012.

12. Art. 50a. The National Council participates in matters of the European stability mechanism. Art. 50b. An Austrian representative in the European stability mechanism may only agree or abstain in voting to: 1. a proposal for a resolution to grant stability aid to a member state in principle, . . . 3. . . . if the National Council has authorised him/her/them to do so on the basis of a proposal of the Federal Government. . . .

Without approval by the National Council the Austrian representative must refuse the proposal for such a resolution.

13. The principal claim was related to a violation of the equality-protection clause, with the ESM being potentially detrimental to the objectives of 'sustainable balanced budgets' and of 'thrift and efficiency'. There was also a claim about an insufficient determination of the transferred competences resulting in a violation of the principle of legality.

14. In concrete, Art 9(2) B-VG, 'Single sovereign competences can be transferred through law or through a treaty that has been approved according to Art. 50 (1) B-VG to other states or interstate institutions'.

15. Even in the Portuguese cases, as mentioned, the argument was that the violation lay in the national legal measures that were, in that respect, not required by ESM-obligations.

16. Article 46 TEU.

REFERENCES

Barrett, G. 2020. "Ireland." In *EMU Integration and National Constitutions*, edited by S. Griller and E. Lentsch. Oxford: Hart Publishing. 2021.

Blöchliger, H. and C. Vammalle. 2012. *Reforming Fiscal Federalism and Local Government: Beyond the Zero-Sum Game, OECD Fiscal Federalism Studies*. Paris: OECD Publishing.

Bundesverfassungsgericht. 2009. "Judgment of the Second Senate of 30 June 2009 - 2 BvE 2/08 -, paras. 1-421." http://www.bverfg.de/e/es20090630_2bve000208en.html.

Bundesverfassungsgericht. 2011. "Judgment of the Second Senate of 07 September 2011 - 2 BvR 987/10 -, paras. 1-142." http://www.bverfg.de/e/rs20110907_2bvr098710en.html.

Bundesverfassungsgericht. 2012. "Judgment of the Second Senate of 12 September 2012 - 2 BvR 1390/12 -, paras. 1-215." http://www.bverfg.de/e/rs20120912_2bvr139012en.html.

Bundesverfassungsgericht. 2012b. Press Release, no. 67, 2012, September 12, 2012.

Bundesverfassungsgericht. 2014. "Judgment of the Second Senate of 18 March 2014 - 2 BvR 1390/12 -, paras. 1-245." http://www.bverfg.de/e/rs20140318_2bvr139012en.html.

Bundesverfassungsgericht. 2014b. Press Release, no. 23, 2014, March 18, 2014.

Constitutional Court of Austria. 2013. "VfSlg 19.750/2013."

Constitutional Court of Belgium. 2012. "Judgment n° 156/2012."

Constitutional Court of Belgium. 2016. "Judgement n° 62/2016."

Constitutional Council of France. 2012. "Décision n° 2012-653 DC du 9 août 2012, Traité sur la stabilité, la coordination et la gouvernance au sein de l'Union économique et monétaire." https://www.conseil-constitutionnel.fr/decision/2012/2012653DC.htm.

Constitutional Court of Spain. 2012. "Judgement, ECLI:ES:TC:2012:9A."
Constitutional Law Committee of Finland. 2011. "Opinion 14/2011."
Constitutional Law Committee of Finland. 2012. "Opinion 13/2012."
Court of Justice of the European Union. 2012. "Case C-370/12", *Pringle*, ECLI:EU:C:2012:756.
Court of Justice of the European Union. 2015. "Case C 62-/14", *Gauweiler*, ECLI:EU:C:2015:400.
Court of Justice of the European Union. 2017. "Case C-493/17", *Weiss et al.*, ECLI:EU:C:2018:1000.
Council of the European Union. 2010. "Decision of the Representatives of the Governments of the Euro Area Member States Meeting Within the Council of the European Union", May 10, 2010. https://register.consilium.europa.eu/doc/srv?L =EN&f=ST%209614%202010%20INIT.
Council of State of the Netherlands. 2012. "Opinion of 1 March 2012", *Kamerstukken*, Parliamentary Papers 33221, 4.
Council Regulation (EC). 1997. "No 1466/1997 on the strengthening of the surveillance of budgetary positions and the surveillance and coordination of economic policies."
De Vries, A. 2014. "Aandacht voor het parlementair budgetrecht in Europees perspectief - Rapport van een werkgroep uit de commissie voor de Rijksuitgaven van de Tweede Kamer der Staten-Generaal", September 9, 2014. https://zoek.officie lebekendmakingen.nl/blg-376413.pdf.
Dijsselbloem, J. 2014. "Raad voor Economische en Financiële Zaken", December 30, 2014. https://zoek.officielebekendmakingen.nl/kst-21501-07-1217.html.
EFSF Framework Agreement. 2010. "EFSF Framework Agreement of 7 June 2010 between the participating Member States and the European Financial and Stability Facility", June 7, 2010. https://www.esm.europa.eu/sites/default/files/20111019_ efsf_framework_agreement_en.pdf.
Euro Area Governments. 2010. "Statement by the heads of state and government of the Euro area", March 25, 2010. https://www.consilium.europa.eu/media/21429/2 0100325-statement-of-the-heads-of-state-or-government-of-the-euro-area-en.pdf.
European Commission. 2012. "Blueprint for a deep and genuine economic and monetary union – Launching a European Debate", November 28, 2012. https://eur-lex .europa.eu/lexuriserv/lexuriserv.do?Uri=COM:2012:0777:FIN:EN:PDF.
European Commission. 2016a. "Communication Towards a Positive Fiscal Stance for the Euro Area", November 16, 2016. https://eur-lex.europa.eu/resource.html?Uri =cellar:30353466-b172-11e6-871e-01aa75ed71a1.0011.02/DOC_1&format=PDF.
European Commission. 2016b. "Decision (EU) 2016/221 of 12 February 2016 amending Decision (EU) 2015/1937 establishing an independent advisory European Fiscal Board", February 12, 2016. https://eur-lex.europa.eu/legal-content/EN/TXT /PDF/?Uri=CELEX:32016D0221&from=EN.
European Commission. 2017a. "Reflection paper on the deepening of the economic and monetary union", May 31, 2017. https://ec.europa.eu/commission/sites/beta-po litical/files/reflection-paper-emu_en.pdf.

European Commission. 2017b. "Communication on further steps towards completing Europe's economic and monetary union: A roadmap", December 6, 2017. https://ec.europa.eu/commission/sites/beta-political/files/reflection-paper-emu_en.pdf.

European Commission. 2017c. "Communication on new budgetary instruments for a stable euro area within the Union framework", December 6, 2017. https://ec.europa.eu/info/sites/info/files/economy-finance/com_822_0.pdf.

European Commission. 2017d. "A European Minister of Economy and Finance", December 6, 2017. https://ec.europa.eu/info/sites/info/files/economy-finance/com_823_0.pdf.

European Commission. 2017e. "Proposal for a Council Regulation on the establishment of the European Monetary Fund", December 6, 2017. https://eur-lex.europa.eu/resource.html?Uri=cellar:050797ec-db5b-11e7-a506-01aa75ed71a1.0002.02/DOC_1&format=PDF.

European Commission. 2017f. "Report from the Commission presented under Article 8 of the Treaty on Stability, Coordination and Governance in the Economic and Monetary Union", February 22, 2017. https://ec.europa.eu/info/sites/info/files/c20171201_en.pdf.

European Commission. 2017g. "The Fiscal Compact: Taking Stock", February 22, 2017. https://ec.europa.eu/info/sites/info/files/1_en_act_part1_v3_0.pdf.

European Council. 2010a. "Conclusions – 28–29 October 2010", November 30, 2010. https://www.consilium.europa.eu/uedocs/cms_data/docs/pressdata/en/ec/117496.pdf.

European Council. 2010b. "Council Regulation (EU) No 407/2010 of 11 May 2010 establishing a European financial stabilisation mechanism", May 12, 2010. https://eur-lex.europa.eu/lexuriserv/lexuriserv.do?Uri=OJ:L:2010:118:0001:0004:EN:PDF.

European Council. 2012. "Treaty on Stability, Coordination and Governance in the Economic and Monetary Union", March 2, 2012. https://www.consilium.europa.eu/media/20399/st00tscg26_en12.pdf.

European Stability Mechanism. 2012. "Treaty establishing the European Stability Mechanism", February 03, 2012. https://www.esm.europa.eu/sites/default/files/20150203_-_esm_treaty_-_en.pdf.

Gérard, P. and W. Verrijdt. 2017. "Belgian Constitutional Court Adopts National Idetntiy Discourse." *European Constitutional Law Review* 13, no. 1: 182–205.

Griller, S., L. Papapdopoulou, and R. Puff. 2020. *National Constitutions and EU Integration.* Oxford: Hart Publishing. 2021.

Griller, S. and E. Lentsch. 2020. *EMU Integration and National Constitutions.* Oxford: Hart Publishing. 2021.

High Court of Ireland. 2012. "IEHC 296 (2012 3772P)", July 17, 2012.

Juncker, J., D. Tusk, J. Dijsselbloem, M. Draghi, and M. Schulz. 2015. "Completing Europe's Economic and Monetary Union", June 22, 2015. https://ec.europa.eu/commission/sites/beta-political/files/5-presidents-report_en.pdf.

Korioth, S. and J. Marx. 2020. "Germany." In *EMU Integration and National Constitutions,* edited by S. Griller and E. Lentsch. Oxford: Hart Publishing. 2021.

Kudrna, Z. and E. Lentsch. 2019. "Constitutional Amendment Index: the procedural requirements of an EMU-induced constitutional change in EU member states" *Zeitschrift für öffentliches Recht*, 2019/3, pp 443–464.

Leino-Sandberg, P. and T. Saarenheimo. 2018. "A fiscal union for the EMU?" *Ademu Working Paper*, March, 2018. http://ademu-project.eu/wp-content/uploads/2018/06/0095-A-fiscal-union-for-the-EMU.pdf.

Lentsch, E. 2017. "Report on the institutional consequences of fiscal and economic integration measures." *EMU Choices Working Paper*, 2017. https://emuchoices.eu/wp-content/uploads/2017/08/Report-on-the-institutional-consequences-of-fiscal-and-economic-integration-measures-upload.pdf.

Lentsch, E. 2018. "Report on the compatibility of reform scenarios with the EU Treaties." *EMU Choices Working Paper, 2018*. https://emuchoices.eu/wp-content/uploads/2018/08/Report-on-compatibility-of-EMU-reform-proposals-with-the-Treaties.pdf.

Maduro, M. 2012. "A new governance for the European Union and the Euro: Democracy and Justice." *Robert Schuman Centre for Advanced Studies Policy Paper*, 2012/11. https://cadmus.eui.eu/bitstream/handle/1814/24295/RSCAS_PP_2012_11rev.pdf?Sequence=1.

Martins A. and J. de Sousa Loureiro. 2020. "Portugal." In *EMU Integration and National Constitutions,* edited by S. Griller, and E. Lentsch. Oxford: Hart Publishing. 2021.

Monti, M. et al. 2016. "Future Financing of the EU: Final report and recommendations of the High Level Group on Own Resources", April 1, 2016. https://ec.europa.eu/info/sites/info/files/about_the_european_commission/eu_budget/future-financing-hlgor-final-report_2016_en.pdf.

Saurugger, S. and C. Fontan. 2017. "Courts as political actors: Resistance to the EU's new economic governance mechanisms at the domestic level", 5 November 5, 2017. https://halshs.archives-ouvertes.fr/halshs-01628964/document.

Supreme Court of Estonia (2012). "Decision 3-4-1-6-12", July 12, 2012.

Thirion, G. 2017. "European Fiscal Union: Economic Rationale and Design Challenges." *CEPS Working Document*, January 20, 2017. CEPS Working Document. https://ssrn.com/abstract=3047087.

Tsebelis, G. 1999. "Veto Players and Law Production in Parliamentary Democracies: An Empirical Analysis." *The American Political Science Review* 93, no. 3: 591–608.

Van Rompuy, H. 2012. "Towards a genuine economic and monetary union", June 26, 2012. https://www.consilium.europa.eu/media/33785/131201.pdf.

Van Rompuy, H., J.M. Barroso, J. Juncker, and M. Draghi. 2012. "Towards a genuine economic and monetary union", December 5, 2012. https://www.consilium.europa.eu/media/23818/134069.pdf.

Woźniakowski, T. 2018. "Why the Sovereign Debt Crisis Could Lead to a Federal Fiscal Union: The Paradoxical Origins of Fiscalization in the United States and Insights for the European Union." *Journal of European Public Policy* 25, no. 4: 630–49.

Chapter 6

Studying Integration and EMU's Choices

Dirk Leuffen and Uwe Puetter

6.1 INTRODUCTION[1]

The Eurozone Crisis has been conceived, at times, as a life-threatening experience for some of the member states' economies, if not for the European Union (EU). As such, the crisis triggered a renewed interest in European integration. Yet, the apparent revival of integration theories was less marked by the demarcation of clear fault lines than during the grand debates of past decades. Today, there is more eclecticism; for example, several contributions seek to bridge or combine the classic grand theories of neofunctionalism and liberal intergovernmentalism (Jones et al. 2016; Schimmelfennig 2015). Others, such as the new intergovernmentalism (Bickerton et al. 2015b), even avoid a clear positioning along the rationalist–constructivist divide. In our view, the softening of the debate is not the consequence of all disputes having been settled. Substantive differences between theoretical perspectives based on varying sets of ontological premises, as formulated for instance by the three institutionalisms (Hall and Taylor 1996; Aspinwall and Schneider 2000), remain – discursive institutionalist analysis of the Eurozone Crisis is a case in point (Crespy and Schmidt 2014; Schmidt 2013). However, different perspectives seem more willing to accept a state of co-existence of potentially antagonistic analytical perspectives, today, and this applies in particular to the study of Economic and Monetary Union (EMU) and the Eurozone Crisis.

The *EMU Choices* research consortium has not been the only collaborative research project on the Eurozone Crisis, but in comparison to other prominent projects, such as ENLIGHTEN, it aimed for a fairly integrated research design as opposed to thematic or pluralistic clustering. By design, it was meant to concentrate a large collaborative effort on the generation of project-wide databases. The consortium integrated scholars from different theoretical, ontological and epistemological camps – stretching across the three institutionalisms and with backgrounds in various integration theories – and combined rigorous analyses of both, dataset and causal process observations (Brady 2010). The consortium, thus, built on the premise that if scientific disputes had not been settled in the past, different approaches to conceiving and studying EMU and its crisis may very well have their raison d'être. Moreover, the expectation was that by integrating a range of perspectives, a more complete picture of the Eurozone Crisis was likely to emerge. The consortium members were actively incited to 'working together' (Poteete et al. 2010) and to reaping the benefits of cross-fertilisation, theoretical diversity and the inclusion of multi-method approaches.

This chapter reviews some of the consortium's theoretical and methodological choices and links these to selected outcomes to evaluate the merits of the pluralistic design selected. It finds that bringing together different approaches has proven to be an effective means for fostering productivity and generating scientific insights. The chapter also discusses the benefits and weaknesses of the different approaches and shows how they can complement each other.

Agreeing on the envisaged division of labour within the project meant that differences regarding the link between ontology and methodology (Hall 2003) could not be sidestepped. Whereas a group of colleagues believed in the merits of recording member state preferences at specific points in time and then comparing and analysing these preferences cross-sectionally, others maintained that decision-making at times of crisis was characterised by large degrees of uncertainty while decision makers were immersed in a dense web of interactions at and across various levels, including feedback loops and equifinality. Temporality emerged as a key point of contention. Temporality is understood here not as the question of how time matters in politics in its own right (cf. Goetz and Meyer-Sahling 2009), but how decision-making is assumed to unfold over time. Those following a stylised but well-structured understanding of European Union (EU) decision-making seek to register diverging preferences of EU member states and organs, which can then be aggregated to explain negotiation outcomes. In Pierson's words (1996), such static approaches work with 'snapshot view[s]' or 'set[s] of consecutive snapshots' (Bulmer 2009) and their overall aim is mostly to generate generalisable explanations, abstracting from the noise of individual cases (cf. on this also Héritier 2007). Others are more interested in understanding how individual decisions came about within a highly intertwined policymaking environment. The interest is thus in 'causes of effects' (Goertz and Mahoney 2012), for which the merits of careful process tracing analyses (Beach and Brun Pedersen 2013; Bennett and Checkel 2015), geared at formulating mechanismic explanations of individual cases, are broadly acknowledged. Following

Blatter and Blume (2008) and Blatter and Haverland (2012), the divide relates to a preference for 'covariational' versus 'causal process' analyses. This terminology is used here to dichotomise different approaches followed by members of the *EMU Choices* consortium.

This review distinguishes between the three steps of *agenda setting*, *preference formation* and *European interactions*. First, *agenda setting* accounts for the importance of the selection mechanisms that determined which issues actually made it to the EU negotiation table. As a second step, *preference formation* is investigated. Concerning preference formation, *EMU Choices* has largely focused on the member state level but also scrutinised the preferences of EU organs and institutions, such as the European Central Bank (ECB) or the European Commission. Third, *European interactions* are explored to avoid a bias towards state centric, bargaining-orientated perspectives that are suggested by the concept of 'interstate bargaining' used in Andrew Moravcsik's 'baseline model' of European integration (Moravcsik 1998; Schimmelfennig and Moravcsik 2009). In short, while the overall research design leans more towards a sequential conceptualisation of EU decision-making – as subsequent stages are being kept analytically distinct, the definition of each stage potentially allows diverging analytical treatment and interpretation. There is also some tension inherent in this approach, which allows, however, for variation in interpreting findings and considering how the different stages are interrelated. For example, European interactions for some can be considered constitutive for preference formation, while others hold that preference formation always precedes interstate interactions.

This chapter shows that the mix of approaches and accounts used in *EMU Choices* complemented each other well and contributed to a more encompassing understanding of the politics of EMU reforms. We, thus, agree with Jupille et al. (2003) that 'theoretical, methodological and carefully structured empirical dialogue' continues to constitute the right way forward for studies of European integration.[2]

6.2 COLLABORATIVE RESEARCH AGAINST THE BACKDROP OF DIFFERENT ONTOLOGIES AND METHODOLOGIES

Many analyses of the Eurozone Crisis discuss its implications for integration theory. However, most of these studies suffer from one of two possible shortcomings. Either, when being too focused on one or just a few cases, they are very limited in the covered empirical scope, or alternatively, when extending the number of cases, they neglect the interwoven mechanisms of decision-making over time and across levels. One solution to the trade-off between depth and width (cf. Leuffen 2007) consists in engaging a larger number of researchers to collaborate on the same topic. The *EMU Choices* consortium was able to account for the multiplicity of policy issues, which fall under the umbrella term 'Eurozone Crisis', and the large number of key political actors (member states, EU institutions, socio-economic actor groups, third countries) by integrating researchers with different interests and expertise. This allowed both, paying stronger attention to process and evolution over time as well as conducting rigorous cross-case comparisons. One group of researchers in the project strongly believed in the merits of tracing how EMU politics at different, often closely interwoven levels developed over time. This echoes Pierson's (1996) observation that 'just as a film often reveals meanings that cannot be discerned from a single photograph, a view of Europe's development over time gives us a richer sense of the nature of the emerging European polity'. This group had strong preferences for qualitative case study approaches, including careful process tracing (Bennett and Checkel 2015) to account for the dynamic interactions and feedback mechanisms across different levels which, in their view, characterised EMU policymaking. This group was also concerned about equifinality (Goertz and Mahoney 2012). In contrast, another group of consortium members was more inspired by covariational logics of inference (Blatter and Blume 2008) and the approaches followed, for instance, by the *Decision-Making in the European Union* (DEU) projects (Thomson et al. 2006, 2012). In their view, by rigorously dissecting the different steps of EMU policymaking and by focusing on just a few key moments of the process, comparability across all EU member states could be achieved and would facilitate the discovery of law-like regularities. While both groups agreed on the necessity of high-quality data collection, they disagreed on the temporal depth of the data to be collected. Eventually, the *EMU Choices* consortium sought to integrate both perspectives. Project members collected data on preferences in conjunction with preselected issues at specific points in time and conducted qualitative interviews and process-tracing analyses, which revealed how these preferences and how the interactions of governmental actors and EU institutions at the European level evolved over time. The research design accounted for a large number of domestic and European actors, including all member states, the key EU decision-making institutions, as well as selected economic actors, such as banks, organised business and trade unions.[3] Different theoretical considerations guided the formulation of research interests and the corresponding methodological choices while the data collection was partially conducted in collaboration. This applied in particular to the EU-wide expert interviews and questionnaires which covered all member states and formed the basis of the larger consortium-wide EMU Positions (Wasserfallen et al. 2019) and EMU Formations (Kudrna et al. 2019) datasets. These datasets certainly represent a unique contribution to *EMU Choices*. In addition, to measuring preferences and saliences, we collected process-tracing information on selected countries and issues; in fact, many colleagues contributed to both types of research simultaneously.

The two diverging ontologies which informed the overall research design of *EMU Choices* remain visible at the stage of the research output. Most publications can be grouped according to the above distinction: First, snapshot analyses, which seek to identify actor positions and outcomes at pre-defined moments in time and within an ideal-typical EU decision-making cycle. Second, analyses which consider feedback loops and actor interactions over time, mostly based on causal process tracing. In the following is compared a meta-analysis selected 'covariational' vis-à-vis 'causal process tracing' contributions to the *EMU Choices* project. This review is structured along the three steps of i) agenda setting, ii) preference formation and iii) European interactions. This tripartite framework acknowledges the strong importance of agenda setting for pre-selecting and pre-structuring EMU negotiations. It also broadens the scope of EU-level interactions beyond the focus on interstate bargaining which would ex ante bias the analysis in favour of liberal intergovernmentalist accounts. European interactions can also include intergovernmental policy coordination, information exchange and joint policy

In most cases, this grouping of *EMU Choices* research output into covariational versus causal process tracing accounts thus entails ontological or theoretical differences, which at least in parts nicely matches methodological emphasis. Covariational accounts import the notion of distinct spheres of EMU politics, notably domestic (or inner-institutional) preference formation and bargaining from liberal intergovernmentalism and rational choice institutionalism. To be clear, not all contributions labelled as 'covariational' in this chapter endorse liberal intergovernmentalism. Some might, for example, equally investigate the relative power and influence of the Commission in EMU crisis politics. Yet, their ontology, the notion of how EU politics are structured in different phases is imported from liberal intergovernmentalism and rational choice institutionalism. In comparison, the dynamic accounts represent supranational, constructivist, historical institutionalist, post-functionalist and new intergovernmentalist understandings of the politics of European integration. Yet, considerable theoretical openness in most of the contributions are also detected and reviewed in the following. Those who applied static perspectives relied to a stronger degree on the EMU Positions and the EMU Formations datasets.[4] Some of those who focused on process orientation used these datasets, too, but engaged in additional qualitative research work and gathered further information through in-depth interviews and analyses of other primary and secondary sources to anchor data points in more profound historical perspectives. Moreover, the datasets also partially included answers to open-ended questions. Yet, this element of the collaborative work effort was less consistently implemented than the structured part of the interview-based country-specific research, on which the datasets were based.

6.3 AGENDA SETTING DURING THE EUROZONE CRISIS

Agenda setting has not been at the heart of classic integration theories, at least not explicitly. Only more recently has it started to capture EU researcher's attention, as highlighted, for instance, by Princen (2009, 2007), who also offers a definition of agenda (Princen 2007), or Alexandrova et al. (2014). It also constitutes an integral part of EU decision-making's formal models (cf. Thomson et al. 2006).[5] New intergovernmentalism, as applied to the European Council and the Eurogroup, expects agenda setting to reflect the quest for consensus. Thus, a high frequency of meetings should be observed, as should a flexible agenda in terms of time allocation and representation of agenda items to include a mix of hard decision issues and background discussion. Finally, agendas are likely to include routine analyses of the economic situation of the euro area and the identification of policy interdependencies by member state representatives, the Commission and ECB (Puetter 2006, 2014; Hodson and Puetter 2016). Yet, new intergovernmentalism does not consider agenda setting in terms of policy preferences. The *EMU Choices* consortium has acknowledged that agenda setting is important for understanding both the politics and the outcomes of EU decision-making during the Eurozone Crisis. Clearly, the crisis itself and external dynamics which triggered or contributed to it, such as the subprime mortgage crisis in the United States, are important background conditions which unveiled shortcomings in the EMU structure (Scharpf 2011, 2013; Moravcsik 2012). Such circumstances correspond to what Princen (2007, 24) would call 'issue formation as external to the political process'. But this chapter is more interested in issues which are 'internal to the political process' (Princen 2007), and thus, more narrowly, in the processes as well as the outcomes that determined which policy suggestions made it to the European negotiation table and importantly, which issues or solutions were dropped before. The importance of this step is accounted for by Wasserfallen et al. (2019), who addressed a choice process to move from the set of 'potential policy proposals' to the 'negotiated policy proposals'.

Most contributions to the project-related special issue published by the *European Union Politics* (EUP) academic journal take the agenda for granted. As Frieden and Walter (2019) in their review of the *EUP* special issue highlight: 'given the nature of the data, most of the contributions in this special issue neglect this issue [of agenda setting, the authors] and focus on the negotiated policy options'. An exception is Degner and Leuffen (2020), who analyse Franco–German cooperation during the Eurozone Crisis. Their process-tracing analysis shows how France and Germany jointly eliminated a number of issues from the European negotiation agenda. For instance, they show that Germany and France jointly prevented any form of debt restructuring for Greece in 2010, and the failure to establish Eurobonds is another quite informative example. Although Eurogroup President Jean-Claude Juncker and the Commission repeatedly attempted to bring Eurobonds to the European negotiation agenda, the European Council never officially discussed this proposal due to German and other Northern states' opposition to it, a choice tolerated by France. Thus, the contribution finds that some member states were in the position to block issues from the official EMU negotiation agenda during the crisis. Since, with respect to most of the policy issues covered in the *EMU Choices* datasets, the Commission does not possess the formal power of agenda setting – in contrast to legislative decision-making in the EU (Schmidt 2000) – it can only voice its ideas, which, however, may or may not be taken into account in the intergovernmental decision-making process which was so important during the Eurozone Crisis. In contrast, within its realm of responsibility, the ECB was able to set the agenda by taking clear stances. This becomes most visible in ECB President Draghi's famous dictum that the ECB will do 'whatever it takes' to save the euro. Degner and Leuffen's (2020) contribution relates to the dynamic account outlined above.

Adopting a covariational perspective, Finke and Bailer (2019) include agenda setting in their formal decision-making models and show that 'formal rules determining agenda setting and veto rights remain relevant even in times of crisis' (ibid.). Their analysis highlights that the Commission's influence varies across institutional settings. In particular, the Commission is far more influential in formal legislative decision-making as compared to more detached forms of intergovernmental negotiations which, for example, led to new international treaties, as in the case of the treaty establishing the European Stability Mechanism (ESM).

That so few contributions to the *EMU Choices* covered agenda setting may be due to the initial project design which favours the construction of DEU-type datasets (Thomson et al. 2012) and relates to the static approach outlined above. Degner and Leuffen's (2020) article also shows that a process-tracing perspective can reveal important insights into temporal sequences. When France and Germany eliminated potential policies from the formal negotiation agenda, they must have had already formed policy preferences on these issues. In another contribution, Degner and Leuffen (2020) take a closer look at intra-German interactions that have led to the German government's demand to drop a number of issues from the official negotiation table, also using a dynamic approach. In short, agenda setting does not preclude preference formation. Likewise, Bojovic, Munta and Puetter (2020) find that, with regard to the role of socio-economic interest groups in relation to the creation of the ESM, some groups considered 'that the ESM was never an important issue on their agenda' (ibid.), which meant that they did form a particular preference on the issue in the first place.

6.4 PREFERENCE FORMATION

The notion of preference formation was at the core of the *EMU Choices* project. This centrality is mirrored by the initial project design, which was, to a great extent, informed by the liberal intergovernmentalist baseline reading of Eurozone Crisis decision-making, as outlined above. As a consequence, a substantive share of the project's resources was invested in collecting information on member state preferences, on preferences of sub-state public and private actors as well as of international institutions, such as the International Monetary Fund (IMF). Moreover, the analysis of preference formation was an important part of the different *EMU Choices* work packages. In the following is a review of a number of examples highlighting the considerations behind the different approaches to studying preference formation.

The concept of preference formation was not only the most central concept in the overall project design, it also became an inevitable focal point for the discussions on ontology and methodology. What is of particular interest, here, is variation in how preference formation features in the project's research output does not simply reiterate well-known differences in theoretical debate but shows that the link between ontology and methodology is far from trivial. The consortium's largest collaborative effort in relation to preference formation centred on data collection. The methodology behind EMU Positions dataset is most closely linked to the rational institutionalist basis of liberal intergovernmentalism's negotiation theory, which also underlines that the methodological choices in itself dictated the scope of our findings (cf. Csehi and Puetter 2017). Importantly, however, the methodological choice impedes an inspection of how these preferences emerged in the first place. The 'liberal' element of liberal intergovernmentalism is thus not tested but only assumed to exist. At the same time, the EMU Formation dataset represents a bridge between the methodological focus implied by the EMU Positions data, on the one hand, and dynamic accounts, on the other. While it does not trace actor influence beyond four selected events in eurocrisis management – in line with common practices of case study research – it can help to reveal insights into political agency at all levels of preference formation, including the domestic arena. Finally, process-orientated methodology, which is at the centre of in-depth case studies, is the preferred choice of constructivist, as well as historical and sociological institutionalist traditions, which are present in *EMU Choices*. Yet, it is an equally applied method to test liberal intergovernmentalist and rational choice institutionalist theory. While the initial assumption was that methodology should follow ontology or theory, a multiplicity of methodological choices were seen as possible, if not inevitable, to expand our knowledge about euro-crisis politics in our collaborative research work. It is, thus, not only the simultaneous application of different methodological perspectives which can make larger-scale collaborative research interesting but also the simultaneous application of both diverging theoretical and methodological perspectives. The following sample contributions from the research output may illustrate this.

The clearest applications of a static perspective in investigating member state preferences formation during the Eurozone Crisis are the contributions by Lehner and Wasserfallen (2019) and by Târlea et al. (2019). Using the EMU Positions dataset, Lehner and Wasserfallen (2019) analyse the dimensions of conflict that structured the negotiations on EMU reforms. With the help of dimension reduction techniques, the authors show that 'the political contestation in the reform of the Eurozone is one dimensional' separating 'advocates of fiscal transfer and discipline' (Lehner and Wasserfallen 2019). Their central finding thus focuses on determining a prevailing pattern in EMU politics during the Eurozone Crisis. The authors' analysis backs similar findings in the Eurozone Crisis study literature, among them many predominantly qualitative accounts. The covariational approach in this case helps to investigate a general feature of Eurozone Crisis politics based on a much larger dataset as used within previous analyses.

With the help of multilevel regression models, Târlea et al. (2019) analyse member state preferences on forty negotiation issues. That analysis corroborates liberal intergovernmentalist expectations as it finds that countries' financial sector exposure matters in relation to the question of whether these countries favoured more or less integrative measures to fight the Eurozone Crisis. In fact, higher levels of interdependence seem to drive preferences for European integration. In contrast, Târlea et al. (2019) provide less support for the argument that political factors, such as public opinion, party politics or the rise of extremist parties, impacted on national preference formation. The covariational account by Târlea et al. (2019) presents a highly encompassing take on national preference formation during the Eurozone Crisis. In a way, it adopts a bird's eye view on national preference formation in Europe. Yet, while having imported key methodological choices from liberal intergovernmentalist thinking regarding the broad pattern of EU politics, the actual analysis backs a liberal intergovernmentalist reading of Eurozone Crisis politics only to a certain extent. In particular, the authors' approach precludes an analysis of the mechanisms which have generated the observed preferences. It remains somewhat imprecise with regard to how states formed their preferences and, in particular, which role interest groups took in the process.

Here is where the project's design foresaw a series of qualitative case studies, developed by individual project teams. What these case studies have in common is a narrower focus and an in-depth perspective on a specific issue and a smaller set of countries. The idea was to give room for theoretical and methodological variation and supplement data from the EMU Position and EMU Formation datasets, which were based on coding and questionnaire interview work, with less structured expert interviews, media research and process-tracing methodology. It is because of this that these qualitative case studies provide very different insights and arrive at diverse conclusions on respective endorsement or rejection of specific theoretical perspectives. From a methodological point of view, the core strength of small-n research in unveiling and tracing causal mechanisms is, thus, meant to supplement and partially challenge findings which emerge from the above outlined covariational accounts (cf. Lieberman 2005).

In their in-depth analysis of preference formation in France during the Eurozone Crisis, Fontan and Saurugger (2020) argue that the clear distinction between domestic preference formation, on the one hand, and interstate bargaining, on the other, by liberal intergovernmentalism does not hold in the context of Eurozone Crisis decision-making. Instead, they combine theoretical insights from new intergovernmentalism and the political-economy literature and advance the notion of feedback loops, which exist between French politics and other EU member states, such as Germany. A central finding is that 'the main European decisions have been taken by French presidents, in coordination with a small group of high civil servants and the main economic interest groups' (ibid.). Moreover, Fontan and Saurugger point to how embedded the respective presidents and their closest advisers are within EU-level policymaking networks, as predicted by new intergovernmentalism. They conclude that 'preference formation, as a process which involves governmental elites, thus, has become transnational' (Fontan and Saurugger 2020).

Uncertainty is another key factor in preference formation in the French case, the authors find. In this context the close contacts between top-level civil servants and financial sector representatives also come into play. However, Fontan and Saurugger emphasise that the very high degree of centralisation and a 'strong degree of economic patriotism' (Fontan and Saurugger 2020) among the French governing elites are country-specific factors which observers have to take into account. Public opinion, in turn, is found not to have mattered substantially in French preference-formation processes.

Bojovic, Munta, and Puetter (2020) engage in a case study on the role of non-governmental actors in preference formation in relation to the creation of the ESM. Similar to Fontan and Saurugger (2020), they make use of data from the open-ended questions in the EMU Formation dataset. In addition, they conducted well over thirty semi-structured interviews with representatives of socio-economic actors and governmental officials in nine Eurozone countries. Finally, they evaluate the peer rankings on actor influence from the EMU Formation dataset. In contrast to the highly centralised political system of France, the evidence from the countries in the authors' sample (Spain, Portugal, Ireland, Austria, the Netherlands, Finland, Estonia, Slovenia and Slovakia) does not suggest a relevant role of socio-economic actors in domestic preference formation. Moreover, it is apparent from the in-depth interviews how little political effort socio-economic actors showed to actively influence government policy on the matter. The limited role of core socio-economic interests (banking, business, trade unions) in influencing governmental preference formation in relation to the creation of the ESM is also apparent from the EU-28 data on peer rankings of actor influence. Moreover, Bojovic, Munta and Puetter review the role of parliamentary interventions and negative public opinion in the studied countries. Here, intervention is focused on obtaining scrutiny rights in relation to ESM-related decision-making at the national level. The actual decision to create the ESM, its size and set up was hardly politically contested, and executive actors enjoyed considerable leeway in these issues.

Degner and Leuffen's (2020) analysis of German decision-making processes shows some important country-specific variation. The authors demonstrate that the German government, indeed, closely followed public opinion at key moments of the Eurozone Crisis. Yet, similar to Bojovic, Munta, and Puetter (2020), the authors find that economic interest groups, only played a secondary role, if at all, questioning a key expectation of liberal intergovernmentalism.[6] In their in-depth case study of preference formation in Southern Europe, Morlino, and Sottilotta (2019), too, reveal the absence of public opinion as a significant factor shaping governmental preferences. More specifically, compared to the German context as revealed in Degner and Leuffen's (2020) account, Morlino and Sottilotta (2019) demonstrate the fundamental antagonism between governments that implemented far-reaching austerity-orientated measures while remaining largely unresponsive to detrimental preferences of their constituencies.

All four case studies reviewed here offer important insights into processes of preference formation. Moreover, they partly challenge a dichotomic understanding of domestic preference formation and interstate bargaining. The careful unpacking of decision-making processes reveals how preference formation evolves over time and is also related to transnational elite interaction.

Moreover, it cannot simply be assumed that domestic constituencies behave in a standardised fashion. Yet, the case study research alone offers no encompassing account on preference formation in relation to EU decision-making across policy sectors and member states. Once again, this highlights that the covariational and causal mechanismic perspectives are complementary and are both able to produce important contributions to our understanding of Eurozone Crisis politics. However, both accounts remain deficient when omitting the other side, and this underlines the value added by pluralistic consortia, such as *EMU Choices*.

The above case studies complement the covariational perspectives, which are based on the project's dataset. Csehi and Puetter (2021) pursue yet a third strategy, which reflects the implicit conversation between the two perspectives within the project. Based on their new intergovernmentalist theoretical perspective, which is closer to those perspectives of most of the process tracers, Csehi and Puetter consider preference formation not to be insulated from EU-level interaction but rather as intertwined. Still, their analysis is based on the EMU Formation dataset rather than on country-specific analysis. Their aim is to determine the broad pattern of preference formation in Eurozone Crisis politics against the background of inconclusive findings of the existing literature on the subject. For this, different integration theories and research perspectives were associated with peer influence rankings as the main resource of the EMU Formation dataset. Given the small number of responses per country in the dataset, the authors decided against studying variation related to the country settings but sought to concentrate on EU-wide dynamics.[7] Influence ratings were triangulated with answers to open-ended questions, which are equally part of the dataset. The findings endorse new intergovernmentalist expectations that central intergovernmental forums, such as the European Council, the Eurogroup and senior expert committees, play a constitutive role for what member states' governments wanted in the euro crisis (Csehi and Puetter 2020). Socio-economic actors, public opinion and even parliaments, when considered across the four decision-making scenarios in the dataset, play a very limited, even negligible role.

Lastly, the study revealed some important open questions relating to preference formation which should be taken up by future research. For example, the study did not arrive at ultimate conclusions regarding the stability of preferences over time. During the course of the Eurozone Crisis, it became apparent that preferences constantly adjusted to a moving target. Thus, preferences do not seem to have been independent of the situation or structure but were adjusted to external constraints; partially, they were informed by high degrees of uncertainty and were subject to interactive feedback processes. Preferences, thus, are not ideal points in an ideal world – and whether learning, updating of information or other mechanisms are dominant remains an empirical challenge.

All of the above case studies also suggest that the engagement of different societal groups, the relevance of public opinion and the configurations of crucial elite networks at the national and EU-level can change depending on the issue, the country context and the timing. There are different explanations for this variation, such as differing electoral calendars (Schneider 2018) or specific conceptions of how citizens react to EU politics (van der Eijk and Franklin 2007). In our view, this lack of stability and the witnessed equifinality constitute major challenges going beyond well-known discussions about the difference between strategic positionings and 'true' ideal points (cf. Bueno de Mesquita 2004; Frieden 1999; Frieden and Walter 2019). Scholars studying the EU must confront this challenge both at the theoretical and empirical levels.

In addition, the role of European interactions – the contacts, exchanges and negotiations between representatives of member states and EU institutions – are found to matter in what used to be referred to as 'domestic preference formation'. The inherent link between these dimensions should be explored in more detail in the future. The following section provides examples for a series of initial findings and conceptualisations of this dimension of Eurozone Crisis politics.

6.5 EUROPEAN INTERACTIONS

From a rational institutionalist perspective, EU-level outcomes result in an aggregation of member state preferences, mediated by decision-making institutions, the relative bargaining power of member states and possibly supranational actors, such as the Commission. Interactions at the European level, therefore, are seen to shape EMU politics in the sense of specific decision-making rules, actor strategies and their resources. The *EMU Choices* research provides an abundance of evidence highlighting that institutions – also in a wider sense – mattered during the Eurozone Crisis. Interestingly, this is underlined most prominently by research following the lines of the covariational perspective. For example, Lundgren et al. (2019) highlight that compromise and reciprocity mattered largely for explaining outcomes during the Eurozone Crisis – somewhat in line with Achen's (2006) compromise model – and that in contrast to conventional wisdom (cf. e.g. Schimmelfennig 2015), Germany did not dominate decision-making. Instead, countries with intermediate positions performed rather well during the negotiations. In line with this, Finke and Bailer (2019) find that both creditor and debtor states faced prohibitively high costs during the Eurozone Crisis and, therefore, states' negotiation powers were limited (cf. also Frieden and Walter 2019); the outsiders, in principle, were in a strong position due to their limited vulnerability, but they were institutionally excluded at least from the core EMU organs.[8] Finke and Bailer (2019), thus, highlight the importance of institutions. Their model distinguishes veto power of individual member states also according to voting rules – unanimity of intergovernmental agreements and qualified majority for legislative decisions under the ordinary legislative procedure.

While the covariational accounts test bargaining models in relation to the negotiation outcome, the process-orientated case studies take a very different look at EU-level interactions. Both of the following contributions adopt a new intergovernmentalist perspective (Bickerton et al. 2015a) in this regard. Fontan and Saurugger (2020) show how the key civil servants who deliver decisive advice in French decision-making are linked with their EU counterparts through the Economic and Financial Committee (EFC) and the Eurogroup Working Group (EWG), which is a key forum for policy analysis and main source of generating policy ideas. This finding is strongly endorsed by Csehi and Puetter's (2021) analysis of influence patterns, as derived from EMU Formation data. The influence of the two senior civil servant committees is rated similarly to the influence of the corresponding principals of these civil servants. Csehi and Puetter also review the role of the Commission. The latter is found to be a steady and relevant yet never decisive actor. This finding is in line with the new intergovernmentalist notion of the Commission as a largely complicit actor to member state governments' dominant role in the Eurozone Crisis (Bickerton et al. 2015a). The focus of the research is not redistributional gains and losses but how the most senior political elites are embedded in a transnational context in which they, rather than negotiating pre-defined preference, generate these policy preferences, at least partially, as jointly analysed policy challenges and identify what their relevant groups see as appropriate fixes. Intense processes of policy coordination generate constant feedback loops between the European and domestic levels, complemented with bilateral intergovernmental interactions by actors such as the French and German governments.

6.6 CONCLUSION

Our review shows that the *EMU Choices* consortium has provided a large scale of diverse empirical evidence, underlining the value addition of encouraging collaboration across major theoretical fault lines. The chapter highlights that the static or covariational approaches were able to formulate and test useful baseline accounts of EMU politics in times of crises. At the same time, the simplifying assumptions underlying such approaches resulted in a certain myopia with regard to questions of actor complexity and interactions over time and across different levels. For instance, the assumption that national preference formation can be conceptualised as a stable and independent process, which is insulated from intergovernmental bargaining and supranational influence, remains open to debate (Csehi and Puetter 2021, cf. 2017). The analysis of decision-making in the context of the Eurozone Crisis showed that iterated interactions in the context of ongoing crisis dynamics erode differences between levels of decision-making. Moreover, financial and fiscal interdependencies seem to inform both preference formation itself as well as interstate bargaining. Our analysis also highlights that agenda setting does not necessarily precede preference formation, as the case of Germany and France, and their capacity to shape the agenda highlights.

Moreover, the role of public opinion and socio-economic actors remains contested. *EMU Choices* shows the room for variation as well as the restrictions of classic liberal intergovernmentalist understandings of two-level games (Putnam 1988), yet our research in itself does not produce an alternative grand theory which could be applied to preference formation across member states and levels of decision-making. Future research should strive for a more careful identification of scope conditions. Moreover, further theorising of how problems in domestic politics become a standalone input in European interactions or, alternatively, how European reactions to domestic contestations of EU policies could amplify rather than pacify conflict and lead to a disequilibrium in European politics are urgently needed (Hodson and Puetter 2019).

A key takeaway from our collaborative work in *EMU Choices* is that, in general, the approaches used, despite their diversity, were still able to communicate. In fact, bringing them together allows for a more encompassing perspective on the politics of EMU reform. Controversial debates are unavoidable in such a collaborative context but can prove to enhance productivity, contribute to sharpening and defending concepts and, if empirical variation emerges, help clarify the scope conditions under which different theories perform best. We stress that the relevant approaches of studying European integration should be seen as complementary rather than competitive (cf. Ioannou, Leblond and Niemann 2015; Hooghe and Marks 2019; or more generally Wiener and Diez 2009). However, the division of labour should be spelt out more carefully to specify 'domains of application' (cf. Jupille et al. 2003). Finally, collaboration can contribute to identifying the blind spots of the various approaches taken. Often, these remain hidden given the foci, interests and – associated with that – the methodologies of the different schools. In order to avoid such bias, more inclusive research designs should be encouraged. Ultimately, as our collaborative work experience also shows, it is about the willingness of individual researchers to engage in cross-fertilisation and multi-method research in a collaborative work context. A careful definition of the division of labour can help. Ambition to reach beyond existing research practice certainly is of use. Yet, the determination to work together is what matters in the end.

NOTES

1. The authors wish to thank the editors, in particular, Fabio Wasserfallen, for helpful comments. All remaining errors are our own.
2. A more critical assessment is put forward by Moravcsik (1999).
3. Again, it should be noted that most research conducted in *EMU Choices* focused more narrowly on the politics of the Eurozone Crisis, rather than on long-term developments in EMU.
4. The *EMU Position* dataset can be accessed at: https://emuchoices.eu/data/emup/. The *EMU Formation* dataset is available here: https://emuchoices.eu/data/emuf/ (accessed 29 February 2020).
5. For a more general perspective, also cf. the Comparative Agendas Project (https://www.comparativeagendas.net/).
6. Note, however, that Moravcsik (2018) more recently acknowledged a particularly strong importance of public opinion for salient issues such as crises (cf. also Degner 2019).
7. For an alternative approach to the analysis of the *EMU Formation* dataset see Kudrna et al. (2019).
8. Even for the creditor states, the costs of failing EMU were prohibitively high (cf. Schimmelfennig 2015).

REFERENCES

Achen, C. H. 2006. "Institutional realism and bargaining models." In *The European Union Decides,* edited by R. Thomson, F.N. Stokman, C.H. Achen, and T. König, 86–123. Cambridge: Cambridge University Press.

Alexandrova, P., M. Carammia, S. Princen, and A. Timmermans. 2014. "Measuring the European Council agenda: Introducing a new approach and dataset." *European Union Politics* 15, no. 1: 152–67.

Aspinwall, M., and G. Schneider. 2000. "Same menu, separate tables: The institutionalist urn in political science and the study of European integration." *European Journal of Political Research* 38: 1–36.

Beach, D., and R. Brun Pedersen. 2013. *Process-Tracing Methods: Foundations and Guidelines.* Ann Arbor: University of Michigan Press.

Bennett, A. and J.T. Checkel. 2015. *Process Tracing. From Metaphor to Analytic Tool.* Cambridge: Cambridge University Press.

Bickerton, C.J., D. Hodson, and U. Puetter. 2015a. "The new intergovernmentalism and the study of European integration." In *The New Intergovernmentalism. States and Supranational Actors in the Post-Maastricht Era,* edited by C.J. Bickerton, D. Hodson, and U. Puetter, chapter 1. Oxford: Oxford University Press.

Bickerton, C.J., D. Hodson, and U. Puetter. 2015b. "The new intergovernmentalism: European integration in the post-Maastricht era." *Journal of Common Market Studies* 53, no. 4: 703–22.

Blatter, J. and T. Blume. 2008. "In Search of Co-variance, Causal Mechanisms or Congruence? Towards a Plural Understanding of Case Studies." *Swiss Political Science Review* 14, no. 2: 315–56.

Blatter, J. and M. Haverland. 2012. *Designing Case Studies. Explanatory Approaches in Small-N Research.* Houndmills: Palgrave Macmillan.

Bojovic, J., M. Munta, and U. Puetter. 2020. "The European stability mechanism and domestic preference formation during the eurocrisis: The role of non-governmental actors." *Political Studies Review,* no. 4: 475–490.

Brady, H.E. 2010. "Data-set observations versus causal-process observations: The 2002 U.S. presidential election." In *Rethinking Social Inquiry. Diverse Tools, Shared Standards*, edited by H.E. Brady, and D. Collier, 237–42. Plymouth, UK: Rowman and Littlefield.

Bueno de Mesquita. 2004. "Decision-making models, rigor and new puzzles." *European Union Politics* 5, no. 1: 125–38.

Bulmer, S. 2009. "'Politics in Time' meets the politics of time: historical institutionalism and the EU timescape." *Journal of European Public Policy* 16, no. 2: 307–24.

Crespy, A. and V. Schmidt. 2014. "The clash of Titans: France, Germany and the discursive double game of EMU reform." *Journal of European Public Policy* 21, no. 8: 1085–101.

Csehi, R. and U. Puetter. 2017. "Problematizing the notion of preference formation in research about the euro crisis." *EMU Choices Working Paper*, October, 2017. https://emuchoices.eu/2017/10/18/csehi-r-and-puetter-u-2017-problematizing-the-notion-of-preference-formation-in-research-about-the-euro-crisis-emu-choices-working-paper-2017/.

Csehi, R. and U. Puetter. 2021. "Who determined what governments really wanted? Preference formation and the euro crisis." *West European Politics,* 44, no. 3: 463–484.

Degner, H. 2019. "Public attention, governmental bargaining, and supranational activism: Explaining European integration in response to crises." *Journal of Common Market Studies* 57, no. 2: 242–59.

Degner, H. and D. Leuffen. 2020. "Crises and responsiveness: Analysing German preference formation during the Eurozone crisis." *Political Studies Review*, 18, no. 4: 491–506.

Degner, H. and D. Leuffen. 20120. "Franco-German cooperation and the rescuing of the Eurozone." *European Union Politics* 20, no. 1: 89–108.

Finke, D. and S. Bailer. 2019. "Crisis bargaining in the European Union: Formal rules or market pressure?" *European Union Politics* 20, no. 1: 109–33.

Fontan, C. and S. Saurugger. 2020. "Between a rock and a hard place: Preference formation in France during the Eurozone crisis." *Political Studies Review,* 18, no. 4: 507–524.

Frieden, J. and S. Walter. 2019. "Analyzing inter-state negotiations in the Eurozone Crisis and beyond." *European Union Politics* 20, no. 1: 134–51.

Frieden, J. 1999. "Actors and preferences in international relations." In *Strategic Choice and International Relations*, edited by D.A. Lake, and R. Powell. Princeton: Princeton University Press.

Goertz, G. and J. Mahoney. 2012. *A Tale of Two Cultures: Qualitative and Quantitative Research in the Social Sciences.* Princeton, Princeton University Press.

Goetz, K.H. and J.-H. Meyer-Sahling. 2009. "Political time in the EU: dimensions, perspectives, theories." *Journal of European Public Policy* 16, no. 2: 180–201.

Hall, P. 2003. "Aligning ontology and methodology in comparative research." In *Comparative Historical Analysis in the Social Sciences*, edited by J. Mahoney, and D. Rueschemeyer, chapter 11. New York: Cambridge University Press.

Hall, P. and R.C.R. Taylor. 1996. "Political science and the three new institutionalisms." *Political Studies* 44, no. 5: 936–57.

Héritier, A. 2007. *Explaining Institutional Change in Europe.* Oxford: Oxford University Press.

Hodson, D., and U. Puetter. 2019. "The European Union in disequilibrium. New intergovernmentalism, postfunctionalism and integration theory in the post-Maastricht period." *Journal of European Public Policy* 26, no. 8: 1153–71.

Joney, E., R.D. Kelemen, and S. Meunier. 2016. "Failing forward? The Euro crisis and the incomplete nature of european integration." *Comparative Political Studies* 49, no. 7: 1010–34.

Jupille, J., J.A. Caporaso, and J.T. Checkel. 2003. "Integrating institutions: Rationalism, constructivism, and the study of the European Union." *Comparative Political Studies* 36, no. 1-2: 7–40.

Kudrna, Z., S. Bailer, S. Târlea, and F. Wasserfallen. 2019. "Three worlds of preference formation in European Union Politics: Evidence from new data on Eurozone Reforms." *EMU Choices Working Paper*, March, 2019. https://emuchoices.eu/wp-content/uploads/2019/03/2018WP_Kudrna_et_al_EMUfpaper.pdf.

Lehner, T. and F. Wasserfallen. 2019. "Political conflict in the reform of the Eurozone." *European Union Politics* 20, no. 1: 45–64.

Leuffen, D. 2007. "Case selection and selection bias in small-n research." In *Research Design in Political Science. How to practice what they preach,* edited by T. Gschwend and F. Schimmelfennig, 145–60. Houndmills: Palgrave Macmillan.

Lieberman, E. S. 2005. "Nested analysis as a mixed-method strategy for comparative research." *American Political Science Review* 99, no. 3: 435–52.

Lundgren, M., S. Bailer, L.M. Dellmuth, J. Tallberg, and S. Târlea. 2019. "Bargaining success in the reform of the Eurozone." *European Union Politics* 20, no. 1: 65–88.

Moravcsik, A. 1998. *The Choice for Europe. Social Purpose and State Power from Messina to Maastricht.* Ithaca, NY: Cornell University Press.

Moravcsik, A. 1999. "'Is something rotten in the state of Denmark?' Constructivism and European integration." *Journal of European Public Policy* 6, no. 4: 669–81.

Moravcsik, A. 2012. "Europe after the crisis. How to Sustain a Common Currency." *Foreign Affairs*, 91, no. 3: 54–68.

Moravcsik, A. 2018. "Preferences, power and institutions in 21st-century Europe." *Journal of Common Market Studies* 56, no. 7: 1648–74.

Morlino, L., and C.E. Sottilotta. 2019. "Southern Europe and the Eurozone crisis negotiations: Preference formation and contested issues." *South European Society and Politics* 24, no. 1: 1–28.

Pierson, P. 1996. "The path to European integration: A historical institutionalist analysis." *Comparative Political Studies* 29, no. 2: 123–63.

Poteete, A.R., M.A. Janssen, and E. Ostrom. 2010. *Working Together. Collective Action, the Commons, and Multiple Methods in Practice*. Princeton: Princeton University Press.

Princen, S. 2007. "Agenda-setting in the European Union: A theoretical exploration and agenda for research." *Journal of European Public Policy* 14, no. 1: 21–38.

Princen, S. 2009. *Agenda-setting in the European Union*. Basingstoke et al.: Palgrave Macmillan.

Putnam, R.D. 1988. "Diplomacy and domestic politics: The logic of two-level games." *International Organization* 42, no. 3: 427–60.

Scharpf, F.W. 2011. "Die Eurokrise: Ursachen und Folgerungen." *Zeitschrift für Staats- und Europawissenschaften* 9, no. 3: 324–37.

Scharpf, F.W. 2013. "The costs of non-disintegration: The case of the European Monetary Union." In *Zur Konzeptualisierung europäischer Desintegration. Zug- und Gegenkräfte im europäischen Integrationsprozess*, edited by A. Eppler and H. Scheller, 163–85. Baden-Baden: Nomos.

Schimmelfennig, F. 2015. "Liberal intergovernmentalism and the euro area crisis." *Journal of European Public Policy* 22, no. 2: 177–95.

Schimmelfennig, F., and A. Moravcsik. 2009. "Liberal intergovernmentalism." In *European Integration Theory*, edited by A. Wiener, and T. Diez. Oxford: Oxford University Press.

Schmidt, S.K. 2000. "Only an agenda setter? The European Commission's power over the Council of Ministers." *European Union Politics* 1, no. 1: 37–61.

Schmidt, V.A. 2013. "Arguing about the Eurozone Crisis: A discursive institutionalist analysis." *Critical Policy Studies* 7, no. 4: 455–62.

Schneider, C.J. 2018. *The Responsive Union: National Elections and European Governance*. Cambridge: Cambridge University Press.

Târlea, S., S. Bailer, H. Degner, L.M. Dellmuth, D. Leuffen, M. Lundgren, J. Tallberg, and F. Wasserfallen. 2019. "Explaining governmental preferences on Economic and Monetary Union Reform." *European Union Politics* 20, no. 1: 24–44.

Thomson, R., J. Arregui, D. Leuffen, R. Costello, J. Cross, R. Hertz, and T. Jensen. 2012. "A new dataset on decision-making in the European Union before and after the 2004 and 2007 enlargements (DEUII)." *Journal of European Public Policy*, 19, no. 4: 604–22.

Thomson, R., F.N. Stokman, C.H. Achen, and T. König. 2006. *The European Union Decides*. Cambridge: Cambridge University Press.

Van der Eijk, C., and M. Franklin. 2007. "The sleeping giant: Potential for political mobilization of disaffection in Europe." In *European Elections and Domestic Politics: Lessons from the Past and Scenarios for the Future*, edited by W. Van der Brug, and C. Van der Eijk, 189–208. Notre Dame, IN: University of Notre Dame Press.

Wasserfallen, F., D. Leuffen, Z. Kudrna, and H. Degner. 2019. "Analysing European Union decision-making during the Eurozone Crisis with new data." *European Union Politics,* 20, no. 1: 3–23.

Chapter 7

Eurozone Politics and Its Implications for Further Reforms

Zdenek Kudrna and Sonja Puntscher Riekmann

7.1 INTRODUCTION

There is no shortage of reform proposals for the completion of the financial, economic and political architecture of the Economic and Monetary Union (EMU). The EU bodies as well as independent experts have presented plentiful reports identifying these changes. Yet, no major reform has been adopted since 2014, and it is not for lack of trying. This chapter summarises the key features of Eurozone politics identified by the *EMU Choices* project and draws their implications for further EMU reforms. Our guiding question is What can make such reforms politically feasible?

We identify eight political and legal constraints on completing the EMU (see Table 7.2) and reconcile them with two reform scenarios. The severity of these constraints implies that the rapid progress of Eurozone reform is unlikely unless fostered by another existential crisis. At the same time, these eight characteristics also indicate pathways for the convergence of policy preferences and potential progress towards EMU reforms. We argue that, on balance, the Eurozone is set on a course of gradual reforms that can cumulatively improve the completion of EMU architecture, albeit at a much slower pace than originally envisaged in Presidents' Reports.

However, gradual reforms keep the Eurozone exposed to the vagaries of economic and political cycles as well as unpredictable exogenous shocks. Any protracted economic recession, financial instability, an insurrection of populist parties in any member government or European Parliament or another unexpected shock may derail gradual reforms. Any such disruption may trigger another existential crisis in which a member government might face the choice between completion of the EMU or the catastrophic break-up of the single currency. This uncertainty preserves the urgency of EMU reforms and imposes a time constraint on gradual reforms that cannot be spread across decades.

The crucial insight into the political feasibility of gradual reforms is that member states' preferences were shaped primarily by fears of financial-sector meltdown. This concern enabled the agreement on reform measures that, together with ECB policies, contained the escalation of the Euro Crisis between 2010 and 2015. However, the same concern about financial stability now undermines Northern support for further reforms, due to a suspicion that any new risk-sharing mechanisms might be (mis)used to pay for legacy losses in Southern banking systems. Yet, a sustained reduction of legacy risks and losses can ease the key reform constraint by providing the basis for the gradual convergence of preferences. De-risking financial sectors can facilitate the shift from a myopic focus on past losses to the fundamental questions of the single currency sustainability.

This chapter starts with a brief outline of the existing EMU reform agenda and two future scenarios for achieving these goals. The next section discusses the eight key characteristics of Eurozone politics and derives their implications for further EMU reforms. Section 7.4 provides a reality check for our analysis, based on expert interviews at member states' delegations in Brussels. The concluding sections derive four policy recommendations and reconcile them with the most recent policy developments to the end of 2019.

7.2 TWO REFORM SCENARIOS WITH DIFFERENT TIME HORIZONS

While Eurozone reforms enacted between 2010 and 2015 mark the most profound deepening of European integration since the Maastricht Treaty, there is also a clear consensus that Eurozone institutional architecture is yet to be completed. In EU parlance, this reform agenda is described as completing the four unions (van Rompuy et al. 2012; Juncker et al. 2015). The economic union focuses on national structural reforms that enable each member state to prosper within the constraints of the single currency. The financial union is to ensure the stability of banks and increased risk-sharing with the private sector through deeper capital markets. The fiscal union is to deliver the sustainability of debts and public expenditures that are precursors for macroeconomic stability. Finally, the political union is to provide democratic legitimacy and accountability adequate for the deeper integration instituted by these reforms.

The EU actors have outlined reform goals in a series of consultative documents, starting with the *Blueprint for a deep and genuine economic and monetary union* (Commission 2012) and the subsequent *Four Presidents' Report* (van Rompuy et al. 2012). Individual reform steps towards the four unions were specified and followed upon in further documents, including the *Five Presidents' Report* on completing the EMU (Juncker et al. 2015), *White Paper on the future of Europe* (Commission 2017c), *Reflection Paper on the deepening of the EMU* (Commission 2017a) and the *Roadmap for a more united, stronger and more democratic union* (Commission 2017b). The *Reflection Paper* provides the most specific proposals for the construction of the four unions (table 7.1) that should replace the 'in-between governance that has emerged from the crisis due to ad hoc measures' (Commission 2017a, 17).

While the agenda of the four unions is clearly established, its progress has stalled. No major element of financial or fiscal risk-sharing has been adopted since 2014 as momentous political and legal constraints either block reforms altogether or reduce their significance to minor changes. These circumstances indicate that the key parameter distinguishing future reform scenarios is going to be time. One scenario should assume that the EU will be able to overcome existing constraints and regain the momentum from the 2010-to-2014 period to progress with the four unions by 2025 as envisaged in the *Presidents' Reports*. The other scenario accepts that political and legal constraints cannot be removed, but some of them may be eased over time, thus facilitating gradual reforms over a much longer time horizon than 2025.

The post-crisis experience suggests that without the pressures of existential crisis, Eurozone reform politics runs into a stalemate, despite the continuous effort of some actors to achieve consensus on the next steps. It seems that fast progress towards the four unions would require the re-emergence of a massive crisis that forces member states to accept risk-sharing to prevent the break-up of the EMU. Relying on extreme events to induce reform is an inherently risky strategy as crisis-induced decisions tend to be improvised, lack legitimacy and be prone to mishaps with potentially catastrophic consequences. Moreover, there is no guarantee that, when faced with the choice between a break-up and risk-sharing, all member governments would be willing and able to choose the latter.

The alternative scenario focuses on gradual reforms, enabled by easing some key constraints. These may cumulatively improve the completeness of EMU architecture but only on time scales reaching far beyond 2025. The most likely mechanism enabling gradual progress is de-risking banking sectors, which would reduce concerns about legacy losses, thus facilitating the preference convergence on the next steps towards completing the Banking Union (see section 7.3.1). The obvious downside of the gradual scenario is that it dramatically prolongs the period that the Eurozone faces shocks with an incomplete set of response instruments. Therefore, EU member states should make the best use of the period of relative economic stability to

Table 7.1 EMU Reform Agenda from the Reflection Paper

Financial Union: Banking and Capital Markets
1. Risk reduction by reducing non-performing loans (NPL)
2. Banking union (BU) completion: creating the fiscal backstop for the Single Resolution Fund (SRF) and the European Deposit Insurance Scheme (EDIS)
3. Capital Market Union (CMU): supranational supervisory framework allowing for the greater diversification of funding and risks
4. Beyond BU and CMU: While acknowledging legal, political and institutional difficulties, the Commission proposes sovereign bond-backed securities, a European safe asset, and a new regulatory treatment of sovereign bonds.

Economic Union: Convergence
1. Multi-annual approach to reforms under the European semester: including better coordination and elaboration of binding standards on social rights to the common consolidated corporate tax base
2. Linking national reforms to EU funding: as a first step strengthening the stabilisation features of the EU budget by, e.g., modulating the co-financing rate according to MS economic conditions
3. Establishing a macroeconomic stabilisation function: the creation of a Eurozone fiscal capacity either based on national contributions as a share of GDP or VAT or on revenues such as excises, levies or corporate tax; introducing the capacity to borrow
4. European Unemployment Scheme: a re-insurance fund for national schemes based on the prior convergence of labour market policies
5. European Investment Protection Scheme for MS investments in infrastructure and skills development
6. Rainy day fund: either based strictly on contributions and thus limited or with the capacity to borrow

EMU Architecture for Fiscal and Political Union
1. European Monetary Fund: built on ESM to provide liquidity assistance to member states and the last resort common backstop of BU
2. European Finance Minister: merging Eurogroup permanent chair with the Commissioner for financial and monetary affairs, who would also chair ECOFIN
3. Legal consolidation: integrating ESM and Fiscal Compact into EU law framework, transforming the Eurogroup into a Council configuration and clarifying relations between Euro Area and non-Euro Area members
4. Euro Area Treasury: tasked with economic and fiscal surveillance (supported by a European Fiscal Board), coordination of the issuance of the European safe asset, macroeconomic stabilisation management, preparing decisions to be taken by the Eurogroup and controlled by the EP

consolidate private and public finances to resolve the stalemate and progress with gradual reforms.

The nature and timing of the next massive shock are generally unpredictable. The last Euro Crisis was triggered by the most severe global financial crisis in eight decades, which started with the collapse of the US financial markets. However, the next crisis may be triggered by another exogenous risk, such as natural disaster, or develop endogenously from prevailing political constellations across the EU. Whereas the EP elections in 2019 did not result in a major upheaval by populist far-right parties, the traditional pro-reform coalition of the EPP (European People's Party) and the S&D (Progressive Alliance of Socialists and Democrats) no longer exists, and majorities have to include other parties. Furthermore, the presence of populists in several member state governments does not bode well for the consensus-seeking in the Council and European Council. Hence, the gradual reform scenario is also time-constrained – the sooner the Eurozone readies for the next shock, the better.

While the Eurozone is better prepared for the next crisis than it was for the last one, the presence of economic, political and other risks implies that there is no room for complacency and postponement. The European Stability Mechanism, the Banking Union and the extraordinary intervention tools of the European Central Bank improved the EMU's resilience. Yet, the Southern member states need to sustain their commitment to economic and financial stability, while the Commission and Northern member states need to keep working on acceptable reform designs even when consensus seems unlikely. The sustained debate about reforms helps to advance the gradual reform scenario, but it also makes the E(M)U better prepared for the crisis scenario because more mature reform proposals could be adopted faster and with lower risk of mishaps or unintended consequences.

7.3 EUROZONE REFORM POLITICS AND THEIR IMPLICATIONS FOR REFORMS

The *EMU Choices* datasets and comparative case studies enabled the systematic analysis of Eurozone reform politics. The previous chapters discussed in detail individual insights that are brought together in Table 7.2. It provides a schematic overview of eight characteristics of Eurozone politics and outlines their implications for the feasibility of future reforms. These findings confirm some common wisdom, help to dispel some popular media myths and reveal mechanisms that can facilitate further reforms.

7.3.1 Financial Stability Shapes National Policy Preferences

Târlea et al. (2019) analyse systematically the observed preferences of EU member states on contested EMU issues and conclude that national positions were informed primarily by the exposure of the domestic financial sector (see

Table 7.2 Key Features of Eurozone Politics and Their Implication

Eurozone Politics' Feature	Implications for Further Reforms
Financial stability is the key determinant of policy preferences	Instrumental for the adoption of crisis-induced reforms between 2010 and 2015; currently undermines Northern support for EMU reforms, but also provides the basis for preference convergence, when Southern banks de-risk
North-South divide of policy preferences	Fundamental obstacle to be overcome either by gradual convergence of preferences or crisis pressure
Single-dimensionality of the policy conflict structure	Prevents package deals across multiple policy dimensions and/or domains; EMU reforms must be compromises between North and South
Franco-German agenda setting reflecting German redlines	Joint proposals have a good chance of acceptance by other EU members, although the tandem can also exclude some proposals from the EU legislative agenda
Balanced bargaining outcomes without German dominance	EU decision rules protect the voice of smaller members, and the Commission remains effective in delivering balanced legislative compromises (which does not prevent asymmetric distributional consequences, though)
Southern European states accepted austerity to stop crisis escalation	Without immediate crisis pressure, Southern states will promote their policy preferences on the EU level more assertively, especially when they resolve their banks
The dominant role of governments and EU institutions in preference formation	Instrumental for the adoption of crisis-induced reforms between 2010 and 2015, but also a source of political backlash in many EU countries where reforms lacked legitimacy

also chapter 2). They have identified a systematic association between the relative size of the national financial system to the national economy – measured by financial-sector liabilities and national balances in the EU TARGET system – and governments' preferences regarding Eurozone reforms between 2010 and 2015. Eurozone governments were more likely to support further integration in fiscal and economic policy when the exposure of their financial sector was substantial. The financial sector exposure was a better predictor of preferences than domestic political factors, such as the ideology of governing parties, the share of Eurosceptics in the parliament or the prevailing public opinion on European integration (Târlea et al. 2019, 8).

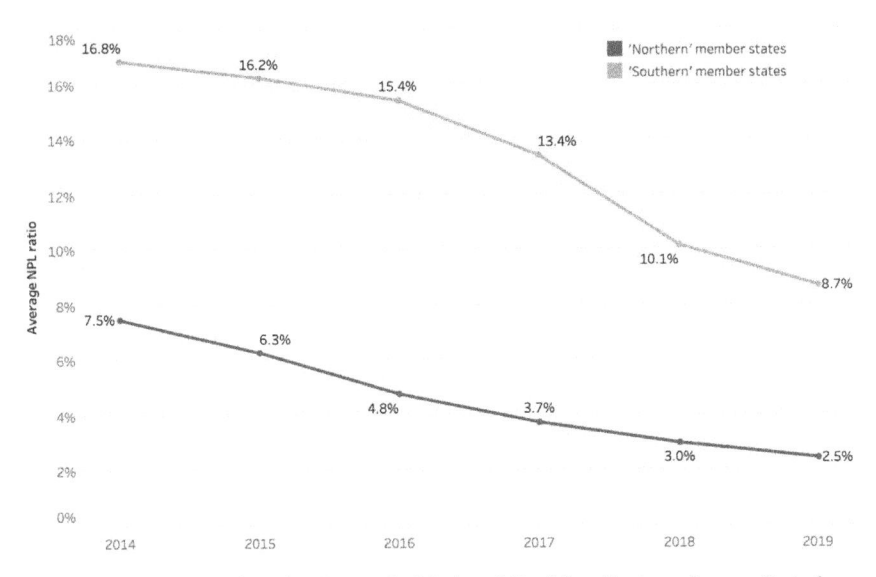

Figure 7.1 Non-performing Loans in National Banking Sectors. Source: Data from EBA risk dashboards (Sep 2014 - Sep 2019).

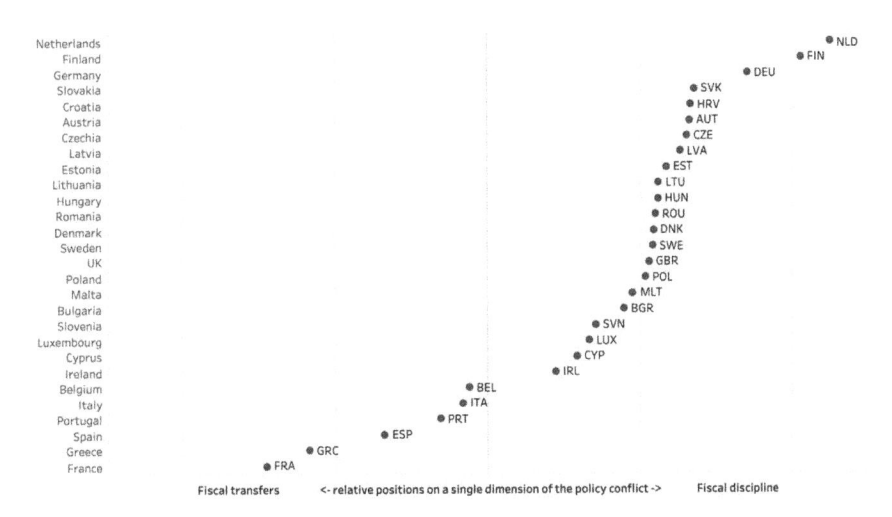

Figure 7.2 Estimated Ideal Points on Eurozone Reforms from 2010 to 2015. Source: Lehner and Wasserfallen (2019) based on EMU Positions data.

The perceived necessity to protect national financial sectors continues to shape national preferences. However, since financial sectors in Northern member states are more stable than in Southern ones (Figure 7.1), the concern over financial stability currently undermines Northern support for further reforms (see section 7.3.2). Member states emphasising fiscal discipline suspect that

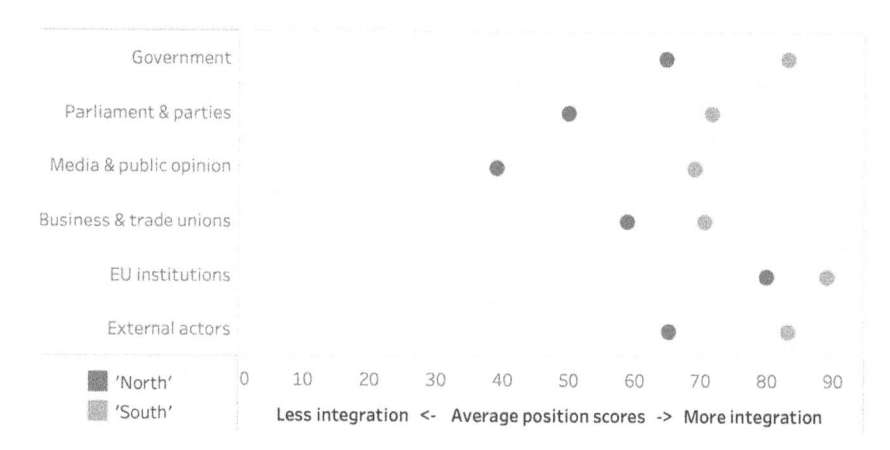

Figure 7.3 Positions of Actor Groups in North and South. Source: EMU Formation dataset. The positions of 'EU institutions' and 'External actors' refer to perception of their positions in member states. For the purpose of this figure, member states to the left of and including Malta in figure 7.2 are coded as South and the rest as North.

any new risk-sharing mechanisms might be used to pay for legacy losses in Southern banking systems. One reason for protracted negotiations of the European Deposit Insurance Scheme or fiscal backstop to the Single Resolution Fund is that the Northern coalition plays for time to ensure that legacy losses are resolved before any further risk-sharing is agreed. They also insist on developing a complex set of financial rules that relate the amount of banks' contributions to the EU mechanisms to their risk-profiles, thus requiring greater contributions from riskier banks, predominantly in Southern economies.

At the same time, the finding that preferences on EMU reforms are strongly shaped by structural economic factors presents an opportunity. The change in the underlying economic characteristics, such as the reduction of risks in Southern banking sectors, can bring about the change of preferences and their convergence on policy compromises. After all, the EMU reform debate cannot dwell indefinitely on decade-old financial losses that are being gradually resolved (see figure 7.1).

The new Commission will have the opportunity to refocus the debate on the issue of long-term resilience and sustainability of the single currency. Closing the gap between financial stability of banks in different countries and reaching an agreement on risk-based contributions should put within reach the Council's agreement on missing aspects of the Banking Union.

7.3.2 The North–South Divide of Policy Preferences

The deep divide of policy preferences is common wisdom among observers of Eurozone politics, which Lehner and Wasserfallen (2019) confirmed in their systematic analysis (see chapter 2). The forty contested aspects of the

Six-Pack, Two-Pack, Fiscal Compact, European Financial Stability Facility, European Stability Mechanism, assistance to Greece and the Banking Union point towards a clear North–South division (see figure 7.2).[1] One pole of the reform debate was occupied by countries such as France, Greece and Spain, while the Netherlands, Finland and Germany represented the other extreme.

These divisions are deep-rooted in the national preference formation process. On average, the position of each group of actors involved in the preference formation was more pro-integration in Southern countries and less in Northern ones (figure 7.3). The difference also applied to the perceived positions of EU institutions in the two groups of countries, respectively.

The North–South divide presents the fundamental obstacle to EMU reforms because both coalitions are rather stable and capable of blocking any proposal (see chapter 2). While the systematic analysis of member state preferences (which underpins figures 7.2 and 7.3) provides a robust aggregate view, it also reduces the visibility of variations across issues and countries (see methodological discussion in chapter 6). As is demonstrated in chapter 5, not all Southern countries are alike with regard to their economic issues and political responses. Moreover, there are member states with aggregated positions close to the middle of the distribution, which masks the fact that they are closer to the Northern end on some issues and to the Southern on others. Furthermore, some countries – prominently Ireland – have shifted their policy positions as economic circumstances improved (see also section 7.4). All these variations to the overall North–South divide may become important pathways for further reforms if they facilitate the formation of new policy coalitions sufficient to pass individual reform measures, despite the stalemate on more ambitious reforms.

7.3.3 Single-Dimensionality of the Policy Conflict Structure

While the North–South divide is common knowledge, the single-dimensionality of policy conflict on EMU reforms is a fundamental insight that could be obtained only through systematic empirical analysis (see chapter 2). The single-dimensional structure provides a straight-forward negotiation space for reciprocity and compromise between the two coalitions that are led by France and Germany (Lehner and Wasserfallen 2019). However, it is rather atypical in the context of EU policymaking, in which most conflicts are multi-dimensional as substantive interests are combined with the left–right ideological orientation of governments or their general preference for more or less integration (see chapter 2 for discussion).

The absence of additional dimensions effectively precludes a formulation of package deals, whereby member governments make concessions on EMU reforms as long as they are aligned with their political orientation or in exchange for benefits in some other policy domain. The single-dimensionality effectively requires governments to negotiate compromises on the given policy issue without recourse to side payments related to other policies. It also reaffirms the North–South divide by indicating less variation across countries and issues that could be exploited to form a consensus on individual issues (see section 7.3.2).

This single-dimensional characteristic implies that negotiations of individual policy issues resemble a zero-sum game between North and South. Thus, it may be easier to negotiate broader reform proposals as was the case during the banking crisis, when, for example, the access to the ESM for bank stabilisation was balanced with a commitment to the development of the Banking Union. Such broad packages are more difficult to negotiate, but at least in principle, provide more opportunities for reciprocity and mutual concessions between the two coalitions.

7.3.4 Franco-German Agenda Setting

The distribution of EMU reform preferences along the single dimension puts France and Germany in a very prominent position to restart their traditional role as the engine of European integration. If they can support any joint proposal, it has a good chance of being accepted because the two countries occupy opposite ends of the preference distribution (see figure 7.2) and, in most cases, serve as a focal point for the two coalitions negotiating a compromise reform design. Moreover, they have developed a unique mechanism of preference formation, whereby French policymakers internalise German red lines when building their policy preferences (see chapter 3). Hence, their initial proposals may tilt towards the German position because French negotiators rely on the subsequent rounds of iterative negotiations in Brussels to rebalance EU compromises (see section 7.3.5).

In the early period of the Eurozone Crisis, Franco-German cooperation facilitated the adoption of intergovernmental policies like the ESM and the Fiscal Compact, but also played an important role for policies like the legislative Six-Pack on economic governance or the complementary Two-Pack (Degner and Leuffen 2019). However, the two countries can also use their agenda-setting power to block EMU reform proposals, as was the case with any form of debt restructuring for Greece (until late 2011) or pre-empting any discussion of Eurobonds. Their unique position thus can cut both ways.

7.3.5 Balanced Bargaining Outcomes without German Dominance

In any case, the agenda-setting power of the Franco-German couple does not readily translate into an unrestrained capacity to determine the outcomes of

EU legislative bargaining. The empirical evidence presented by Lundgren et al. (2019) demonstrates that the EU decision-making system preserves the voice of all member states and balances the positions of individual countries and coalitions (see chapter 2). The average negotiation success – understood as whether or not a country gets what it wants in EU legislative bargaining – was evenly distributed across member states and their coalitions (figure 7.4). Most member states were able to achieve some of their goals, but none got its way all the time.

The relative symmetry of reform outcomes dispels the media myth that Germany, perhaps together with France, dictates the content of EMU reforms. As argued in the previous section, these countries are instrumental in setting the reform agenda, but the specific parameters of the reform legislation depend on the balance of preferences among all member states. The relative power of large member states does not dictate outcomes, which also bodes well for their legitimacy as they do not systematically favour any country (Lundgren 2019).

7.3.6 Southern Europe Accepted Austerity to Stop Crisis Escalation

While the EMU reform legislation was balanced, the economic consequences of the Euro Crisis were not. The crisis impacted Southern

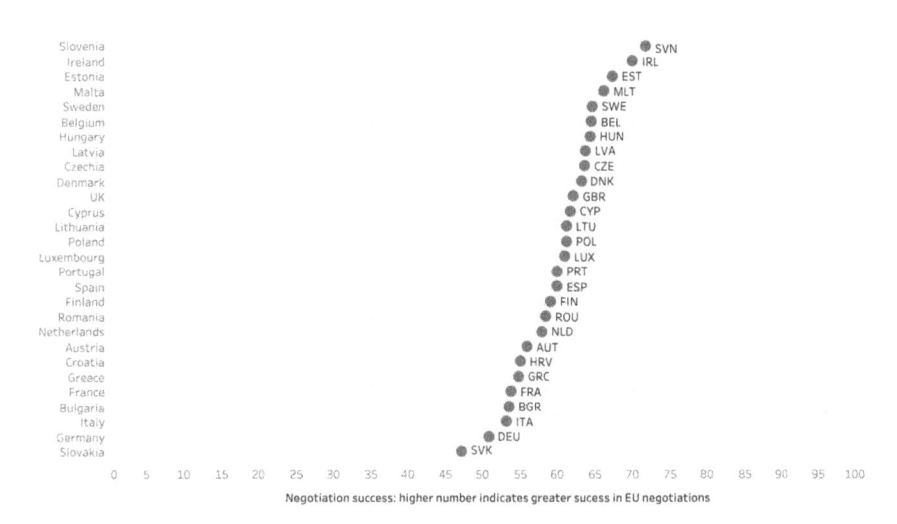

Figure 7.4 Average Negotiation Success of Member States. Source: Lundgren et al. (2019). Average negotiation success of EU member states during Eurozone reform negotiations, 2010–2015. Negotiation success (0–100) measured based on how frequently a member attained its preferred outcome.

economies much more dramatically and forced their governments to adopt policies that they, and the majority of their voters, had consistently opposed in the past. As case studies in chapter 4 document, while the reasoning differed across the Southern countries, all governments accepted the overriding priority of stopping the crisis' escalation, even if they faced electoral consequences later on. For example, Sottilotta (2019) details that Italian support for austerity policies cannot be explained by the traditional demand of technocratic elites for external constraints on economic policy. It was policymakers' concern about financial stability and the perceived need to avoid a formal bailout that induced Italy to strengthen the Stability and Growth Pact with the Fiscal Compact as well as the Six- and Two-packs (Sottilotta 2019).

Without the pressure of the escalating crisis, the Southern coalition is likely to be more assertive in pursuing its policy preferences. If this is done in the context of its compliance with the reformed macroeconomic and financial stability criteria, the countries will have a strong case. At some point, the Northern countries will have to accept that financial risks have been resolved; thus, the new risk-sharing mechanisms, such as EDIS, will support the long-term stabilisation of EMU without the risk of using them to cover legacy losses. However, if Southern countries try to reassert their influence, while some of them breach the stability criteria, the divide with the North will only deepen, thus prolonging the time needed for preference convergence.

7.3.7 The Dominant Role of Governments and EU Institutions in Preference Formation

National policy positions were influenced primarily by governments and EU institutions that are more influential than other political or business actors. Kudrna et al. (2019) analysed EMU Formation data and confirmed this executive bias (figure 7.5). While in most EU countries, parliaments were involved, their influence was relatively low. Public opinion and business actors were involved only in member states with established practices of economic policy coordination or those most affected by the crisis (although even there their actual influence was minimal, as documented in chapter 4).

Given the long-term impact of recent EMU reforms on the economic policy of member states, the influence of political and social actors in formation preferences was very limited. The dominant role of government and EU actors was instrumental in relatively rapid adoption of reforms during the Euro Crisis but also paved the way for a populist backlash against the EU in many countries. The Eurozone reform politics needs a wider source of legitimacy in national systems as well as at the EU level as envisaged by the political union proposals.

Figure 7.5

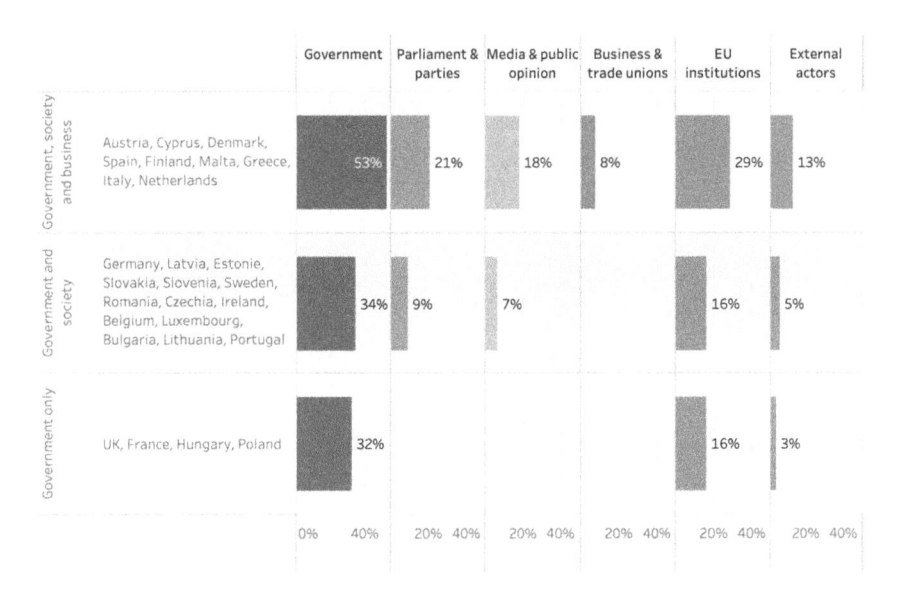

Group	Countries	Government	Parliament & parties	Media & public opinion	Business & trade unions	EU institutions	External actors
Government, society and business	Austria, Cyprus, Denmark, Spain, Finland, Malta, Greece, Italy, Netherlands	53%	21%	18%	8%	29%	13%
Government and society	Germany, Latvia, Estonie, Slovakia, Slovenia, Sweden, Romania, Czechia, Ireland, Belgium, Luxembourg, Bulgaria, Lithuania, Portugal	34%	9%	7%		16%	5%
Government only	UK, France, Hungary, Poland	32%				16%	3%

Figure 7.5 **Actors Influencing National Positions.** Source: Kudrna et al. (2019); weighted averages of influence scores from the EMU Formation dataset.

7.3.8 Constitutional Reviews Impose Constraints on Further Reforms

The recent EMU reforms were challenged in national constitutional courts as well as in the EU's Court of Justice. Member states' constitutions guarantee national identity and sovereignty, which were affected by new constraints on national parliaments' budgetary decision-making autonomy and budgetary responsibility. While no constitutional infringements were ascertained to date, these rulings clarified relevant constitutional options, limits and obstacles that will shape any further transfers of competences to the supranational level (see chapter 5).

In the view of constitutional courts, neither the Fiscal Compact nor the ESM went far enough to render the resulting obligations unconstitutional. However, further EMU reforms may cross such a limit and thus require a constitutional amendment. Moreover, the recent EMU reforms also stretched their Treaty base considerably, and further reforms are likely to require changes of EU treaties (Lentsch and Griller 2019). Should that happen, the substantive limits imposed by the recent rulings will be exacerbated by demanding procedural requirements that national legal systems impose on the EU treaty change and constitutional amendment (figure 7.6). The combination of substantive and procedural legal constraints increases the complexity of national as well as EU-level negotiations by providing their opponents with additional opportunities for legal challenge.

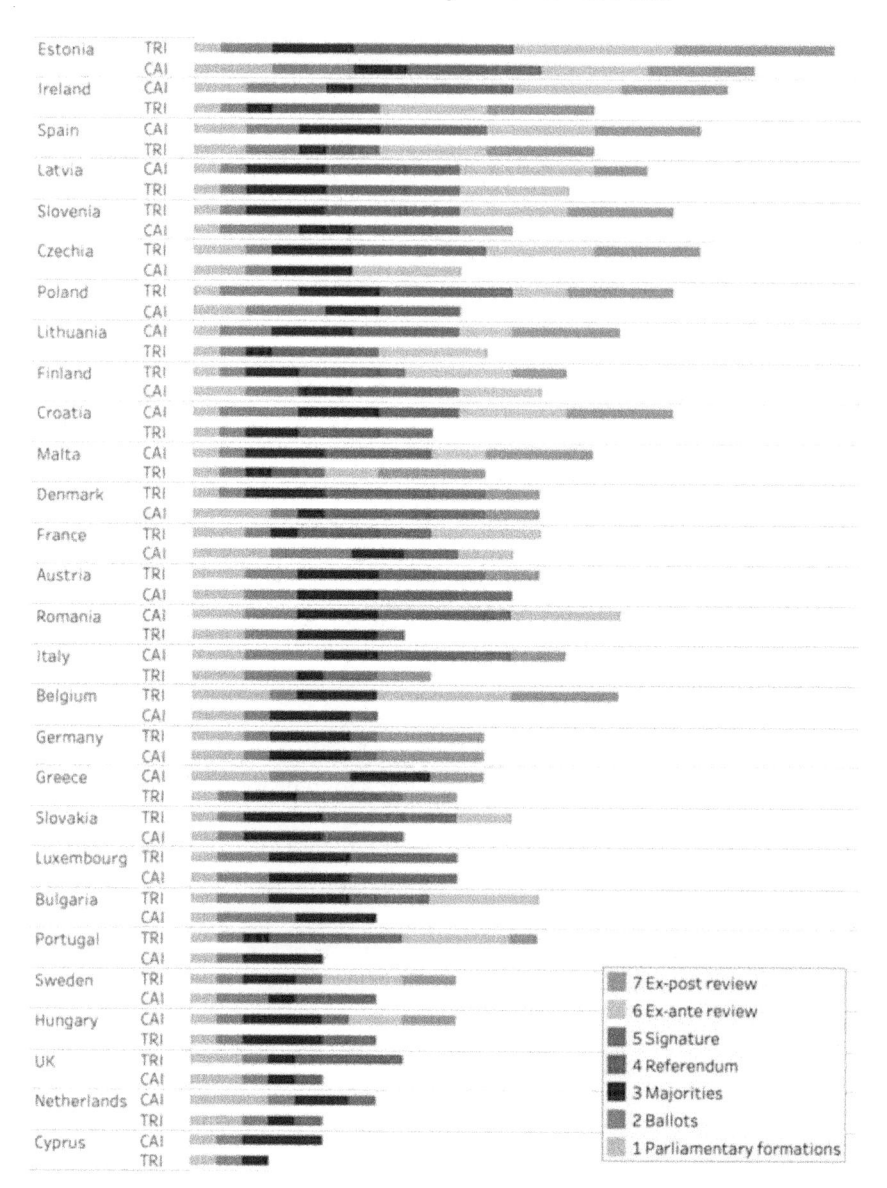

Figure 7.6 Procedural Requirements of EU Treaty Change (TRI) and National Constitutional Amendment (CAI). Note: See chapter 5 for index specification. Source: Kudrna and Lentsch (2019).

Overall, the key characteristics of Eurozone politics impose a complex set of hurdles that undermine the political feasibility of any reform proposal. Member states need to overcome the North–South divide and negotiate compromises on the single dimension between the two coalitions. They also need to navigate legal limits and engage national parliaments, public, businesses and labour unions to gain legitimacy beyond governments and EU institutions. Achieving this in the times of normal consensual politics, rather than during an escalating crisis, is never going to be quick.

The ideal reform proposal for further sharing of fiscal or financial risks across the Eurozone should build on the achievements of Southern member states in resolving legacy losses in their financial sectors and economies. The Commission's proposal should build on the joint Franco-German position that is representative of the two sides of the divide. Once such a proposal actually enters EU legislative negotiation – via ordinary legislative procedure or otherwise –there is a good chance the final legislation will be a balanced compromise.

While restarting the traditional Franco-German 'engine' of European integration could increase the chances of progress, recent experience is not encouraging. President Macron has attempted to relaunch the collaboration by stipulating several proposals (2017, 2019), but his attempts were disappointed by the muted response from the German chancellor. The protracted negotiations of the German coalition government in 2018 and the subsequent decision of Angela Merkel to step down as CDU chair have undermined expectations for the new initiatives. Whether the appointment of Ursula von der Leyen as Commission president will be conducive to changes in the German position remains to be seen.

Extrapolating from the key characteristics of Eurozone politics is a difficult task, by definition. However, the slow progress of EMU reforms in the last five years supports the view that the political and legal constraints are binding. Despite numerous proposals submitted and adopted by the Commission and many attempts at political restarts, no major milestone has been reached. This conclusion supports the prominence of the gradual scenario in the foreseeable future.

7.4 REALITY CHECK AT MEMBER STATES' REPRESENTATIONS

The *EMU Choices* consortium has conducted a survey of well-informed officers at national representations in Brussels to confront our findings with the reform expectations in member states. In the summer of 2018, nineteen semi-structured interviews with representatives and deputies from Comité des représentants permanents (COREPER) were conducted (Warren et al. 2019). Our questions focused on the expectations of which reforms outlined in the Commission's (2017) Reflection Paper (see table 7.1) are likely to be adopted in the next five years. Table 7.3 briefly summarises our findings of the prevailing consensus and expectations of progress.

Table 7.3 Perceptions of Preference Convergence

EMU Reform Initiative	Views of COREPER Members
Risk reduction by reducing non-performing loans (NPL)	Broad consensus on the policy. Significant progress is seen as likely in the next five years by most member states.
Creating the fiscal backstop for the Single Resolution Fund (SRF)	Consensus, including Germany and France, but not Nordic-Baltic-plus countries. Progress not seen as likely within five years.
Adopting the European Deposit Insurance Scheme (EDIS)	Germany and Nordic-Baltic-plus countries block the proposal, although agreeing to the principle. Agreement not seen as likely within five years.
Capital Markets Union (CMU)	Broad consensus on Commission proposals and progress seen as likely within five years.
Sovereign bond-backed securities or other forms of European safe asset	Some Southern countries support it, France and Germany are undecided, and Nordic-Baltic-plus countries oppose it. Progress not likely within five years.
Multi-annual approach to reforms under the European semester	Broad consensus on the policy. Significant progress is seen as likely within the next five years by most member states.
Binding standards on social rights	Member states are united in opposition. Agreement not seen as likely within five years.
The common consolidated corporate tax base	Polarising issue. Agreement not seen as likely within five years.
Establishing any form of Eurozone macroeconomic stabilisation (via fiscal capacity or borrowing such as European Investment Protection Scheme, European Unemployment Scheme or Rainy day fund)	Some Southern countries support it, Nordic-Baltic-plus countries strongly oppose it. Agreement not seen as likely within five years.
European Monetary Fund	Significant reform unlikely over the next five years, although the minor transformation of ESM possible, especially if SRF backstop adopted.
Legal consolidation: integrating ESM and Fiscal Compact into EU law	High variance in positions, depending on the preferred legal model for surveillance and financing mechanisms. Germany supports consolidation more than France. Some agreement is expected within five years.

The interviews indicate expectations of some progress with less controversial reforms focusing on the development of Capital Markets Union, European Semester and legal consolidation of intergovernmental treaties to EU law. These aspects of the EMU governance framework are important, but advance Eurozone's financial stability or resilience only indirectly. The same applies to the potential transformation of the ESM to the European Monetary Fund, which entails mere governance rearrangement unless complemented by some form of additional fiscal risk-sharing.

Overall, there are very limited expectations of convergence on the more substantive EMU reforms. While there has been clear progress in the reduction of banking sector risks over the last few years (figure 7.3), there is a prevailing concern about banking sector stability in the Southern member states (Warren et al. 2019). Many of these economies improved the resilience of their public finances as well as financial sectors, but their achievements are overshadowed by Italy. The current government in Rome is ambivalent about its commitments to public spending limits and sustained resolution of legacy losses in the banking sector. Given the size of the Italian economy, the progress of others seems insufficient for greater convergence on EMU reforms.

The *EMU Choices* survey also indicates political shifts in member state support for further reforms. While the North–South cleavage remains dominant, other coalition patterns seem to be emerging from current debates (see Warren et al. 2019). The most prominent one is the role of Hanseatic League (often referred to as Nordic-Baltic-plus) of countries that are taking more polar positions than Germany on reform proposals.[2] The emergence of this coalition is also related to Brexit as these countries often sided with the UK on financial and economic matters and on maintaining the rights of the Eurozone non-members (Warren et al. 2019). They will no longer be able to rely on the large member state to represent their position in Brussels, and their informal collaboration aims at preserving their voice collectively. Hence, somewhat paradoxically, Brexit may actually deepen the North–South divide because the UK has – from its opt-out position – supported reforms stabilising the Eurozone. With the UK's departure, the EU will lose a centrist voice in EMU debates (see figure 7.2), which has actively contributed to the formation of reform compromises, despite its frequent opposition to EU decisions on financial regulation (see Chapter 3).

7.5 POLICY RECOMMENDATIONS

The key characteristics of Eurozone politics are stacked against further reforms. While all stakeholders agree that the institutional architecture of the single currency remains incomplete and in need of reforms outlined in the

Presidents' Reports, the futile debates of the last five years were dominated by mistrust and myopic focus on legacy losses. While navigating political and legal constraints remains difficult, progress is not impossible. However, it will be one delivered by a cumulation of gradual reforms over a long period. Unless there is another existential crisis forcing decisions between further reforms or catastrophic break-up, substantial steps towards the economic, financial, fiscal and political unions by 2025 remain unlikely. The normal, non-crisis politics of Eurozone reform is going to move slowly.

At the same time, the systematic empirical analysis of recent reforms yields several policy recommendations that can enhance the progress of gradual reforms and prepare alternatives for more turbulent times. The North–South divide is fundamentally rooted in mistrust, that Eurozone members will not maintain their commitments to rules designed to prevent macroeconomic or financial instability. Hence, the first step is to rebuild trust by respecting the limits imposed by the reformed Stability and Growth Pact and continue to improve the soundness of national financial sectors. The second step is to search for the politically feasible reform designs that can be passed within the prevailing political and legal constraints. While the first recommendation should narrow the North–South divide by reducing mistrust and shifting the attention from crisis legacies to the long-term stability of the single currency, the second one should maximise the use of political opportunity thereby created.

However, the Commission cannot plan only for the sunny times of sustained economic and political stability that are necessary for the gradual reform scenario. There need to be alternative policies for crisis situations that may come on the heels of deep economic recession, another financial meltdown or populist challenge. Therefore, the Commission should define crisis reform scenarios that would have to be adopted to stop another escalating Euro Crisis, and that also serves as a benchmark for the progress of gradual scenario. Finally, there is always a need for innovative economic ideas that could improve the Eurozone architecture, while fitting within the political and legal constraints better than the existing proposals. Hence, the Commission should continue to support research on monetary unions, including unorthodox and controversial ideas about their break-up.

7.5.1 Maintaining and Improving Economic and Financial Stability

The first recommendation builds on the insight that member states' preferences on EMU reforms are shaped by the fears of the financial meltdown. While it enabled member states to agree on recent EMU reforms, it also serves as a justification for Northern foot-dragging on the obvious reform steps, such as the European Deposit Insurance Scheme (EDIS). This objection can be overcome by demonstrable achievements in reducing risks in the financial sector, which – together with maintaining SGP limits – helps to rebuild trust and refocus the reform debate from the past problems to future challenges.

The current period of sustained economic growth enabled member states to improve their public finances and, by and large, comply with the SGP limits. In 2018, all Eurozone members bar Cyprus complied with deficit criteria, and in 2019, no member state is under the excessive deficit procedure (Commission 2019). At the same time, France, Belgium, Cyprus, Italy and Greece struggle to comply, and a worsening economic climate is going to make it even harder. Similarly, Eurozone members made major progress in de-risking their financial sectors. Since these are dominated by banks, the reduction of legacy losses is about the restructuring of non-performing assets and improving financial stability indicators. The Commission, the European Banking Authority and the European Central Bank in its capacity as Eurozone banking supervisor, closely monitor the de-risking of banking portfolios (see Commission 2017d). While there has been sustained progress (see figure 7.3), the ratios of non-performing loans in Greece and Cyprus remain extreme, at above 40 and 20 per cent, respectively (EBA 2019). Even without these two countries, the Southern average ratio is still double the Northern rate. Overall, the macroeconomic and financial stability needs, and gets, continued attention before the convergence of risk indicators between the two country groups can pave the way for the convergence of preferences on further EMU reforms.

The focus on financial stability is also justified by the fact that the EDIS proposal, while side-lined to technical committees, is more advanced than other proposals from the *Presidents' Reports*. Even though our survey indicated scepticism about its adoption within the next five years, it is still the most likely next step. It also seems that more technical and narrowly defined financial reforms are more politically feasible than larger fiscal risk-sharing instruments, such as common unemployment insurance or some form of a common counter-cyclical fund, despite the greater opportunities of the latter for broader package deals.

7.5.2 Developing Gradual Reform Designs

The reform agenda of deepening financial, economic, fiscal and political unions was outlined in numerous reports. However, all proposals, including the fiscal back-up for bank resolution fund or the common deposit insurance, were side-lined. The Commission strives to increase the chances of their adoption by reducing the scope of risk-sharing, watering-down controversial provisions, postponing deadlines and resorting to changes in economic governance. While this increases the gap from those initial ambitions, the cumulation of modest reforms can gradually improve the completeness of the

EMU architecture. Consequently, the Commission and member states should continue the reform debate, despite its modest results and the shift of political attention to other crises.

While this recommendation is self-evident, it is also rooted in the insights from our analysis of Eurozone politics. The political and legal constraints on reform summarised in section 7.3 justify a continuous search for feasible solutions that are acceptable to both sides of the divide and do not require treaty or constitutional changes. Moreover, the single-dimensionality of the policy conflict on EMU reforms also implies that connecting multiple reform proposals, such as those clearly favoured by the North and those supported by the South, can enhance political feasibility. The single-dimensionality makes package deals across multiple policy domains unlikely but does not exclude package deals within the EMU reform domain if such an opportunity arises.

7.5.3 Preparing for Crisis-Induced Reforms

The gradualist scenario assumes that the E(M)U will be able to avoid another existential crisis for sufficient time to complete its reforms. However, the Commission should develop another set of reform designs that could be adopted in crisis circumstances. Such policy proposals are likely to differ from the gradualist reforms because they need to deliver drastic change to stop the crisis from escalating. If member states ever face the stark choice between the completion of EMU or its catastrophic disintegration, they may accept far-reaching reforms.

Preparing for the alternative course of action is a prudent strategy under any circumstances. However, this recommendation also addresses several insights from our analysis. First of all, clearly defined proposals can serve as a useful reminder of potentially drastic choices between major risk-sharing reforms or break-up in the escalating crisis. It is both a benchmark for the progress of gradual reforms and a corrective against ever greater watering-down of proposals as the EU strives to find political agreement (see section 7.4).

Second, the executive bias in national preference formation deprived recent reforms of much political legitimacy. Governments and EU bodies pushed them through with limited public debate, while parliaments, public opinion and business actors often accepted them as necessary, without challenging them. This contributed to political resentment of the EU and Eurozone, fuelling protest votes by populist parties in many countries. Putting forward plans for crisis-induced reforms would provide national parliaments and social actors with an opportunity to discuss a Plan B. These discussions would provide a degree of legitimacy, should the crisis reform ever be implemented under extreme time pressures of another escalating crisis.

7.5.4 Supporting Innovative Economic Thinking

The *EMU Choices* project has analysed the politics of past reforms and extrapolated insights for the four unions defined in the *Presidents' Reports*. Taking the fundamental components of these reforms as given overlooks the possibility that there are innovative policy designs, which could navigate the political and legal constraints better than the existing ones. Consequently, the Commission should continue to support economic research in this area, even though other EU crises push for a shift to other research priorities.

The concept of quantitative easing serves as a reminder that a relatively novel and untested policy tool can play a fundamental role in containing crises and essentially saving the single currency. After all, it was the commitment to do 'whatever it takes' (Draghi 2012), backed by unorthodox monetary policy tools, that was instrumental for containing the ever-escalating crisis. However, the Commission should support not only academic research into ways of improving the resilience of the EMU but also into potential break-up scenarios. During the crisis and afterward, various ideas were put forward for dismantling of euro or introducing parallel currencies, such as the mini-bots in Italy. While these concepts generally underestimate catastrophic risks, they should be evaluated by systematic research, and the knowledge so gained should be integrated into the planning for crisis-induced reform designs.

7.6 RECENT DEVELOPMENTS AND REFORM SCENARIOS

The analysis of political and legal constraints that Eurozone politics imposes on further EMU reforms is based on data covering 2010 to 2015. Another four years have passed, which enables us to discuss findings of this book, including our scenarios and policy recommendations, in the context of the most recent reform experience. While it is true that no major reform was completed by the end of 2019, it would be premature to conclude that the reform process has stalled completely. At a closer look, there is some evidence that economic stability and continued negotiations have delivered gradual preference convergence on some reform measures. The gap between Northern and Southern positions has narrowed, and 2020 may see the adoption of some reforms.

Comparing the current EMU reform agenda (see table 7.1) with the expectations of well-informed national representatives in Brussels (see table 7.3) reveals that there are three types of reforms proposals: easy, impossible and plausible. First, there are relatively uncontroversial reforms, such as consolidation of the ESM and Fiscal Compact to EU law, changes to the governance of the European Semester or progress towards Capital Markets Union, which do not involve risk-sharing issues and are likely to be adopted. Second, there are major reforms, such as European safe assets, macroeconomic stabilisation mechanisms and measures enhancing the political legitimacy of the Eurozone that involve dramatic sharing of risks and sovereignty. Their chances of adoption within the term of the next Commission are minimal, unless there is a shift to some crisis-induced scenario. Finally, there are three reforms that include some element of risk-sharing but are not completely out of reach by 2024. These potentially plausible cases include some form of EU funding for national structural reforms and the two missing pieces of the Banking Union: the fiscal backstop of the Single Resolution Fund and the common deposit insurance.

Two of the following cases demonstrate that member state preferences gradually converge, albeit at the glacial pace. This convergence is driven by the sustained financial and macroeconomic stability, combined with policy entrepreneurship by the Commission and expert groups in Brussels. Any progress between 2015 and 2019 required a lot of searching for a politically feasible policy design that could be adopted by the divided Council without the pressure of the immediate crisis.

The EU funding for reforms was initially proposed as the Convergence and Competitiveness Instrument (CCI) in 2012 (Commission 2012, 21–23; 2013; van Rompuy et al. 2012, 13–16). It was intended as a potential compromise between Southern countries that expected a Eurozone-wide macroeconomic stabilisation tool, and Northern states were at best willing to consider some support for structural reforms necessary to stabilise individual economies. Formally, the CCI was to provide EU funding for the implementation of country-specific recommendations from the European Semester, with the key policy innovation being an enforceable contract between the Commission and member governments. However, no agreement was achieved even on the key parameters, such as whether the funding should be a loan or grant, or how could a contract be credible and legitimate at the same time (see Rubio 2013; van Rompuy 2013; D'Alfonso and Stuchlik 2016).

Consequently, the CCI was neither developed as a new fiscal tool nor integrated into the 2014–2020 multi-annual financial framework (MFF). Except for a small pilot scheme providing technical assistance,[3] the convergence and competitiveness proposals dropped off the EU agenda until the negotiations of the next MFF. It made its return when the Commission draft of the 2021–2027 MFF included a reform delivery tool with an allocation of €22 billion. The Eurogroup agreed to include the instrument in the EMU reform programme and restarted negotiations about the Budgetary Instrument for Convergence and Competitiveness (BICC). At the end of 2019, all delegations accepted the allocation and co-financing rules; therefore, it is now certain that BICC will be part of the EMU toolbox (Dias and Zoppe 2020; Council 2019a). While the overall budget remains subject to agreement on the whole MFF, the financial capacity of the new tool will be about 0.1 per cent of Eurozone GDP per year.

The Single Resolution Fund (SRF) was introduced to cut the link between the solvency of large systemic banks and individual member states. If all preventive measures fail, the SRF can provide common EU resources for bank restructuring, thus avoid a situation when a member state may be unable to secure necessary resources by sovereign borrowing. The SRF is funded by bank levies, and its gradual build-up should reach the target amount of about €55 billion in 2024. While this suffices for the resolution of one large cross-border bank (EPSC 2015, 2), it is not large enough to break the state-bank solvency link during financial crises.

The initial discussions of a single resolution mechanism indicated that member states would provide further guarantees or direct credits to backstop SRF in case more funding was needed. However, this decision has been postponed up until the completion of the SRF in 2024. Since the SRF funding is governed by intergovernmental agreement, the Commission was in no position to make the formal proposal and broker compromises. However, its internal think-tank outlined potential solutions as either providing guarantees for the SRF to borrow on private markets or relying on the ESM to provide a credit line (EPSC 2015). The former was more in line with the initial logic of providing additional risk-sharing over and above existing mechanisms, but the convenience of the latter prevailed. At the end of 2019, member states agreed to instruct respective boards of ESM and SRF to develop a credit line backstop up to €68 billion (Centeno 2019). The agreement is expected to be signed as part of a package of related ESM changes in 2020.

The BICC and SRF backstop demonstrates that some preference convergence between the North and South is possible. It is slow, but it allows gradual progress through patient negotiations. At the same time, making these two proposals politically feasible required abandoning the idea of providing additional risk-sharing for the Eurozone. Both outcomes represent new forms of risk-sharing but within the limits of existing ESM and MFF. While they do not provide any fresh resources, they can still improve the resilience of the EMU. Both reforms shifted some decision-making powers to the supranational level. The pre-arranged credit line allows SRF to mobilise resources faster, which may be important in a crisis. Similarly, BICC provides the Commission with a stronger role in approving funding for reform projects than in structural funds that serve similar purposes.

The negotiations of the common deposit insurance were not conclusive by the end of 2019. However, they still provide important insights into the gradual reform scenario. The scheme was announced as a part of the Banking Union, which – alongside the ECB commitment to 'do whatever it takes' – was instrumental in stopping the crisis escalation in summer 2012. The Commission proposed the introduction of a mutual borrowing mechanism among individual national schemes already in 2010, but member states sidelined this option by making it voluntary. The Commission made the next attempt in 2015 by proposing the EDIS. It proposed the introduction of a fully mutualised scheme governed by the existing Single Resolution Board phased-in over eight years. It limited EDIS benefits to countries that comply with EMU rules and fund their national deposit scheme adequately. The EDIS contribution was to be calculated using the risk-based methodology, reducing contributions by safer, more stable banks. Despite these overtures, Germany and other Northern states opposed the proposal.

In 2017, the Commission tried to restart negotiations by backtracking from full mutualisation and proposing a co-insurance model while also replacing the fixed schedule with conditional timing based on the reduction of legacy losses (Commission 2017e; Schnabel and Véron 2018). However, the most important obstacle to the EDIS adoption remains the risk-based formula for calculation of banks' contributions to the scheme. Numerous working groups are collecting data and testing various approaches but were not able to reach a compromise by the end of 2019 (Centeno 2019; Council 2019b).

The gradual strategy is yet to lead to a compromise on EDIS, but there was also an attempt to speed up the process by formulating a grand bargain on the completion of the Banking Union. In November 2019, the new German Minister of Finance, Olaf Scholz, proposed a four-point plan to lift the deadlock (Scholz 2019; BMF 2019). First, he asked for common insolvency and resolution procedures for small banks outside of SRM reach, which would prevent member governments – so far including Italy and Germany – from bending the rules (see Noonan 2020). Second, he insisted on further de-risking of banking sectors. However, apart from reducing the non-performing assets, he proposed new risk-weighting of sovereign bonds based on their concentration in banks' portfolios. This aspect would be hard to accept, especially in Italy, where domestic banks buy and hold a large proportion of national debt. Thirdly, Scholz signalled German openness to accept EDIS, if watered-down further from co-insurance to re-insurance model, whereby EDIS only provides liquidity to national deposit insurance but needs to be repaid in full afterward. While re-insurance would be a progress, it provides only temporary risk-sharing, putting weaker banking systems at a disadvantage. Finally, for good measure, Scholz also suggested adding the common corporate tax base to the package deal to prevent arbitrage.

The deal would be difficult to accept for Southern countries that rely on their banks to buy their sovereign bonds. However, even before national representatives could discuss the merits of the proposal, Scholz's domestic position was severely weakened by his loss of leadership contest for the Social Democratic Party. It turned out that there was no consensus in Berlin, and Scholz was no longer in a position to foster one. This attempt at a grand bargain confirmed the informed scepticism of COREPER members (see section 7.4), and EDIS talks quickly returned to the technical level discussion of risk-based contribution formula.

While the outcomes of the three reform cases differ, they all illustrate that a gradual reform strategy can navigate its way through Eurozone politics that is biased towards deadlock. Despite all political and legal constraints that this book documented empirically, EMU reforms remain on the agenda and show marginal signs of progress.

The three reform cases also support a limited generalisation about the coping mechanism that the Commission and EU expert bodies rely on in navigating political and legal constraints. The comparison of initial policy designs with those from the end of 2019 reveals the key parameters of the gradual approach (table 7.4). The most obvious is the gradual watering-down of risk-sharing elements. The end goal of the EDIS proposal was reduced from full mutualisation to co-insurance in the Commission's proposals and to mere re-insurance in the Scholz version. Similarly, SRF backstop and BICC proposals also backtracked from the initial ambition of providing additional risk-sharing tools to operating within existing frameworks of ESM and MFF, respectively. The same trend is observable in the timing of reforms: while initial proposals included ambitious schedules, the most current ones shy away from any deadlines. At the same time, the decision on the SRF backstop was initially postponed up until 2024, so adopting the scheme in 2020 is an improvement of sorts.

Table 7.4 The Stylised Comparison of Reform Designs

Proposal	Initial Design	End of 2019 Design
EDIS	Fully mutualised EDIS	Co-insurance EDIS
	Risk-based contributions	Risk-based contribution
	Phased-in within eight years	No set deadlines
SRF backstop	Additional risk-sharing via guarantees or credits from member states	Risk-sharing through ESM up to a pre-set limit
BICC	Binding reform contracts with the Commission	Commission approval based on Eurogroup priorities
	Funding in addition to existing EU budget	Funding from the EU budget

7.7 CONCLUSION

This chapter has summarised political and legal constraints on EMU reforms that were empirically analysed in the previous chapters. The overall picture clearly demonstrates that Eurozone politics is heavily biased against changes that include any element of risk-sharing. This is confirmed by the survey of Brussels insiders as well as the most recent policy developments until the end of 2019.

The data and analysis from the *EMU Choices* project systematically document that there are no easy ways to jumpstart or speed up Eurozone reforms. The EU is reduced to painstaking negotiations of marginal reforms that may complete the architecture for the single currency, but more likely in decades than years. The only alternative is a crisis-driven scenario brought about by exogenous shock. This may be a positive shock in the form of new, pro-European governments in the key member states that would be able to reshape some political constraints. However, most shocks large enough to dislodge the status quo are likely to be negative, such as the return of the Euro Crisis due to a deep recession.

Crisis scenarios are obviously very risky and prone to mishaps. There is no guarantee that the ECB and EU governments will be able to orchestrate the turning point, as was the 'whatever-it-takes' statement combined with the Banking Union commitment in summer 2012. Moreover, if the crisis is to enable any reform progress, it needs to change the single-dimensionality of Eurozone politics, thus rearranging the North–South coalitions along multiple dimensions and opening space for some kind of package deal or grand bargain. A new crisis that merely deepens existing divides can only increase the probability of catastrophic failure.

At the same time, the E(M)U is better prepared for the next crisis than in 2008. At the very least, the combination of existing stabilisation mechanisms, such as the European Stability Mechanism and the Single Resolution Mechanism made the Eurozone much more resilient. The same applies to all other reforms supporting macroeconomic and financial stability. The availability of these mechanisms makes it easier to scale them up if future crises challenge the viability of single currency again. Moreover, the advanced state of debate about further reforms spanning all four unions also makes the EU better prepared to act swiftly to implement additional risk-sharing and stabilisation tools in the hour of need. While, so far, effects of the COVID-19 crisis on the EMU arrangements remain to be seen, and the old North–South divide again dominates public debates, political advocacy for the use of existing crisis instruments, such as the ESM, as well as for their enhancement may vindicate our concluding statement.

NOTES

1. The North–South divide is a simplifying metaphor established in the media. It is not geographically correct and oversimplifies the distribution of policy preferences (see chapter 2 for more precise discussion). However, we use these references because they are familiar, but they should not be taken literally.
2. While other countries join the positions of the Hanseatic League, the core is formed by Denmark, Estonia, Finland, Ireland, Latvia, Lithuania, the Netherlands and Sweden.
3. The Commission created the Structural Reform Support Programme to preserve and develop the know-how from the implementation of structural reform in Greece and Cyprus. It was uncontroversial as it focused on technical assistance and used only €150 million from existing budgetary reserves. Nonetheless, it demonstrated the benefits of joint formulation of reform projects successfully enough to have its budget doubled within a year and tripled again in the 2021–2027 MFF (Kurnai 2018).

REFERENCES

BMF. 2019. "Position paper on the goals of the banking union: BMF – non-paper." *Bundesfinanzministerium*. http://prod-upp-image-read.ft.com/b750c7e4-ffba-11e9-b7bc-f3fa4e77dd47.

Centeno, M. 2019. "Letter of the President of the Eurogroup to the President of the Euro Summit." https://www.consilium.europa.eu/media/41643/20191205-letter-president-of-the-eurogroup-to-cm.pdf.

Commission. 2012. "A Blueprint for a deep and genuine Economic and Monetary Union." *The European Commission*, November 28, 2012. http://eur-lex.europa.eu/Lex-UriServ/LexUriServ.do?uri=COM:2012:0777:FIN:EN:PDF.

Commission. 2013. "Towards a Deep and Genuine Economic and Monetary Union – The introduction of a Convergence and Competitiveness Instrument." *The European Commission*, March 20, 2013. https://eur-lex.europa.eu/legal-content/EN/ALL/?uri=CELEX:52013DC0165.

Commission. 2015. "Proposal for a Regulation of the European Parliament and of the Council amending Regulation (EU) 806/2014 in order to establish a European Deposit Insurance Scheme." *The European Commission*, November 24, 2015. https://eur-lex.europa.eu/legal-content/EN/TXT/?uri=CELEX:52015PC0586.

Commission. 2017a. "Reflection paper on the deepening of the EMU." *The European Commission*, May 31, 2017. https://ec.europa.eu/commission/sites/beta-political/files/reflection-paper-emu_en.pdf.

Commission. 2017b. "Roadmap on further steps towards completing Europe's EMU, December 6, 2017." https://ec.europa.eu/commission/publications/completing-europes-economic-and-monetary-union-factsheets_en.

Commission. 2017c. "White Paper on the future of Europe." *The European Commission*, March 1, 2017. https://ec.europa.eu/commission/future-europe/white-paper-future-europe-and-way-forward_en.

Commission. 2017d. "Banking sector and financial stability: European semester thematic factsheet." October 16, 2017. https://ec.europa.eu/info/sites/info/files/file_import/european-semester_thematic-factsheet_banking-sector-financial-stability_en_0.pdf.

Commission. 2017e. "Proposal for a Council Regulation on the establishment of the European Monetary Fund." *The European Commission*, December 12, 2017. https://eur-lex.europa.eu/legal-content/EN/TXT/?uri=CELEX%3A52017PC0827.

Commission. 2019. "Communication on 2019 European Semester." *The European Commission*, June 5, 2019. https://eur-lex.europa.eu/legal-content/EN/TXT/?qid=1560257977630&uri=CELEX:52019DC0500.

Council. 2019a. "Term sheet on the budgetary instrument for convergence and competitiveness (BICC)." *The European Council*, October 10, 2019. https://www.consilium.europa.eu/en/press/press-releases/2019/10/10/term-sheet-on-the-budgetary-instrument-for-convergence-and-competitiveness-bicc/.

Council. 2019b. "Strengthening of the Banking Union - Progress report. The European Council", November 25, 2019. https://data.consilium.europa.eu/doc/document/ST-14354-2019-INIT/en/pdf.

D'Alfonso, A. and A. Stuchlik. 2016. "A fiscal capacity for the euro area? Options for reforms to counter asymmetric shocks." *European Parliamentary Research Service*, September, 2016, PE 589.774. http://www.europarl.europa.eu/RegData/etudes/IDAN/2016/589774/EPRS_IDA(2016)589774_EN.pdf.

Degner, H. and D. Leuffen. 2019. "Franco-German cooperation and the rescuing of the Eurozone." *European Union Politics* 20, no. 1: 89–108.

Dias, C. and A. Zoppe. 2020. "What do we know about the BICC today?" *EGOV Support Unit Briefing*, February 6, 2020. https://www.europarl.europa.eu/RegData/etudes/BRIE/2019/634359/IPOL_BRI(2019)634359_EN.pdf.

Draghi, M. 2012. "Speech at the Global Investment Conference in London", July 26, 2012. https://www.ecb.europa.eu/press/key/date/2012/html/sp120726.en.htm.

EBA. 2019. "Risk dashboard: 2013 to 2019." *The European Banking Authority.* https://eba.europa.eu/risk-analysis-and-data/risk-dashboard.

EPSC. 2015. "Strengthening the EU's Financial System: Bridge Financing Options for the Single Resolution Fund." *The European Political Strategy Centre of the European Commission*, Issue 2. https://ec.europa.eu/epsc/sites/epsc/files/5p_note_bridgefinance.pdf.

Juncker, J.C., D. Tusk, J. Dijsselbloem, M. Draghi, and M. Schulz. 2015. "Completing Europe's economic and monetary union", June 22, 2015. https://ec.europa.eu/commission/sites/beta-political/files/5-presidents-report_en.pdf.

Kudrna, Z. 2018. "Making the politically unfeasible feasible: The Commission's approach to EMU reform design." *EMU Choices Working Paper*, December, 2018. https://emuchoices.eu/wp-content/uploads/2018/12/Kudrna-2018-feasibility-WP-1.pdf.

Kudrna, Z. and E. Lentsch. 2019. "Legal indices of procedural requirements for constitutional and treaty changes in the European Union." *EMU Choices Working Paper*, 2019.

Kudrna, Z., S. Bailer, S. Târlea, and F. Wasserfallen. 2019. "Three worlds of preference formation in European Union Politics: Evidence from new data on Eurozone Reforms." *EMU Choices Working Paper*, March, 2019. https://emuchoices.eu/wp-content/uploads/2019/03/2018WP_Kudrna_et_al_EMUfpaper.pdf.

Lehner, T. and F. Wasserfallen. 2019. "Political conflict in the reform of the Eurozone." *European Union Politics* 20, no. 1: 45–64.

Lentsch, E. and S. Griller. 2019. "Who is afraid of Treaty reforms? EMU Choices Policy brief n. 2." *EMU Choices Working Paper*, February 24, 2019. https://emuchoices.eu/2019/02/24/who-is-afraid-of-treaty-reforms-policy-brief-2/.

Lundgren, M., S. Bailer., L.M. Dellmuth, J. Tallberg, and S. Târlea. 2019. "Bargaining success in the reform of the Eurozone." *European Union Politics*, 20, no. 1, 65–88.

Macron, E. 2017. "Sorbonne speech, English version." *Ouest France*, September 26, 2017. http://international.blogs.ouest-france.fr/archive/2017/09/29/macron-sorbonne-verbatim-europe-18583.html.

Macron, E. 2019. "Dear Europe, Brexit is a lesson for all of us: it's time for renewal, English version." *The Guardian*, March 4, 2019. https://www.theguardian.com/commentisfree/2019/mar/04/europe-brexit-uk.

Morlino, L. and C.E. Sottilotta. 2019. *The Politics of the Eurozone Crisis in Southern Europe: A Comparative Reappraisal*. London: Palgrave Macmillan.

Noonan, L. 2020. "EU regulator call for clearer rules on rescuing banks." *The Financial Times*, February 9, 2020. https://www.ft.com/content/0cb5d87e-4434-11ea-a43a-c4b328d9061c.

Rubio, E. 2013. "Which financial instrument to facilitate structural reforms in the Euro Area?" *Notre Europe -Jacques Delors institute*, Policy paper 104. https://institutdelors.eu/en/publications/which-financial-instrument-to-facilitate-structural-reforms-in-the-euro-area/.

Schnabel, I. and N. Véron. 2018. "Breaking the stalemate on European Deposit Insurance." *Bruegel*, March 5, 2018. http://bruegel.org/2018/03/breaking-the-stalemate-on-european-deposit-insurance/.

Scholz, O. 2019. "Germany will consider EU-wide bank deposit reinsurance." *The Financial Times*, November 5, 2019. https://www.ft.com/content/82624c98-ff14-11e9-a530-16c6c29e70ca.

Sottilotta, C.E. 2019. "Italy: Vincolo esterno or muddling through?" In *The Politics of the Eurozone Crisis in Southern Europe: A Comparative Reappraisal*, edited by L. Morlino and C.E. Sottilotta. London: Palgrave Macmillan.

Târlea, S. et al. 2019. "Explaining governmental preferences on Economic and Monetary Union Reform." *European Union Politics* 20, no. 1: 24–44.

van Rompuy, H. 2013. "State of play of the consultations with Member States and institutional actors: Summary note prepared by the Cabinet of the President of the European Council", June 28, 2013. https://www.consilium.europa.eu/uedocs/cms_data/docs/pressdata/en/ec/137665.pdf.

van Rompuy, H., J.M. Barroso, J.C. Juncker, and M. Draghi. 2012. "Towards a genuine Economic and Monetary Union", June 26, 2012. https://www.consilium.europa.eu/media/33785/131201.pdf.

Warren, T., S. James, H. Kassim, S. Puntscher Riekmann, S. Saurugger, and S. Hargreaves Heap. 2019. "A new equilibrium? The changed politics of eurozone reform." *Paper presented at the 9th SGEU Conference*, Sciences Po Paris, June 13–15 2018.

Wasserfallen, F., D. Leuffen, Z. Kudrna, and H. Degner. 2019. "Analysing European Union decision-making during the Eurozone Crisis with new data." *European Union Politics* 20, no. 1: 3–23.

Appendix

EMU Choices Data Portals

The *EMU Choices* project has compiled four datasets:

1. *EMU Positions* covers forty-seven issues and provides systematic data on 2010–2015 Eurozone reforms;
2. *EMU Formation* covers positions and influence of twenty-three national and international actors involved in the formation of national preferences;
3. *EMU Historical* summarises positions for the 1992–2010 period; and
4. *EMU Legal index* provides data on procedural constraints member states impose on treaty changes and constitutional amendments induced by EMU reforms.

Each dataset is made available through data portal that allows users to:

- Interact with the data to get insights and learn about the structure and coverage of each dataset;
- Access detailed codebook explaining the data collection process;
- Download aggregated datasets used in underlying research for this book; and
- Download a non-aggregated dataset for research purposes (these dataset are also available from zenodo.org).

A.1 EMU POSITIONS DATA PORTAL

The *EMU Position* data report positions of member states and EU institutions as well as salience scores for forty-seven contested issues related to EMU reforms between 2010 and 2015.

Appendix

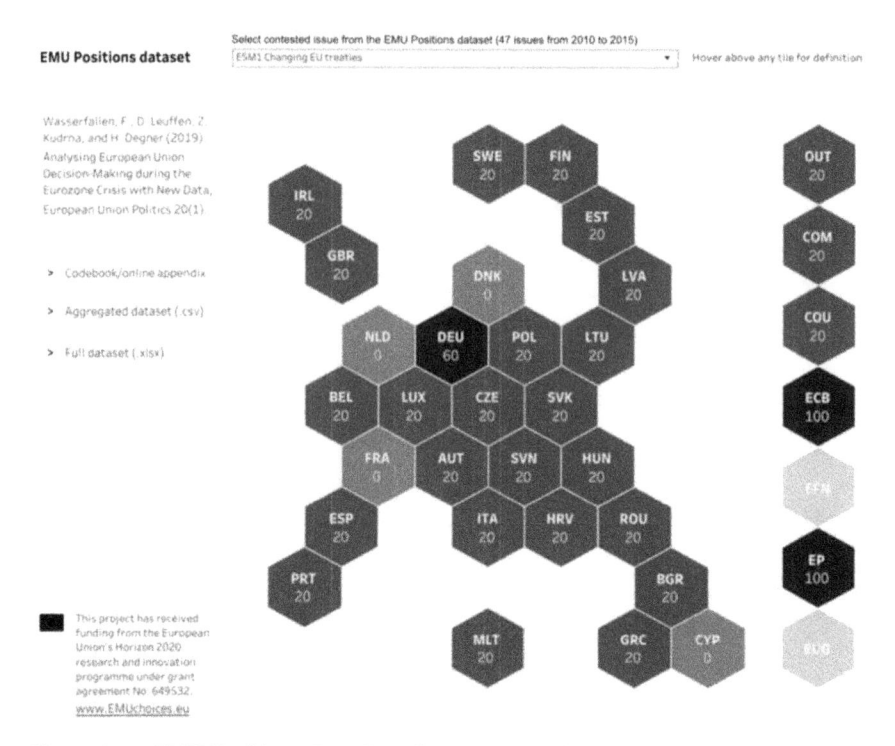

Figure A.1 EMU Positions Data Portal. Source: emuchoices.eu/data/emup/.

EMU Positions data were collected in five steps:

1. Identify and select the most important policy proposals officially negotiated during the Eurozone Crisis. These included support for Greece, the European Financial Stability Facility (EFSF), the European Stability Mechanism (ESM), the Six-Pack on fiscal and economic governance, the Two-Pack on the coordination of national budgets, the Fiscal Compact, the Banking Union, the Financial Transaction Tax, Eurobonds and the Five Presidents' Report.
2. Identify and select the most contested policy issues within these ten proposals based on official EU documents and reports from reputable media,
3. Code the preferences of all twenty-eight EU member states and six EU institutions for the forty-seven issues based on document analysis of official and media reports. The position scores range between 0 and 100.
4. Validate issue definitions, policy spaces, and the coding of positions by structured interviews with twenty-nine experts personally involved in the given negotiations and gather salience scores from these interviews.

5. Aggregate the data using data-quality ratings and alternative aggregation procedures (winner-takes-all, weighted-average, decision-tree method).

A.2 EMU FORMATION DATA PORTAL

The *EMU Formation* data report position and influence scores of twenty-three different actors in all twenty-eight EU member states on four contested issues related to EMU reforms between 2010 and 2015.

EMU Formation data were collected using the following procedure:

1. Develop a questionnaire that combines structured and open questions. Train over twenty interviewers across *EMU Choices* consortium to ensure consistent conduct of interviews according to a clear manual.
2. Conduct 141 interviews in all 28 member states with expert interviewees selected on the basis of their involvement in the relevant decision-making process (mostly from ministries, but also from national parliaments, permanent representations, media or academia).

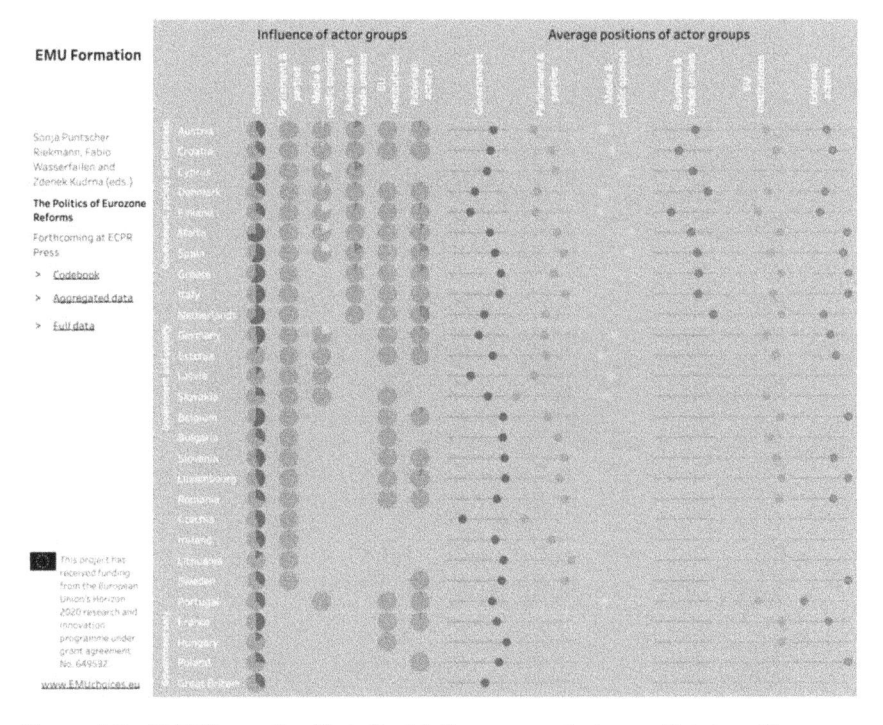

Figure A.2 EMU Formation Data Portal. Source: emuchoices.eu/data/emuf/.

156   *Appendix*

3. Transcribe interview summaries and enter coded answers to structured questions to a dataset. Both positions and influence scores are coded on 0 to 100 scale.
4. Aggregate data by weighted average, using data-quality ratings as weights and excluding scores for actors that were not reported by at least two interviewees.

A.3 EMU HISTORICAL DATA PORTAL

The *EMU Historical* data report positions of member states on forty-one contested issues related to EMU reforms between 1992 and 2010.

EMU Historical data were collected in five steps:

1. Identify key events in the EU's fiscal integration debate between 1992 and 2004. These include Maastricht Treaty, Stability and Growth Pact,

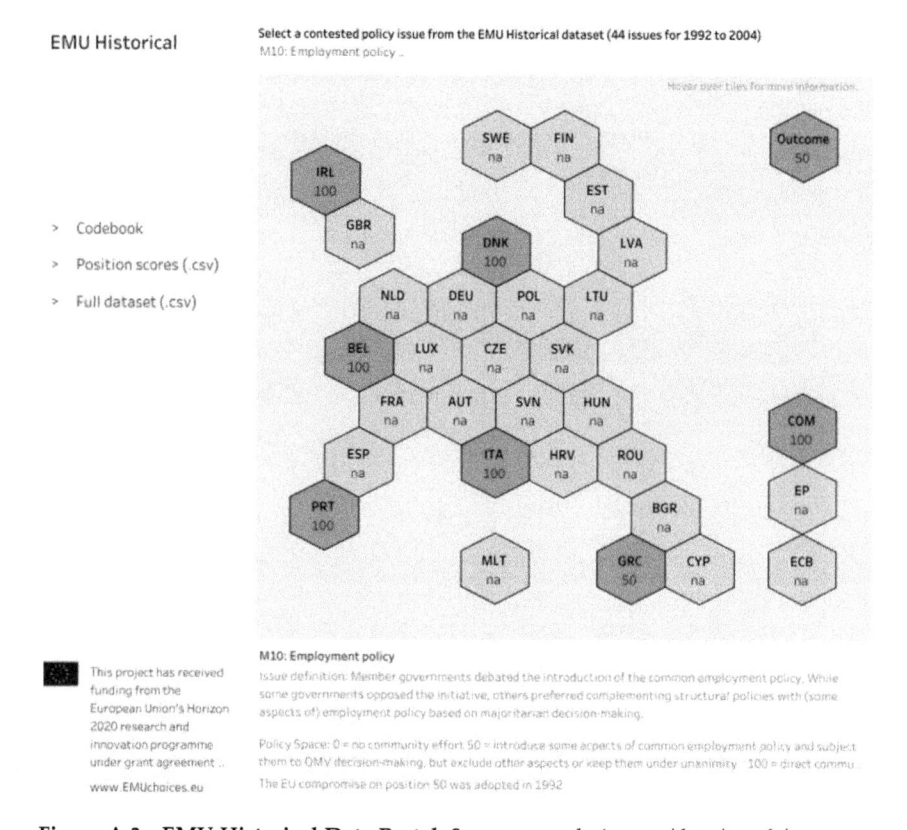

Figure A.3   EMU Historical Data Portal. Source: emuchoices.eu/data/emuh/.

Amsterdam Treaty, Nice Treaty, Constitution, Stability and Growth Pact reform and Lisbon Treaty.
2. Gather primary sources available from the Council Secretariat as well as prominent academic analysis of the key events.
3. Analyse these sources iteratively to identify contested issues that have been discussed repeatedly during the key fiscal integration events.
4. Code the preferences of EU member states and three EU institutions for the forty-four issues related to four key event. The position scores range between 0 and 100.

A.4 EMU LEGAL INDEX DATA PORTAL

The *EMU Legal Index* data report procedural requirements imposed by member states (1) on the adoption of the EU Treaty change, and (2) on the adoption of the national constitutional amendment induced by EMU reforms.

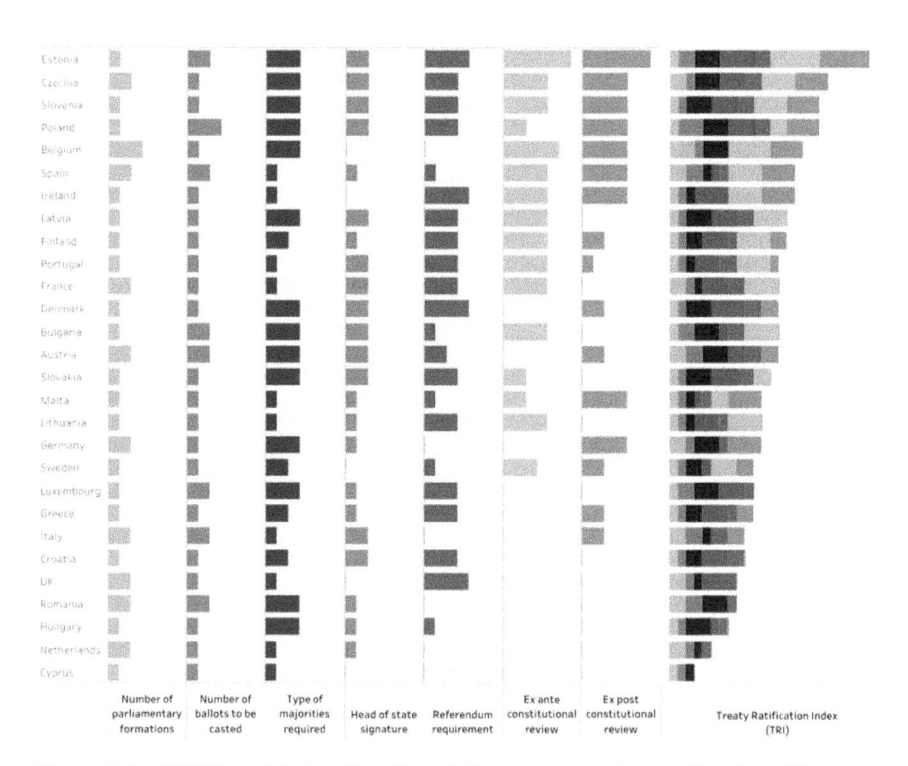

Figure A.4 EMU Legal Index Data Portal. Source: emuchoices.eu/data/emuli/.

The *EMU Legal Index* data can be used to compile four indices capturing procedural requirements imposed on the four decisions. Data provide stylised, comparative information on the role of the following seven potential veto points:

1. Parliamentary formations: How many parliamentary formations must decide on the adoption of EMU-induced constitutional amendment?
2. Ballots: How many ballots are the relevant parliamentary formations required to cast for the adoption of EMU-induced constitutional amendment?
3. Majorities: What are the majorities required for the adoption of EMU-induced constitutional amendment?
4. Head of state: Is the signature of the head of state required for the EMU-induced constitutional amendment?
5. Referendum: Is any referendum possible or mandatory for the adoption of EMU-induced constitutional amendment?
6. Ex-ante constitutional review: Is ex-ante constitutional review required for the EMU-induced constitutional amendment?
7. Ex-post constitutional review: Is ex-post constitutional review required for the EMU-induced constitutional amendment?

Index

References to tables or figures are *italicized*

agenda (setting), 7, 9, 13, 24–26, 35, 66, 70, 105, 107–10, 117, 124, 125, *126*, 128, 132, 133, 143, 144, 147

austerity, 6, 8, 25, 49, 60, 62, 65, 67, 68, *72*, 73, 75, 91, 113, *128*, 133, 134

Austria, 4, *21*, *23*, 69, 84, *84*, *85*, 86, *88*, 90, 92, *96*, *97*, 98n12, 113, *129*, *133*, *135*, *136*, *154*, 155, 156, *157*

bargain, 10, 146–48; bargaining, 2, 3, 7, 9, 13–15, 20, 22, *23*, 24–27, 35, 36, 39, 42, 43, 46, 50, 66, 75, 105, 107, 112, 113, 115–17, *128*, 132, 133; Nash Bargaining Model, 25

Banking Union, 6, 8, 10, 14, 20, 44, 49, 75n5, 83, 125, *126*, 127, 130–32, 144, 146, 148, 154

Belgium, 21, *21*, *23*, 44, 84, *84*, *85*, 86, *88*, 91, *96*, 97, 129, 133, 135, 136, 141, *154*, 155, 156, *157*

BICC. *See* Budgetary Instrument for Convergence and Competitiveness (BICC)

Brexit, 4, 139

Budgetary Instrument for Convergence and Competitiveness (BICC), 9, 144, 145, 147, *147*

Bulgaria, *21*, 23, *84*, 92, *96*, 97, 129, 133, 135, 136, 154, 155, 156, *157*

Commission, 2, 5, 6, 10, 14, 18, 19, 22, 25–27, 38, 41, 42, 44, 46, 48, 64, 66, 75n3, 82, 87, 93, 105, 107–9, 115, 116, *126*, 127, *128*, 130, 137, *138*, 140–47, *147*, 149n3

compromise, 3, 7, 9, 14, 22, 24, 25, 35, 43, 44, 45, 46, 73, 115, *128*, 130, 131, 132, 136, 137, 139, 144, 145, 146

concession, 7, 14, 22, 24, 131, 132

constitutional review, 84, 85, 87, 92, 93, 94, *94*, *95*, 97, *128*, 135, 158; constitutional hurdles, 83, 93; constitutional limits (limitations), 83, 84, *88*, 92

contested issue, 13, 21, 26, 50, 57, 58, 66, 68, 69, *74*, 75, 75n5, 93, 113, 117, 127, 130, 153, 154, 155, 156, 157. *See also* dataset *specific entries*; policy issue

Council (of the European Union), 2, 17, 18, 19, 38, 42, 65, 66, 69, 73, 82, 86, 89, 98n5, 108, 109, 114, *126*, 127, 130, 144, 157

Council of Ministers, 17, 127

159

Court of Justice of the European Union (CJEU), 90, 92, 135
creditor country (state), 26, 115, 118n8
crisis (-driven/induced) scenario, 10, 127, 144, 148
Croatia, *21*, 23, 96, 97, 129, 133, 135, 136, 154, 155, 156, *157*
Cyprus, 8, 21, *21*, 23, 58, *61*, *62*, *63*, 65, 66, 68, *70*, 71, *72*, 73, 74, *74*, *84*, *96*, 97, 129, 133, 135, 136, 141, 149n3, *154*, 155, 156, *157*; CYP (*nation score*), *70*, *72*
Czech Republic, *21*, 23, 84, *96*, *97*, *129*, *133*, *135*, *136*, *154*, *155*, *156*, *157*

debt brake, 34, 41, 44, 67, 68, 71, 72, *72*, 73, *74*, 86
debtor country (state), 19, 25, 26, 115
Denmark, *21*, 23, 47, *84*, 92, *96*, 97, 129, 133, 135, 136, 149n2, *154*, 155, 156, *157*
de-risking. *See* financial stability

economic interest, 14, 17, 18, 20, 27, 34, 35, 49, 58; economic interest groups, 20, 35, 36, 49, 110, 112, 113
EMU Choices project, 2, 3, 4, 8, 9, 13, 15, 20, 27, 34, 40, 42, 47, 48, 50, 60, 68, 75n2, 93, 103, 105, 106, 107, 108, 109, 110, 111, 114, 115, 116, 117, 118nn3–4, 123, 127, 137, 139, 143, 148, 153, 155
EMU Formation data(set), 2, 7, 13–15, 17, 18, 27, 60, 110, 112–14, 116, 118n7, *130*, 134, *135*, 153, 155, *155*
EMU Historical data(set), 2, 153, 156, *156*
EMU Legal Index (dataset), 2, 8, 93, 94, *96*, *97*, 153, 157, *157*, 158
EMU Positions dataset, 2, 13, 15, 16, 18, 21, 25–27, 68, 106, 107, 110, 111, *129*, 153, 154, *154*
ESM, 1, 6, 9, 10, 41–45, 48, 58, 64, 69, 70, *70*, 71, *74*, 75, 75n5, 82–84, 87, *88*, 89, 90–93, 98n11, 99n13, 99n15, 109, 110, 113, *126*, 132, 135, *138*, 139, 143, 145, 147, *147*, 148, 154. *See also* European (Financial) Stability Mechanism
Estonia, *21*, 23, 84, *84*, *88*, 91, 92, *96*, 97, 113, *129*, 133, 135, 136, 149n2, *154*, 155, 156, *157*
Eurobonds, 7, 45, 48, 109, 132, 154
Eurogroup, 2, 18, 38, 41, 108, 109, 114, 116, *126*, 138, 144, *147*
European Central Bank (ECB), 2, 6, 10, 14, 18, 26, 41, 44, 46, *61*, 64, 65, 105, 108, 109, 124, 127, 141, 146, 148
European Commission. *See* Commission
European Council. *See* Council
European Court of Justice (ECJ). *See* Court of Justice of the European Union (CJEU)
European Deposit Insurance Scheme (EDIS), *126*, 130, 134, *138*, 140, 141, 146, 147, *147*
European Financial Stability Facility (EFSF), 13, 20, 75n5, 87, *88*, 89, 130, 154
European (Financial) Stability Mechanism, 1, 13, 20, 34, 58, 87, 98n11, 109, 127, 131, 148, 154; European stability, 41, 98n12. *See also* ESM; financial stability
European Monetary Union (European Monetary Fund/Economic and Monetary Union /monetary union), 1–3, 13, 15, 44, 58, 69, 72, 75, 81, 93, 98n5, 103, 123, 124, *126*, *138*, 139, *See also* Treaty on Stability, Coordination and Governance
European Parliament (EP), 18, 19, 44, 60, 66, 89, 123, *126*, 127, 128
Eurozone Crisis, 2–5, 15, 16, 19–21, 24, 26, 33, 42, 49, 50, 57, 59, 66–69, 73, 74, *74*, 75, 103–6, 108–17, 118n3, 132, 154
Ex-ante review, 87, 94, *94*, *95*, *136*, 158

Ex-post review, 48, 94, *94*, *95*, *136*, 158

finance minister (ministry), 10, 14, 17, 18, 40, 46, 48, 82, *126*, *138*
financial assistance (treaties), 41, 57, 82, 83, 87, *88*, 92
financial stability, 3, 9, 69, 87, 93, 124, 127, *128*, 129, 130, 134, 139–41, 148. *See also* ESM; European (Financial) Stability Mechanism
Finland, 21, *21*, 23, 44, 69, 84, *84*, *85*, 87, *88*, 90–92, *96*, 97, 113, *129*, 131, *133*, 135, 136, 149n2, *154*, 155, 156, *157*
Fiscal Compact, 13, 20, 42, 45, 47, 48, 68, 69, 71, 73, 75n5, 87, *126*, 130, 132, 134, 135, *138*, 143, 154
fiscal competence, 93, 97
fiscal discipline, 1, 6, 16, 20, 21, *21*, 25, 59, 64, 81, 83, 129
fiscal integration, 81–84, 91, 93, 156, 157
fiscal transfer, 6, 20, 21, *21*, 111
Five Presidents' Report. *See* Presidents' Report
France, 5, 7, 8, 14, 21, *21*, *23*, 25, 34, 40, 41, 43–48, 50, *84*, *85*, 86, *96*, 97, 109, 112, 113, 116, 117, *129*, 131–33, *133*, 135, 136, *138*, 141, *154*, 155, 156, *157*
Franco-German cooperation, 7, 24, 25, 44, 51n3, 109, *128*, 132, 137

Germany, 5–8, 10, 10n1, 14, 19, 21, *21*, 22, *23*, 24, 25, 34, 40–48, 50, 51n3, 61, *61*, 64, 67, 69, 71, 75n4, 84, *84*, *85*, 87, *88*, 89, 90, 92, *96*, 97, 109, 112, 113, 115–17, *128*, *129*, 131–33, *133*, 135, 136, 137, *138*, 139, 146, *154*, 155, 156, *157*. *See also* Franco-German cooperation
gradual (-ist scenario/strategy/reform), 9, 10, 82, 123–27, *128*, 137, 140–43, 145–47. *See also* crisis(-driven/induced) scenario
Great Britain, 7, 8, *21*, 23, 34, 40, 42, 45–50, 51n2, 68, 84, *96*, 97, 129, 133, 135, 136, 139, *154*, 155, 156, *157*
Greece, 8, 13, 34, 21, *21*, 22, *23*, 40–42, 45, 48, 49, *61*, 62, *62*, *63*, 64–67, 69, *70*, 71, 72, *72*, 73, 74, *74*, 75, 75n3, *84*, 87, *88*, 89, *96*, *97*, 109, *129*, 131, 132, *133*, 135, 136, 141, 149n3, 154, *154*, 155, 156, *157*; HEL (*nation score*), *70*, *72*
Grexit, 62, 72

Hungary, *21*, 23, 96, 97, 129, 133, 135, 136, 154, 155, 156, *157*

institutionalism, 24, 36–39, 46, 107
integration theories, 8, 9, 39, 75, 103–5, 107, 108, 110, 111, 114, 117
interest groups, 16, 18–20, 27, 35, 36, 48, 49, 110, 112, 113
intergovernmentalism (liberal intergovernmentalism/new intergovernmentalism), 4, 8, 14, 33, 35–38, 46, 58, 66, 75, 103, 107, 108, 110, 111–14, 116, 117; intergovernmental bargaining (coordination/agreements), 14, 20, 25, 26, 36, 42, 43, 46, 83, 84, 87, 97, 107, 109, 114, 116, 117, 132, 139, 145. See also inter-state (interstate) bargaining
International Monetary Fund (IMF), 6, 41, 45, 64, 87, 110
inter-state (interstate) bargaining, 2, 13, 14, 15, 20, 27, 35, 105, 107, 112, 113, 117. See also intergovernmentalism, intergovernmental bargaining
Ireland, 21, *21*, 23, 62, 84, *84*, 85, *88*, 90, 92, *96*, 97, 113, *129*, 131, *133*, 135, 136, 149n2, *154*, 155, 156, *157*

Italy, 8, *21*, 23, 44, 60, *62*, *63*, 64, 66, 67, 69, 70, *70*, 71, 72, *72*, 73, 74, *74*, 75, 75n4, 84, *84*, *96*, 97, 129, 133, 134, *135*, 136, 139, 141, 143, 146, *154*, 155, 156, *157*; ITA (*nation score*), 60, 68, *72*, 75n2

Latvia, *21*, 23, 84, *84*, *96*, 97, 129, 133, 135, 136, 149, 154, 155, 156, *157*
Legal index. See EMU Legal Index (dataset)
legislative bargaining (instances of legislative politics, proceedings/ negotiations on EU level in general/ordinary legislative procedure), 4, 5, 7, 18, 24, 26, 38, 109, 116, *128*, 132, 133, 137; legislation, 1, 8, 17, *72*, 73, 75n5, 84, 86, *126*, 133, 137. See also European Parliament (EP); treaties *specific entries*
liberal intergovernmentalism. *See* Intergovernmentalism
Lithuania, *21*, 23, 84, *84*, *96*, 97, 129, 133, 135, 136, 149n2, *154*, 155, 156, *157*
Luxembourg, 21, *21*, 23, 44, *84*, *96*, 97, 129, 133, 135, 136, 154, 155, 156, *157*

Maastricht (Treaty), 2, 6, 43, 60, 69, 81, 124, 156
Malta, 8, *21*, 23, 57, 58, 59, 61, *61*, *62*, *63*, 65, 66, 68, 69, *70*, 71, *72*, 73, 74, *74*, *84*, *96*, 97, 129, 130, 133, 135, 136, 154, 155, 156, *157*; MLT (*nation score*), *70*, 71, *72*
media, 5, 7, 18–20, 27, 51n5, 112, 127, *130*, 133, 149n1, 154, 155
memorandum of understanding (MoU), 6, 64, 65, 67, 69
method, 1, 2, 3, 9, 21, 37, 38, 94, 104–7, 110, 111, 112, 117, 131, 146, 155

national constitutional law, 8, 81–87, 92, 93, 97, 135, *136*, 157; constitutional courts, 2, 3, 5, 7, 8, 41, 42, 83, 84, *85*, 86, 87, *88*, 89–92, 135
national government, 5, 7, 18, 19, 20, 81, 89, *130*. *See also* government specific entries
national legislature. *See* national parliament
national parliament (domestic parliament/member state/MS parliament), 7, 17, 18, 27, 37, 38, 41, 42, 47–49, 58, 59, 60, 62, 66–68, 73, 75, 85, *85*, 86, 87, *88*, 90–93, *95*, 97, 114, *126*, *130*, 134, 135, *136*, 137, 142, 155; parliamentary (*parliamentary proceedings*), 17, 51n5, 58, 66–68, 74, 86, 88, 91, 92, 94, *94*, *95*, 97, 113, 158. See also European Parliament (EP)
national preference formation. *See* national parliament; preference formation
nation score, 15, 60, *70*, *72*, 127, 135, 153–57. *See also* position *specific entries*
negotiation, 8, 13–22, 24–27, 35, 38, 40, 42, 43, 45–50, 57–62, 66–71, 73, 74, 75, 90, 104, 105, 107–11, 115, 116, 130–33, *133*, 135, 137, 143–46, 148, 154; outcome, 14, 22, 25, 26, 104; success, 133, *133*; theory, 110. See also intergovernmentalism, intergovernmental bargaining; legislative bargaining; preference formation
Netherlands, 4, 21, *21*, 23, 44, 47, 48, 67, *84*, *88*, 91, 92, *96*, 97, 113, *129*, 131, *133*, 135, 136, 149n2, *154*, 155, 156, *157*
new institutionalism. *See* Institutionalism
new intergovernmentalism. *See* Intergovernmentalism
North-South divide (North-South cleavage/North-South coalition), 5, 6, 9, 10, *128*, 129, 130, *130,* 131, 132, 136, 139, 140, 148, 149n1

ordinary legislative procedure. *See* legislative bargaining

Parliament. *See* European Parliament (EP)
Parliamentary. *See* European Parliament; National parliament
Poland, *21*, 23, 47, *96, 97, 129, 133, 135, 136, 154, 155, 156, 157*
policy issue, 3, 5, 6, 26, 47, 50, 66, 75n5, 106, 109, 132, 154. *See also* contested issue; *EMU Positions* dataset
Portugal, 8, *21*, 23, 61, 62, *62*, *63*, 64, 66, 67, 70, *70*, 71, *72*, 73, 74, *74*, 84, *84*, 91, *96*, 97, 99n15, 113, *129*, 133, 135, 136, 154, 155, 156, *157*; POR (*nation score*), 64, *70, 72*
positions. *See* Nation score
power (formal power), 14, 25, 26, 35, 37, 41, 42, 44, 66–68, 83, *85*, 86, 87, *88*, 89–92, 109, 116, 126, 132, 145
preference formation, 2, 3, 7–9, 13–20, 27, 33–43, 45–50, 57–59, 66, 68, 69, 74, *74*, 75, 75n5, 105, 107, 110–15, 117, *128*, 131, 132, 134, 142. *See also* contested issue; national preference formation
Presidents' Report, 5, 123, 125, 140, 141, 143, 154
procedural limits (procedural hurdles/procedural constraints/procedural requirements), 2, 8, 93, 94, 95, *95*, 96, *96*, *97*, 135, *136*, 153, 157, 158. *See also EMU Legal Index* (dataset)
public opinion, 7, 14, 16–19, 27, 39, 41, 47–49, 58, 59, 68, 111–15, 117, 118n6, 128, *130*, 134, 142

rational choice, 24, 34, 37, 107, 111
rescue, 1, 6, 8, 10n1, 34, 41, 45, 47, 70
responsibility, 8, 10, 37, 59, 82, 87, 89, 92, 109, 135
responsiveness, 14, 57, 59, 73, 74, 75
reverse qualified majority voting (RQMV), 34, 41, 44, 51n3

Romania, *21*, 23, 84, 92, *96, 97, 129, 133, 135, 136, 154, 155, 156, 157*
Slovakia, *21*, 23, 84, 96, 97, 113, *129, 133, 135, 136, 154, 155, 156, 157*
Slovenia, 21, *21*, 23, 84, *84*, *85*, *96*, 97, 113, *129*, 133, 135, 136, 154, 155, 156, *157*
Single Resolution Fund (SRF), 9, *126*, 130, 138, 144–47, *147*
Single Resolution Mechanism (SRM), 145, 146, 148
Single Supervisory Mechanism (SSM), 6, 83
Six-Pack, 1, 13, 20, 75n5, 84, 87, 130, 132, 134, 154
Spain, 8, *21*, 23, 44, 45, 47, *61*, *62*, *63*, 64, 66, 67, 69, 70, *70*, 72, *72*, 73, 74, *74*, 75, 84, *84*, *85*, 86, *96*, 97, 113, *129*, 131, *21*, 23, 96, 97, 129, 133, 135, 136, 154, 155, 156, *157*; ESP (*nation score*), *70, 72*
Stability and Growth Pact (SGP), 1, 20, 51n3, 57, 81, 83, 134, 140, 141, 156, 157
supranational actor (SN agent/SN institution/SN player), 2, 14, 18, 26, 27, 38, 44, 50n1, 59, 66, 115, 117, *130*
Sweden, *21*, 23, 45, 47, *96, 97, 129, 133, 135, 136*, 149n2, *154, 155, 156, 157*

temporality, 104
Treaty on Stability, Coordination and Governance (TSCG), 34, 44, 48, 58, 83, 84, *84*, 85–87, 92, 93, 98nn7–8. *See also* Stability and Growth Pact (SGP)
Two-Pack, 1, 13, 20, 130, 132, 134, 154

United Kingdom (UK). *See* Great Britain

veto (player/points/position/power/rights), 24, 25, 42, 46, 47, *88*, 89–91, 93, 94, *94*, 95, 96, 109, 116, 158
vincolo esterno, 60

About the Editors and Contributors

EDITORS

Zdenek Kudrna, former research fellow, Salzburg Centre of European Union Studies, University of Salzburg.

Sonja Puntscher Riekmann, former Jean Monnet Professor and director of the Salzburg Centre of European Union Studies, University of Salzburg.

Fabio Wasserfallen, professor of European Politics at the University of Bern.

CONTRIBUTOR DETAILS

Stefanie Bailer is professor of political science at the University of Basel. Her research interests encompass decision-making at the European and international level, parliamentarians and parliamentary careers in Western European parliaments, and negotiations in the European Union and international organisations. Her research has been published in *European Journal of Political Research, International Political Science Review, European Union Politics, Journal of Common Market Studies, Journal of European Public Policy*, among others.

Stefan Griller is professor of European Law and deputy director of the Centre of European Union Studies at the University of Salzburg. He held positions at the Institutes of European Law and International Law in Vienna and Bratislava, the Diplomatic Academy Vienna and the Institute of Public Administration in Maastricht/Luxembourg.

Shaun P. Hargreaves Heap is Professor of Political Economy at King's College London. His research is in macroeconomics and experimental economics. He is currently working on a project in experimental economics that examines how group identifications affect redistributive preferences.

Scott James is a Reader in Political Economy at King's College London. His work relates to the politics of financial regulation, theories of business power, and the role of economic ideas. His most recent book (with Lucia Quaglia) on the 'UK and Multi-Level Financial Regulation' was published by Oxford University Press in 2020.

Hussein Kassim is Professor of Politics at the University of East Anglia and ESRC Senior Fellow under 'The UK in a Changing Europe' initiative. His research is on EU institutions and the EU administration, relations between the EU and the member states, and EU policy and regulation.

Zdenek Kudrna leads the Regulatory Strategy team at the New Zealand Treasury. From 2015 to 2019, he has implemented the Horizon 2020 research project *EMU Choices* at the University of Salzburg. He has also been an advisor to the World Bank, IMF, UNDP and Czech Ministry of Finance.

Elisabeth Lentsch was post-doc researcher at the University of Salzburg. She worked in the Horizon 2020 Project "EMU Choices – The choice for Europe since Maastricht" from 2015–19. Elisabeth Lentsch investigated the legal development of legal framework of the European Economic and Monetary Union and the legal feasibility of EMU reform scenarios. She coordinated the project network of national constitutional lawyers dealing with fiscal and economic integration.

Dirk Leuffen is professor of international politics at the Department of Politics and Public Administration and a principal investigator at the Cluster of Excellence on the Politics of Inequality at the University of Konstanz, Germany. His research interests include the study of (differentiated) European integration, fairness and decision-making in the European Union and more generally the interplay between domestic and international politics.

Leonardo Morlino is Professor Emeritus of Political Science at LUISS, Rome. He is the author, co-author or editor of more than 45 books and author or co-author of more than 230 journal essays and book chapters, published in English, French, German, Spanish, Hungarian, Chinese, Mongolian, and Japanese. His most recent books include: *Equality, Freedom, and Democracy. Europe After the Great Recession* (Oxford UP, 2020), *Comparison. An Methodological Introduction for the Social Sciences* (Barbara Budrich, 2018), *The Impact of Economic Crisis on South European Democracies* (Palgrave, 2017), *The quality of Democracy in Latin America* (IDEA, 2016), in addition to being one of the three co-editors of the *Handbook of Political Science* (3 voll., Sage Publications, 2020).

Uwe Puetter is professor of empirical research on Europe at Europa-Universität Flensburg and visiting professor at the College of Europe in Bruges. His research focuses on the European Council and the Council and wider processes of EU institutional change in the era of new intergovernmentalism.

Sonja Puntscher Riekmann was professor of European politics and director of the Centre of European Union Studies at the University of Salzburg and the Co-coordinator of the Horizon 2020 research project *EMU Choices*. She held positions at the University of Vienna, the University of Innsbruck and the Humboldt University of Berlin.

Sabine Saurugger is professor of political science and director of Sciences Po Grenoble. Her research focuses on theories of European integration, European public policies and the politics of law. Results of her research have been published in journals such as the *European Journal of Political Research, Journal of Common Market Studies, West European Politics, Political Studies, Journal of European Public Policy* and Revue française de science *politique.* More recently, her co-authored book *The Court of Justice and the Politics of Law* has been published in the European Union Series with Palgrave (2017).

Cecilia Emma Sottilotta is an Assistant Professor of International Relations and Global Politics at the American University of Rome. Her most recent books include *Rethinking Political Risk: Concepts, Theories, Challenges* (Routledge, 2016) and *The Politics of the Eurozone Crisis in Southern Europe: A Comparative Reappraisal* (Palgrave, 2019, co-ed. with Leonardo Morlino).

Jonas Tallberg is professor of political science at Stockholm University, where he coordinates the research group on global and regional governance. His primary research interests are global governance and European Union politics. His publications on EU politics include the monographs *Leadership and Negotiation in the European Union* (2006) and *European Governance and Supranational Institutions* (2003), as well as articles in journals such as *European Union Politics*, *International Organization*, *Journal of Common Market Studies*, *Journal of European Public Policy*, and *West European Politics*.

Thomas Warren was a Senior Research Assistant at the University of East Anglia from 2017–18 as part of the Horizon 2020-funded 'EMU Choices' project. His research explores EU integration, political economy and ideas.

Fabio Wasserfallen is professor of European politics at the University of Bern, where he is also Co-Director of the Institute of Political Science. Together with Sonja Puntscher Riekmann, he has coordinated the Horizon 2020 project *EMU Choices*. Previously, he was professor of comparative politics at Zeppelin University, associate professor of political economy at the University of Salzburg and Fung Global Fellow at Princeton University. The findings of his research have been published in journals such as the *American Political Science Review*, *American Journal of Political Science*, *British Journal of Political Science*, *European Journal of Political Research*, *European Union Politics* and *Journal of European Public Policy*.

Milton Keynes UK
Ingram Content Group UK Ltd.
UKHW021535050924
447875UK00001B/111

9 781910 259764